GW00480542

NEW
- PEZ

CORNWALL
COUNCIL

24 HOUR RENEWAL HOTLINE 0845 607 6119
www.cornwall.gov.uk/Library

tree
Productions Inc.

For Tracey Rogers ~ The Queen of Monaco
Wish you were here.

Cruiser

\krü-zer\

- A motor-powered ship intended for cruising
- One who plays at courtship

Chapter One

VANDANA

Every story starts somewhere.

Mine, tragically, begins headfirst in a toilet.

"Jesus, V! How many drinks did you have tonight?" asks Derek, my considerably less-wasted husband. He's been holding my topknot ponytail out of the line of fire like a concerned spouse should, but now that the worst is over, I hear it. The judgment in his voice. The lack of warmth.

Maybe it's my imagination.

Or the fact I'm hammered and not wearing it well.

I'm panting and lightheaded, hugging the throne dressed in Balmain, half a mil in borrowed rubies, and what's left of my pride. Thank god Derek got me home in time. If the staff at the Peninsula Hotel in Beverly Hills had found me splayed out in their lobby like a *Girls Gone Wild* hot mess, I'd never live it down.

"I'm sorry, babe." I prop myself up against our bathroom wall to catch my breath. "I ... I don't know what got into me tonight. I just wanted to celebrate. Guess I went a little overboard." I muster a smile, but Derek's face might as well be up there on Mount Rushmore—that's how stony his expression is.

"Now we know who ate all the caviar," he mutters, like he hasn't heard anything I've just said. He flushes away the final remnants of my evening and crouches down in front of me. "C'mon, my little drunk. Off to bed."

In one graceful flourish, because he's always balanced and even-keeled, Derek hoists me up. This is where we're supposed to hug, and I say thank you. Thank him for coming to a client launch party. Thank him for being by my side after coming home for the first time in four months. But his moody silence during the limo ride to the event keeps looping in my mind. How he kept checking his phone when he thought I wasn't looking. The kiss on my cheek in front of a client. There was no feeling behind any of it.

The real issue isn't how many glasses of champagne I've had tonight.

The real issue is why I grabbed every flute that went by on a silver tray in the first place.

As I wobble on bare feet and scour the marble floor for my shoes, I feel the weight of Derek's gaze. "They're downstairs," he says. "You could barely walk straight. Do you want me to unzip you?"

It's our routine. Me, forever in and out of gowns and cocktail dresses. Derek, always zipping me up and down. Slipping back into familiar territory almost makes me forget he was away for so long. But the look in his steel-blue eyes—usually intense from thinking about schedules and conflicts he has to manage—is far away, and it has been all night. I want to chalk it up to the 'recalibration period.' After six years of living with a first assistant director, I'd finally gotten used to Derek being away for weeks and months at a time on film sets. It's a pattern we've managed to work around, although it always takes a few days to get back into the rhythm of our marriage.

But tonight, the distance between us seems greater than when he was halfway around the world in South Africa. We've been fighting every day since he came home last Saturday. Stupid arguments over nothing. Me not putting sugar in his coffee. That I didn't take his car in for an oil change like he'd asked me to. Switching up the brand of toilet paper.

A big no-no, apparently.

Not wanting to make a big deal out of anything else right now, I turn my back and Derek yanks my zipper lower. I wait for the usual boob grope or neck nuzzle. Nothing. Wriggling the beaded Lycra past my shoulders, I pause. Inhale the scent that's been bothering me all evening.

Don't. Don't. Don't.

"Is that a new cologne?" I ask.

"Yeah," he says, not meeting my eyes. "I grabbed a random at duty-free."

"Oh. Hugo Boss will be crushed. You've been so devoted."

"I can have more than one."

Now's not the time to dissect his use of a new fragrance. And the longer I look at him, the more fidgety he becomes.

"What?" he asks, bristling again.

"Nothing."

Or maybe it's your long walks every morning without replying to any of my texts.

Usually I visit Derek's film set once or twice, but his grueling schedule and my work commitments made it impossible this last time. The time zone difference didn't help either. His texts came in when I was asleep. Our Facetimes were short, one of us inevitably having to end the call early. Derek insists it was just one of those jobs, and I'd consider believing him if it wasn't for his hair.

He's rocked the same buzzcut for years. The ongoing joke has always been that he likes to stoke my Adam Levine fantasy because with cropped hair Derek does look like him, minus the tattoos and brown eyes. Except he doesn't look like Adam tonight. Or himself. Bleached strands shoot through his dark brown hair, courtesy of four months in sunbaked Cape Town. It's longer too, curling past his ears onto his velvet tuxedo collar.

Derek doesn't like hair touching his ears. Never has.

"If it's nothing," he says, "then it's time to take that monkey suit off." He shrugs out of his Tom Ford blazer and dumps it on my side of the vanity in what feels like a punctuating gesture. We bickered over him dressing up for the event, and only when I reminded him that I bought the tux for these specific occasions did he cave. "I hope I lived up to your expectations tonight, V. Aside from the champagne over-load, you were great. The queen of public relations perfect, as always."

His smile is as thin as the compliment, and when he turns to leave, I feel the night slipping away even further. "Don't fall asleep, 'kay?" I ask, reaching for his arm. "Let's cuddle for a bit."

Having never been a cuddler, Derek regards me with a peculiar look. "Might want to rinse off first," he says, wrinkling his nose. "You smell a little ripe."

The door bangs shut behind him, and boozy self-pity surges in my throat. If that's his version of a rally, we're deeper in the hole than I imagined. I'm the first to admit our once-active sex life has seen better days, and a lot of it has to do with me. But Derek also promised he would never do back-to-back films and then promptly went AWOL for eight of the past twelve months. Since he's come home, the only action between us has been one half-hearted erection dozing against my butt.

And that didn't amount to anything.

Absence hasn't made either of our hearts grow fonder.

I crank on the shower, ready to wash away an evening that refused to do me any favors. Under a blast of hot water, throbbing head resting against the tiles, I decide the tonic will be a quiet weekend, just the two of us. There isn't much going on at work tomorrow since it's Friday, and I can leave early. I'll cancel Saturday brunch with my besties, June and Flynn. Derek and I can be together and enjoy our morning coffees in bed. Laugh over some on-set horror stories he always comes home with and hasn't yet told me. What I crave is sheet-gripping sex but that feels like a long shot. Step one is rekindling the spark between us.

I can do it.

Through sheer willpower, I'll turn this around.

There is no calamity I can't manage.

After the long shower, I bundle into a robe and find Derek still dressed and perched on the side of our California King bed. He's usually the first one under the covers, constantly telling me to hurry up. A beam of cold, slanting light from the floor lamp hits his face at an odd angle and makes it looks like he's frowning.

Because he is.

Hard.

"Everything okay?" I ask.

Derek sighs and pushes the heels of his hands into his eyes. It's so quiet I can hear the TV that's still on downstairs and the gurgle of the fountain in the garden.

"We need to talk," he says.

My legs, fingers, brain—everything starts to tingle.

In couple's vernacular, *we need to talk* means only one thing.

Somewhere, in the darkest part of my mind, this conversation has always lurked. Derek works with the most beautiful women on the planet, all of them vain and vulnerable, and incredibly needy. He sees them at their most raw. And in various stages of undress. I read the script for *Tangled Roots*, his last project. I knew it was a starring vehicle for nubile newcomer Fiona Lynn-Meyers. Knew she'd be naked for at least ten pages. One page of script equals one minute of shooting. And if the scenes need to be reshot, as the emotional ones do…

I sit heavily beside him on the bed. "It's Fiona, right?"

It's a stupid, stupid thing, needing to know. But I have to. If we're going to end things, I could at least save some face if his fling is with a busty, twenty-four-year-old ingenue and not the weird craft services girl. Or worse, a production assistant.

There can't be anything worse, right?

Derek's hands fall into his lap. He stares blankly at the Elizabeth Taylor Warhol print he bought me for my thirtieth birthday. *You have the same eyes*, he'd said. *Soulful and beckoning.*

"I love you, Vandana," he says, choking up. "I need you to know that. I'll always love you."

With the finality of his words, my stomach pitches. "Do I know her?"

Derek looks at me straight on, the way he does when he wants to make sure I'm listening, which, truth be told, sometimes I'm not. All I see are his blurry pupils, washed with tears of pain.

And fear.

"It's not a woman," he says.

Yup, turns out there's worse.

Chapter Two

It's quiet this morning in the offices of Sevruga, the luxury PR company I co-founded with my partner, Vaughn. On casual Fridays, no one shows up before ten a.m. That's usually when I wake up, but after tossing and turning all night, I gave up on the notion of sleep. Derek was already gone when I came downstairs to make coffee. The only sign of him was the cashmere throw draped along the sofa where he'd slept.

I don't want to think about where he went.

I don't want to think.

I'm a ghost of myself this morning, fighting back tears and this close to indulging in scream therapy.

Damn you, Alistair Noelle.

I scroll through his Instagram feed a fifth time but the only photos of him and Derek from South Africa are group shots with the crew. Never together, just the two of them. He's been careful, like Derek.

Alistair's a grip, one of those guys on set who pushes the dolly or moves cranes. I remember him clearly. Hard to forget the only man at the wrap party last year who wore a kilt, gladiator sandals and nothing else. He had this Viking quality to him, strutting around with two blonde braids hanging down his back and drinking out of a deer-horn beer stein. Quick to smile, he approached me guilelessly, flirted even.

Looking back, it's impossible to say if he and Derek were ever in the same space that night. I barely saw Derek. The club they'd rented out for the night was packed, and for most of the evening, I hung out in a private booth with the director, and long-time friend, Stryker Talone. I kept a low profile because wrap parties are strange, incestuous things. One final, drunken blowout for cast and crew who had been under pressure together for months. I let Derek work the room and wasn't looking for signs of infidelity. But he and Alistair had already been involved.

That's what Derek told me last night.

It's been almost a year.

I toss my iPhone onto my desk, massaging the throb in both temples. I'm running on three hours of sleep and a quattro Americano. Forget about the plans to reconnect with Derek this weekend. Project number one is re-evaluating my life.

"Hey, Vans!" a familiar voice shouts from down the hall. "Are you actually here?"

I jolt upright in my chair. Vaughn Scriller is the only person who calls me Vans, or should I say, the only one who gets away with it. Moreover, why is he here? His wife Lindsay is supposed to be dragging him off on vacation, their first getaway in five years. Their flight leaves in three hours. I compose myself and poke my head into the hallway.

His face lights up when he sees me. "Ha! I knew I smelled your perfume."

Vaughn's a youthful fifty-five, one of those distinguished, timeless men with salt-and-pepper hair and beard who only look better as they age. Better yet, we look good together, and that goes a long way toward caché in this town.

"What's going on?" I ask. He should not be in workout gear or toting his Tumi briefcase. "Don't tell me you bailed? Lindsay will have my head."

"No, the trip is still on. Unfortunately," he grumbles. "That's why I

8

need to take some files with me. Fend off the boredom. I was about to call you, but since you're here…" He waves at me to join him in his office.

"Give me a sec."

If my compact mirror isn't lying, concealer hides most of the traces of my sleepless night. But Vaughn is my first test. Can I make it through a conversation without breaking down? The short walk from my corner office to his suddenly feels much longer. I take my usual seat on the sofa and watch Beverly Hills traffic through the floor-to-ceiling window as Vaughn flips through files in his cabinet.

"How'd it go last night?" he asks. "Sorry I was a no-show. Lindsay dragged me to Saks to buy us safari outfits." He turns his head so he can roll his eyes at me.

"It went great. Everyone loved the free pair of shoes. I think this line is going to blow up."

Akari is a Japanese designer known for eye-popping dresses that the glitterati snatch up faster than limited edition Vuitton, and now she's expanding into shoes. At fifteen-hundred a pair, the influencers and curated media in attendance last night at the Peninsula drooled over the luxe freebies. She texted me this morning with the good news that her spring line sold out.

Vaughn slams the filing cabinet drawer shut and mutters, "Where did I put that fucking thing?"

"Most people would sound happier going on a month-long, first-class safari in Africa," I say.

"Most people would be thrilled to find a twenty on the sidewalk," he sasses back. "You know how uptight I get when I don't have my finger on the pulse."

"It's only four weeks; you'll survive. And maybe you'll actually enjoy yourself."

"Christ, I hope so." His watchful eyes dart from the Bauhaus coffee table I found for him to the nook with club chairs where he illegally vapes and savors small batch whiskey. He doesn't always do work in here, something I've had to skate around when Lindsay texts me asking where he is. "For crying out loud," he says, moving his briefcase to one side. "Right in front of my face." He rips the top page off a legal pad sitting on his desk and walks it over to me. "Here. Happy Friday."

"Morgan de Rohan-Chabot," I read out, Vaughn's tidy printing so much better than my illegible scrawl. "Who's he?"

"It's *Sha-bow*," he corrects, "which means he's probably French and pretentious as fuck. Some hotshot yacht designer. He wanted to meet earlier this week and I forgot. He sounds legit. Money to burn."

"Interesting. We don't have any clients in that market."

"Exactly," he says. "That's why you need to have dinner with him tonight."

"What?" I'm already halfway to my living room couch with a bucket of KFC and a sappy Hallmark movie to cry my eyes out to. My brain is filled with rocks. The last thing I need is a night of schmoozing. "No, I can't. I—"

"Yes, you can," he interrupts. "And you will. He's only got one more night in town and asked to meet with you specifically."

"Why me?"

Vaughn tilts his head, a *You're really asking me that?* expression all over his face. "Because you're built like Gisele and make Kate Beckinsale look like the girl next door. Back in her prime, of course." He winks and saunters back to his desk, jamming files into his bag. "He's staying at the Fairmont in Santa Monica. It's your 'hood, so probably better you than me anyway. I'm too old to be dealing with hyphenated Monaco princelings."

A tingle runs up my spine. "He lives in Monaco?"

One of my dream destinations. Derek promised to take me there for our anniversary, but that was last year, before work took over his life.

"Apparently. And he mentioned something about you traveling there for an event. November, I think." Vaughn's unusually distracted today. He never lets important details like that slide.

"Why wouldn't he hire someone from Europe?" I ask.

Vaughn pauses his busy work to give me his full attention. "Is everything okay? Or have you forgotten we are the fucking best when it comes to luxury PR? *That's* why he's after us. You've been itching to land a monster client for months. This is an opportunity on a silver platter, darlin'. And I'll only say this once," he adds, in a fatherly tone, "but you haven't had your head in the game lately."

We share revenue fifty-fifty, although our bonuses are based on the billings we bring in as individuals. Vaughn reels in most of our big fish clients. All of them men, the old boy's network. I'm no slouch in securing new business, but he's right. I've lost focus and can't pinpoint the reasons why. Morgan sounds like a potential whale. One I can land on my own. But tonight of all nights?

"Okay, okay. I'll meet with him."

"Great," he says. "I'll check in with you next week to see how it went."

"How? You'll be off-grid on safari."

He pauses, *so* busted. "Lindsay doesn't know about the sat phone, okay? Don't spill the beans." In reaction to my suspect look, he quickly adds, "Technically, it's not a lie if she doesn't know about it."

I wave a warning finger at him. "If you start calling every day, I'm going to ignore you."

"Vans," he says, "you know it's never a crisis of belief between us. I trust you more than I trust my own children." Our mutual gazes zero in on the silver photo frame atop his desk. Janelle and Aaron in younger, less troubled years. Back when they both held so much promise. Vaughn's ability to avoid what he doesn't want to deal with is legendary, but both kids landing back on the streets is taking a toll. It's written all over his face. "I'm trying, okay?" he says, quietly. "This holiday is me trying. A month is insane though. How many fucking elephants can one man look at?"

Hollow fear shines in his eyes. A man about to leave behind the only thing that keeps him afloat.

"I know you're trying," I say, making my way over to console him. "But for Lindsay's sake and yours, forget about work. I've got your back."

After our quick hug, he pecks me on the cheek. "This place would fall apart without you. That husband of yours is one lucky son of a bitch. Did he go with you last night?"

The persistent pulse at my temples fires harder. "Yeah. Why?"

"Because he's been MIA for the past four months and most of this year. He needs to man up and take the reins."

I laugh tonelessly. "Is it just me, or did my mother reincarnate into you?"

"Listen up," he says. "I know you can do it all, you're a flawless fucking machine, but the point is, you shouldn't have to."

The softness in his voice, the truth in what he says; my lip trembles as I try to keep it together. "Maybe when you come back from vacation, I'll go on one," I say. "I could use a break."

Vaughn searches my face and must attribute the emotions I'm hiding to work. "If you don't want to deal with yacht boy, I'll figure it out. Say the word."

"It's fine," I reassure him.

My business is the last thing standing. Hell if I'm going to let that crumble too. And there's no way I'm telling him about Derek. Not before his trip. He'll use it as an excuse not to go, and Lindsay will be crushed. She confided in me that this is her last-ditch attempt at fixing their marriage.

With a final, mournful sweep through his office, Vaughn slings the Tumi over his shoulder and sighs. "Talk to Quigley for some intel before you head out tonight. He knows all about yacht boy. Damn near pissed himself when I told him he might become a client."

Quigley, aka Thomas Quigley, aka TQ, is our devoted assistant. A forty-year-old Peter Pan, with a sly sense of humor and a fine collection of Bespoke suits which has had many a man's hand down the pant fronts. Some even with his approval.

"Morgan swings for the other team?" I ask.

Vaughn scoffs. "Hardly. According to TQ, he's got quite the reputation as a lady-killer. You know what to do. Wear a low-cut blouse and get 'er done."

A chauvinist, a sexist, and unafraid to be both in today's PC world, Vaughn never fails to remind me how closing deals with men is just a flash of boob away. Sleeping your way to the top, or at least to the next level, still happens in LA. It will happen for time eternal. I'm not one of those woke women—juicing, unshaven man-haters waving placards at rallies—but I draw the line at poor ethics.

"You of all people should know I don't do business that way," I reply in my best reprimanding voice. Vaughn's made the odd drunken overture and felt the sting of my rejection every time.

At the very least, he owns it.

"Why do you put up with me?" he asks, serious for once.

"Because you're brilliant in ways I'm not. Because together, we're better." And before he can come up with another excuse to delay his departure, I shunt him out of the office he practically lives in with a playful shove. "Go," I say. "And don't you dare call me next week. I'll handle Mr. de Rohan-Chabot all on my own."

Chapter Three

FROM MY HOUSE, THE DRIVE TO THE FAIRMONT HOTEL TAKES FIVE minutes. But I'm nervous and leave too early. I've got time to kill so I idle on Second Avenue and recap everything TQ and I discussed earlier in the afternoon. The quick and dirty? Morgan's only thirty-four, insanely talented and infamous. Not just for his client list, which reads like a *Who's Who* of global movers and shakers.

"The CFO of Deutsche Bank. Russian business tycoons. Royalty." TQ listed these off on his fingers.

"Is *he* royalty?" I asked. "I assume yes if he's named his company Royal Morgan Yachts."

"After centuries of dirty inbreeding, isn't half of Europe royal?" he joked. "I do know his family comes from serious money. His father also built boats. Surprisingly, being rich and idle isn't baked into their DNA."

"Interesting. Do they work together?"

"No, his father retired. Now it's just Morgan and his millions. Or billions." The perennially single TQ made a sad face. He was very disappointed Morgan doesn't swing for his team.

"So why is he infamous?" I asked.

"Attitude, for one thing. He's got a massive chip on his shoulder, coming from money, the fact his father was in the biz. Everyone thinks he had a leg up, didn't have to try hard, yadda, yadda, yadda. The usual bitchiness."

"Any successful man swings it around," I said. "Is that all it takes these days to be infamous?"

But I'd lost TQ's attention. He gazed reverentially at my Apple monitor, moisturized chin in hand. I'd Googled Morgan, as you do, and the photos that had popped up made it hard to look away. I failed algebra but recognize mathematically perfect beauty when I see it. The golden ratio. People say the same thing about my face, but they never notice my eyebrows aren't perfect mirror opposites, or that I have a little ski jump at the end of my nose.

"By the way," TQ said, elfin eyes all dreamy as he pointed at the screen, "he is as hot as he looks in these photos. I was at this swank party in London last year, and guess who rolls in?" I leaned back with a smile, waiting for the details. All the great TQ stories start with him at a party. I swear, half the gossip in LA comes from him walking through the dingy doorways of after-hours clubs. "As luck would have it," he continued, "I could only admire him from a distance. Women were hanging off him like monkeys on a tree. That's mainly why he's infamous. His sobriquet is the Cruiser, and I'm pretty sure that doesn't come from his love of fine sailing vessels."

"Sobri-what?" I asked.

"Nickname, mon ami." He tossed his coiffed golden hair in a gesture that perfectly matched his haughty accent.

"So he's a rich playboy."

"You say that like it's a bad thing."

"Are you jealous I get to meet him?" I teased.

"Of course I am," he sniffed. "And since I'm *not* invited, can you do me one favor and get a guesstimate?" He leaned forward and his voice took on a conspiratorial tone. "It was too dark in the club for a proper look. I'm praying he's undersized. Something—anything—to make him less attractive."

I rolled my eyes and laughed. "Sorry, I'm not scoping out some stranger's crotch. Not even for you."

"Fine," he said, acting all put upon. "We'll assume he's hung like a donkey. Cue my weeping."

"You can come along to take notes."

"No, no, no," he said, and held up his hands in mock protest. "I'll let *you* drown in all that male virility."

I glanced back at my monitor. Based on everything TQ had just revealed, chances are Morgan's inflated ego will drown me before his virility ever has a chance. Even a 2D image of the man oozed hubris.

"Do not fret, sunshine," TQ said, always my biggest cheerleader. "You'll handle him like you handle everything in your life—impeccably. Seriously, I don't know how you make it look so easy. Badass employer. Adorable husband. Perfect hair." He sighed, a man fresh out of superlatives. "If you weren't so loveable, I'd truly hate you."

I made a funny sound, like I'd tried to laugh but choked instead. I could not bring myself to say it. The ugliness of telling him my life wasn't so perfect had to happen, just not tonight.

TQ misread my ambivalence and grabbed both my hands in his. "On behalf of the deprived gay man population in Los Angeles, you go, girl. School his Euro ass about who wears the PR pants in America. Forget that rascal Vaughn. May I present…" He rolled his arm with a flourish. "*The* Vandana Hillman."

The Vandana Hillman is currently sitting in her Range Rover, having serious second thoughts. My afternoon cram session on yacht design helped, but I'm still woefully uneducated. Making a good first impression is critical. One sniff of weakness is all it takes for the powerplays to start. I hate to say it, but men do get pleasure from one-upmanship.

After a final check in the rearview mirror I silently thank Lillia, my facialist, for squeezing me in last minute. At the very least, my game face has never looked better.

Go. You got this.

Once I get to the Fairmont, a brooding valet pockets my ten like he's somehow gone out of his way to earn it, and my heartbeat quickens the closer I get to the restaurant. As I wait for the hostess, I scan the bar but don't see Morgan. We exchanged texts earlier, confirming time and place, and I'm checking my phone for an update when a twenty-something with enough piercings on her face to set off an airport screener sashays over.

"Hey," she says, all laid-back Valley girl. "I'm Dakota. Table for one, or are you meeting someone?"

"I'm meeting someone. But I don't think he's here yet."

"Oh jeez," she replies, voice dropping low. "Tinder date? Hate those."

"He's a guest at the hotel," I reply, mildly irritated she thinks I'm single, even though I guess I technically am. "Morgan de Rohan-Chabot."

"Oh. Are you Vandana?" She does a miserable job hiding the fact she's hoping I'm not. After I say yes, what's left of her smile slides off her face. "He's on the patio. Follow me."

The Bungalow, one of several eateries in the hotel, is a funky space styled in boho LA beachside and draws a monied, on-the-make crowd. More than a few appreciative heads turn to drink me in. In a tailored, black silk shirtdress and nude wedges, I'm flashing a little extra leg. (Yes, Vaughn, you are more right than wrong.)

Dakota catches wind of the attention coming my way and apparently decides it's better to join forces. "Your friend's got a great accent," she says. "Where he's from?"

"Monaco, I believe."

Her eyes widen. "Seriously? So love to hit that place one day. Looks epically romantic. Are you two…"

"No," I say, although part of me wants to say yes. She's got the determination of a girl too young to know she's angling for a man beyond her pay grade, and it's making me feel older than thirty-three. Not that I consider her competition. She's pretty and all, if you're into shaved heads and pale goths, and no offense to Dakota's artistic choices, but something tells me she'll one day regret the snake tattoo crawling up the back of her leg.

Momentarily lost in the detail of said snake, I crash into the suddenly stopped Dakota. We're on the fringes of the patio and she discreetly points to my left.

"That's him," she whispers.

It's quiet for a Friday, with only a few guests scattered at various tables. When I reflect back on this night though, I'll be hard pressed to remember anyone else being there at all. I wouldn't go so far as to say Morgan's sitting on one of the sofas flanking our table, because sitting is what mere mortals do. He *presides* over the entire patio like a god in his kingdom. His gaze is on the Pacific Ocean across the street, and I say nothing for fear of interrupting what feels like an intimate moment for him. But Morgan senses my presence like an animal attuned to being in the crosshairs of a rifle. His head swivels, eyes locking onto mine.

"Mademoiselle Hillman?" he asks, rising to his full and daunting height.

The fluttery feeling in my stomach looking at his photos online? Yeah, well, that was nothing. If Adam resembled Morgan, then Eve would've dropped her fig leaf in a heartbeat. Apple or no apple.

Morgan is original sin in the flesh.

"Uh … yes," I say. "Hello."

Before my tongue fully untangles, he leans in for a double kiss, one on each cheek. "Bonsoir," he says, his voice sultry and oh-so debonair. "You look lovely."

His stylish scruff of beard tickles my skin, but the rush of heat on my face has everything to do with his soft lips and intoxicating scent. He smells exactly like the ocean. The good bits. Salt and sand and sunshine.

"Can I get you two drinks to start?" Dakota asks, her flirty smile meant only for Morgan.

He casts a questioning glance my way. "If you're a wine drinker, they have a Barolo that's outstanding."

My cheeks are still warm from his kisses. Might as well make them flush more with a great red. "I never say no to a nice wine."

"If I didn't drink it all last night," he jokes to Dakota, "please bring us two bottles of the Giacomo Conterno. And the food I ordered."

"Right away," she replies, although she lingers a touch too long before finally leaving.

Can't say I blame her.

Magnetic and majestic, Morgan is a force of beautiful nature with skin the color of honey-dipped bronze. Women here pay top dollar to glow as he does, but I get the sense he just rolls out of bed, runs a hand through his dirty blond hair, and goes about his day all tanned, tousled, and perfect.

And sexy AF.

His long-sleeved sweater clings to every muscle of his swimmer's physique, and whatever animal donated its wool to create it must have been hand-fed the rarest grains and rocked to sleep every night. The butterscotch knit looks like spun gold. With white jeans cuffed above his ankles and wearing no socks in velvet loafers—it's a look very few men have the confidence to pull off.

But he doesn't lack confidence.

It's all right there, in his *yes-I-am-that-attractive-so-stare-all-you-want* stance.

Morgan gestures for me to take a seat. "Après vous, please."

I settle onto the sofa and he takes a seat opposite me, sliding a full water glass in my direction. "I hope you don't mind me taking liberties on ordering food. I guessed on a couple of things and am curious to see if I'm right."

"Great wine *and* a culinary adventure," I say. "Now you've piqued my interest."

"That makes two of us."

His finely curved mouth breaks into a seductive and imperious smile. A story or three those lips could tell, I'm sure. Something about his specific brand of refined, European hotness intimidates me, and imagining his carved body without the sweater on isn't helping. I place my handbag on the table as a barrier of sorts. Never before has three feet of wood-slat table felt so necessary.

Any closer to him and I'm not sure what I might do.

Focus, Vandana.

"I appreciate you finding time in your schedule to meet," I say. "We're very intrigued with your work."

He tilts his head in an assessing gesture. "It's quite all right to say you are intrigued. Since you're the only one here."

His bluntness comes out of nowhere, and the electricity of it crackles on my skin. Blithe disregard for social niceties is so the opposite of ass-kissing LA.

"It's a euphemism," I clarify. "The collective 'we'?"

"Yes, I hear it all the time," he says, with an air of dismissiveness. "Odd, considering how independent Americans like to be."

If there's a slag in his observation, it's buried deeply by that very charming accent. Chip on his shoulder? More like an old-growth Redwood.

"Well, I'm sure the French have a far more lyrical way of expressing business speak," I counter.

He wordlessly studies me during a pause that seems to go on forever, and I realize that being countered is foreign territory. But I hold my ground, and his eyes are breathtaking as they fixate on mine. Dark caramel with flecks of gold. There's a restlessness in them, a fire I imagine is eternally stoked.

I shift on the sofa and hope it looks nonchalant instead of uncertain.

It's been a long time since I was this self-aware around a man.

"*We* can talk cultural differences another night," he finally says. "I'd like to hear more about you."

With elegant authority, he drapes an arm along the back of the sofa. His fingers drum lightly along the weathered wicker and the silver of his chunky Hublot watch gleams in the soft light. I'd given this meet and greet an hour, max. But the night is young, he's ordered two bottles of wine, and is clearly in no hurry to talk shop. Maybe this is the assuredness of someone who knows he's stupid handsome and can bend the agenda of anyone merely by living and breathing.

I reach for my water glass and take a deep swallow.

I might be here for a while.

Chapter Four

I KEEP MY BIO BRIEF. AN ORANGE COUNTY GIRL, BORN AND RAISED IN Laguna Beach. A father whose network of car dealerships inspired my interest in business. I graduated magna cum laude from Stanford, and two years later, founded Sevruga with Vaughn after being introduced at a cocktail party. He was a senior executive at another PR firm and was ready to branch out on his own.

"It's been a good fit," I say, picking at the olives that arrived with our wine. "We complement each other."

"I was told you two are the best," Morgan says.

"We like to think so." Smiling, I take a sip of the Barolo. Rich and massively structured, it is very good wine. "It sounds like you've made quite the name for yourself as well. What inspired you to become a yacht designer?"

Morgan leans in for an olive, and it borders on erotic as he removes the pit from his mouth with nimble fingers.

God. How to scrub that vision from my brain.

"The ocean is where I feel the freest," he says, leaning back to swirl his wine. "I was born on a boat and christened with saltwater. I learned to swim before I could walk."

"Sounds like destiny, then. In a way."

He shakes his head. "That implies forces beyond my control decided for me, when it's the opposite. If you don't pursue what you're most interested in, what's the point?"

His declaration reverberates deep under my ribcage. I zigged instead of zagged in my career and it's worked out, but there comes a time when that's not enough. The way Morgan looks at me, it's like he knows.

"I understand your father was a boat builder," I say, moving right along. "Did he encourage you to follow in his footsteps?"

"I've never followed anyone," he says, sounding offended at the suggestion. "That's why my boats are as unique as they are."

The man speaks the truth. His yachts are jaw-dropping. The beautiful lines of the exteriors seem to be an extension of him, but all that magnificence comes from an interior place.

"Tell me what inspires your designs," I ask. "From in here."

I lay a hand over my heart and prove he's not the only one who can play the eye contact game. Or games in general. His earlier comment about being born on a boat and so forth felt like sound-bites. Rote answers he's given a million times. I've interviewed hundreds of clients, and I know when they're keeping things surface and safe. Working together effectively means digging deeper. But based on how he angles his body away from me, deeper isn't where he wants to go.

"A well-designed yacht is like a woman," he says, his eyes roaming over my bare legs. "Deceptively simple lines but underneath the surface, they're infinitely more complex. The challenge is wrangling that complexity. The challenge is what interests me."

"Deceptively simple," I repeat. Wow. Had he really just said that? "Forgive me for not agreeing with that part of your design mantra—as it relates to women."

A ghost of a smile flickers on his face. "You're forgetting infinitely complex."

"What you're saying is, women inspire your designs?"

"I enjoy the symmetry and curves of the female form immensely. Very inspirational," he adds, tipping his wineglass in my direction.

Well. What to say to that?

Dakota saves me, reappearing with impeccable timing. She unloads her tray of arugula salads, seared halibut cheeks and a platter ringed with crackers. Nestled in the center is a bowl heaped full of shiny grey pearls.

"I ordered the caviar especially for you," Morgan says. "I figure if someone names their company Sevruga, high-end caviar is a must."

Huh. Just when I'm ready to dislike him. "Thank you," I say. "That's very thoughtful. And you guessed right."

Dakota beams at Morgan. "Do you need anything else?"

Morgan dismisses her with a wave of his hand and tops up our wine. "Bon appétit," he says. "Please, start."

I didn't realize how hungry I am, and it's hard to remain ladylike as I dig into my biggest weakness. While I nibble away, Morgan picks up the conversational thread. Born in the South Pacific on his parents' sailboat, he didn't touch land until his first birthday. An only child, he spent his formative years learning the ropes of boat design from his father and started his own company at twenty. Royal Morgan Yachts now employs ten staff and will hire more next year, pending a few contracts.

His beguiling accent leaves me in a trance. He could read *War and Peace* and make it sound like saucy pulp fiction. With the Barolo starting to go to my head, it's hard not to sink into the cushions and let the night drape around me. Luxuriate in the silent warmth from the heat lamps and the simple pleasures of good wine and caviar.

But I am here for a reason.

When he wraps up his life story and steals a bite of fish, I shift back into gear. "I know you don't have all night, and I want to make sure all your PR questions get answered. I can give you a brief over-view on how we work with clients."

He uncorks the second bottle of Barolo with the wine opener Dakota brought earlier. "Take your time. I have no other commitments. And this needs to breathe."

For the next thirty minutes, I'm a passionate public relations crusader. I tell him how it's a form of storytelling. How we're not involved in, nor do we create advertising for clients. We persuade opinions through earned exposure. "Think of it like this," I add. "With PR you don't control the message, the media does. But that doesn't mean we let them run with unmanaged narratives. We're very hands on. Our focus is primarily on events and interactions designed to plant a flag in the public's mind about who you are. We earn trust and build on it."

Morgan eyes me over his glass of wine. I can tell he's not sold. In fact, no one's ever seemed less interested in what I have to say. "Does it matter what the public thinks of me? My work speaks for itself."

"Well, you called me," I say to jog his memory. "It must matter on some level."

"Do you care what people think about you?"

"This isn't about me."

"But do you?" he presses.

Of course I care. More than I ever let on. "It's my business to care."

He stabs at his salad, taking time to chew and swallow. "To be upfront, this missive has more to do with the opinions of my senior staff." He pause, smiles thinly. "To smooth my edges, so to speak."

Interesting. In other words, he's not here because he wants to be.

"There are three important European yacht shows in the fall," he goes on to explain. "Cannes just finished. Genoa and Monaco are up next. I'm in the mix for a lucrative contract, one of my boats is up for an award, and we're expanding our design services. There's a lot going on. The consensus is I need someone to oversee the bigger picture. When you come to Monaco next week, I'll—"

"Excuse me," I interrupt. "Did you say next week?"

He dabs his mouth with a napkin. "Yes. Didn't Vaughn relay the message?"

"He mentioned a future date but nothing specific."

"Is there a problem?"

Other than my personal life in tatters? Bloody Vaughn and his distractedness. Now I hope he calls me so I can chew him out.

"No problems," I lie. "But I haven't had time to immerse myself in your company or the industry. PR doesn't happen overnight, and this is practically no notice. I just want to manage expectations. And you haven't asked about our terms."

"I'm sure they're reasonable," he says, pouring more wine into his glass before moving onto mine. I'm over my limit and feeling it, so I cover the glass with my hand. Maybe it's the lanterns hanging in the tree nearby or the glow of the half-moon, now high above us. The circle of skin where my wedding band sat for six years pops bright white against my tan. Few people would notice a ring of pale skin. Morgan catches it, however, and we study each other for a length of time that feels a lot longer than the eight seconds it actually is.

I had yanked the ring off before leaving the house tonight, one of those dark, depressing moments with too many questions and no answers. That simple act of removing what had symbolically bound Derek and I felt like a small reclamation of self. Staring at my ringless hand now, it all comes rushing back.

The unknown path my life is on.

Morgan clocks the shift in my body language and sets the bottle down. "Shall we go to my room and finish up the night?"

I blink, not sure I've heard him correctly. "Finish what?"

He tilts this head. "Isn't there one more step between you and me?"

I'm trying hard to keep a neutral expression stamped on my face, but wow. I'm naive about some things, clearly, but not innuendo. This guy is so used to women throwing themselves at him, he doesn't even have to try hard.

I gather my boozy thoughts, a harder-than-expected task. "Just to be clear, this meeting is purely business."

To my great horror, he chuckles. "Perhaps *I'm* not being clear. Did you bring a contract with you? There's a desk in my room and proper lighting. Better suited for me to review your terms, if that's important to you."

Oh. Shit.

Shitty shit shit shit.

The best thing, the only thing, is to pretend those words hadn't left my mouth. "I didn't bring a contract with me, but my assistant can email you first thing Monday."

Have I saved myself? I hope so. I feel my face cramping from the endless smile. Morgan appears unruffled, but in the small pause, I swear I see it: a flash of uncertainty materializing as one line on his otherwise smooth forehead. Or maybe I don't, because I'm tired and tipsy and while a blurred line is a dangerous thing, everything is kind of blurry right now. Before my sensibilities corrupt further, Dakota pops back around, mentioning it's last call; they're closing early tonight for a staff event. I'm surprised to notice we're the only ones left. Morgan asks if I'd like an espresso or aperitif. I'm not keen to lay awake all night replaying what just happened, so I say no and he settles the bill, offering to walk me out.

What a relief to stand. Back on solid ground after such a mortifying wobble on my part. We make our way to the valet area while Morgan chit-chats about LA traffic and weather. If he's trying to make this less painful for me, it's not working, but kudos to him for the attempt.

Back outside, the moon is white and clear in a blue-black sky. It's a few degrees chillier without the heat lamps, and I unpack the pashmina always stored in my bag for nighttime. Morgan offers to drape it around my shoulders and his hands touching my body sends a little charge shooting through me. He makes no move to step back when he finishes the task, and the combination of his body heat and my half-drunk state makes rational thought close to impossible. As I struggle for any conversation starter, a light breeze kicks up.

"Mmm." Morgan inhales deeply. "Night jasmine. So potent. Sensual, don't you think?"

I steal a glance at him. With hands in his pockets and an air of panache to his stance, I can see him on a prow of a boat, the wind in his hair, destination unknown. With that image, some vague, distant yearning rumbles in my belly.

"I've never heard it described that way."

The valet pulls up and Morgan shadows me, offering a hand to help me into the car. Surrounded by familiarity and the sad reality of the here and now, my compass resets. I can't jet off to Europe. I need to run the office and patch my life back together. Yes, Morgan is a great opportunity, but the timing sucks. Maybe one of our junior staff can step in.

"Thanks again for dinner," I say. "Timing wise—"

Just as I turn my head, Morgan leans in for the double kiss thing. Our mouths collide with one hundred percent contact. In shocked reaction his mouth inflames against mine. I can taste wine on his lips, and underneath that, his sweet, singular flavor of sin. It's seriously improper to stay glued to him, but tell that to the arrow of thrill rocketing through me.

Much to my embarrassment, it's him who breaks our kiss.

"I guess that's what you call perfect timing," he says, making light of it.

"Um…" My brain reels with all sorts of indecency. I was this close to open mouth territory. "What I meant to say is, I'm sure you're in discussion with a few firms, and—"

"I'm not talking to other firms," he interrupts, "and I'm not taking no for an answer, Mademoiselle Hillman."

He's practically in the car with me, mere inches all that separates us. Energy crackles like bolts of lightning.

This is where I say no. Don't call me, I'll…

"You can call me Vandana."

Right. So much for that.

"Very well, Vandana." He smiles and nods gallantly. "Enjoy the rest of your evening. I'll call you tomorrow to finalize."

The door closes with a powerful push of his arms. I start the car, beep once and watch the rearview mirror until Morgan disappears into the inky night. Cruising home along Ocean Avenue, I keep licking my lips, his taste still humming on them. My thumping heart refuses to quiet.

Morgan is danger, trouble with a capital T.

I feel it in my very soul.

What the hell am I getting myself into?

Chapter Five

In my freefall back to earth, I rush past stars and darkness and crash breathless from an annihilating orgasm. As my bedroom ceiling slowly comes back into focus, all my wicked fantasies of Morgan linger in the afterburn. The slow and pounding assault. His refusal to let me take the lead. Those lips feasting on mine. He feels so real, I half-expect to see him panting beside me. Instead, Derek's immaculate side of the bed sits empty, as it has been for too many months. A week ago, his arrival was the only thing on my mind.

How quickly things change.

Rolling off the wet spot, I ignore the guilt creeping into my afterglow and fumble for my phone on the bedside table. No text, no nothing from Morgan. Did I play it too cool last night? In the end I didn't say no, but I didn't say yes, either. Jesus. Vaughn's right. My head's not in the game. What kind of fool doesn't jump on a trip to Monaco?

No, I'm sorry, I really don't go for that sort of thing.

On top of it all, I inferred impropriety on his part! I managed to skate my way out of that, barely, and then…

If only that stupid kiss didn't happen.

You mean, if you didn't dry hump his mouth?

Yes, okay, maybe that.

The thing is, Morgan didn't get any less attractive throughout the evening. And if this morning is any indication, he's not easy to forget. Confident but not swaggering. Intelligent and intimidating. Immensely interesting.

He could still call. It's only 10:15.

I know things are bad when my inner voice takes over. Instead of succumbing to it and spinning endlessly in conjecture, I drag my still quaking booty into the shower. It's brunch day, and June and Flynn will be here at eleven. By 10:55, I'm showered and dressed, with the best of Trader Joe's ready-to-eat covering the kitchen island. Flynn arrives first at eleven on the nose. Punctual as a Swiss train, she's also reliably sensitive and caring.

I can forgive the patchouli.

"Hi, hi, hi!" she gushes, locking me in a bear hug before I have a chance to shut the door. As America's favorite self-help guru, Flynn is very touchy-feely, and she rocks me back and forth like she's comforting a devoted fan. "It's been a week and feels like forever. Everything okay?"

She ends the embrace and stands back, still holding onto my hands. Flynn's clever green eyes never miss a thing and under their scrutiny, my chin wobbles. I've never kept drastic news from either of my best friends for this long.

"Not really."

"Uh-oh," she says. "I *knew* something was up when you invited us here."

Our weekly brunches are ironclad, unless extenuating circum-stances crop up. Derek coming home last Saturday took me out of the mix, and they'd understood. But swapping the Beverly Hills hot spot we've been dying to get to for a gathering at my house is super suspect. I don't cook. I can boil an egg if need be, but why go to all that effort? My lack of culinary skills aside, Flynn and her uncanny internal radar pick up on the unusual silence. When he's not working, Derek is a homebody. The TV or Pandora, sometimes both, are on.

The pieces fall into place for her.

"It's Derek, right?" she asks, crestfallen. I nod, mute, and the tears I'm fighting against start to dribble down my cheeks. "Ah crap, bella. C'mere," she says, drawing me back into her arms.

I'm full-on bawling into Flynn's tumble of chestnut curls when June barges through the door. She's out of breath, perpetually late, but closer than family. At the sight of my teary face, she knows immediately. Her frosted blue eyes flash, then harden. Unlike her fellow British counterparts, June is not about the stiff upper lip. She wears her heart on her sleeve and is the most passionate and intense person I know. Do not mess with her or her peeps unless you want a serious arse kicking.

Kicking off her magenta stilettos, she swoops in to join our hug. "That fucking wanker," she scowls. "If he's broken your heart, I'm murdering him."

Sometimes all a girl needs are her best friends, a glass of wine, and an emotional breakdown. After my teary-eyed confessional, June uncorks a second bottle of Pinot Grigio and tops us all up. My impromptu smorgasbord is surprisingly ransacked, and Flynn sifts through the remaining tortilla chip shrapnel.

"I'm still in total shock mode," she admits. "Didn't you say you two were like, fucking all the time?"

I wipe my nose with a Kleenex, adding it to the crumpled pile beside me. "We were," I say cagily, aware I let them both believe things were better than they were. We're all guilty of keeping up appearances and I wasn't above a bit of boasting, especially in the early days. Back then, Derek and I were unstoppable when it came to sex. On my office desk. In the back seat of his souped-up Barracuda. I married him because he was the kind of guy who fingered me under my dress at the movies and went down on me in an airplane bathroom. Adventurous sex has always been my MO, and I considered my relationships successful with that box ticked. But Derek and I were mismatched on other fundamentals. I realized that a year into our marriage. And did nothing about it for all the wrong reasons.

"Have you discussed living arrangements?" June asks, settling back onto one of the kitchen stools. Shoes off, she barely 5'6, and her steady rotation of come-fuck-me heels, Marilyn Monroe curves bursting out of tight dresses, and bombshell beauty fools men into thinking she's a pushover. But beneath her platinum blonde waves lies a brilliant business mind. I can see it grinding away.

"No. And we need to. He's staying with a friend for now. A film guy." Flynn and June exchange pointed glances. "Not *that* guy," I add, although taking Derek's word at this point is probably not the smartest move.

"If you need to crash at my place," June offers, "it's not even a question."

"Same," Flynn pipes in. "Mi casa es su casa. Just like old times."

Their solidarity makes my heart swell, and it doesn't feel like fourteen years have passed since we were roomies at Stanford. With my flair for events, June's cooking skills, and Flynn's ability to talk anyone into anything, the parties at our Palo Alto house were legendary. We ruled the Stanford dating and entertainment scene. When we went out, we went out together, and other women would throw up their hands in surrender whenever our trio descended on a party. As on old boyfriend once joked, *With you three, all a man's gotta do is pick his poison.*

Back then, I was always the dumper, never the dumpee. Maybe that's why I feel strangely unhinged.

"And what about work?" June asks, with her usual one-track mind. There's a reason why she's a millionaire. "With Vaughn away, can you handle everything?"

I perk up, suddenly remembering. "Oh my god. Speaking of Vaughn, I forgot to tell you about last night."

When I'm done detailing the Morgan scenario, June is aghast. "He invited you to his room? That's so inappropriate."

"Right?" I reply, careful to match her tone. I kind of left out, by accident, the part about Morgan and me kissing. "Like it's normal to sign a contract in some stranger's bedroom."

Flynn, already on her phone, checks Morgan out online. "Ah, hello? You forgot to mention he's fucking *stunning.*" Her finger whips along the iPhone screen. "But what is up with his feed? Is this for real?"

"The cats?" I ask.

June peers over Flynn's shoulders and laughs. "Crikey. Okay, maybe you should have gone to his room. Kidding! Seriously though. Is this how Monégasques fill their days? Boats, beaches, and pussies?"

The Royal Morgan Yachts feed is exactly as June describes. Insane yachts. Sultry lagoon destinations with water the color of jade and sapphires. And photos of various cats. Yes, cats. It took me a long time to fall asleep last night, taking it all in. Being a cat lover is a surprisingly humane wrinkle in Morgan's prickly layers.

Flynn sets down her phone. "Bizzaro-land."

"Maybe it's some kind of code only yacht people understand," June offers, dragging a cracker through a smear of hummus.

I shrug. "Maybe he's just into cats."

"Makes sense. You are one fabulous pussy," June says, winking.

Flynn chuckles and hoists up her maxi dress to arrange herself cross-legged on the stool. A celebrity with an open-book policy when it comes to healing and overcoming trauma, she's surprisingly private about her own life. But she loves nothing more than hanging out and dishing about the men in our lives. "Okay. Now that we know he's basically, like, the tenth wonder of the world—"

"Eighth," June interrupts. "There's only seven right now."

"*Whatever.* This isn't Jeopardy." With a shake of her head, Flynn turns to me. "Aside from the creepy, hotel-room move, what's your gut telling you?"

I take my time answering, arranging my Kleenex wads into a triangle. "I don't know. It's a great opportunity but it feels ... a little rushed."

"Is it truly over with Derek?" June prods. "This isn't some midlife crisis, he-she-it exploring thing?"

"Even if it was, I'm not going back. Not after this."

June turns to Flynn, her sly smile broadening. "Then I say we put money down."

Flynn suppresses a laugh, but not fast enough. "I'm in for a hundred that she crumbles in the first week."

"Hey," I protest. "This is not Friday night at Stanford. He's a potential client."

"Right." June smirks because she can always read me like a book. "What's the longest you've ever held out?"

"I dunno. Three dates?"

"More like one," she corrects. "And this bastard is hot as stink." She guzzles the last of the wine and gives me her infamous know-it-all look over the top of her glass. "I know why you didn't say yes. You're worried you might bend your own rules."

My face reddens at the thought of my vibrator working overtime this morning. "First of all, I'm still married. And second, it's not even a done deal. Morgan hasn't signed anything."

"Didn't he say he wasn't taking no for an answer?" June reminds me, sounding gleeful that I'm in the hot seat for a change. I rode her ass relentlessly two years ago until she separated from her useless husband. The darling of the start-up world, she has a knack for finding the right companies at the right time and turning them into hot commodities. She also has a knack for dating losers.

"And technically, you're single," Flynn chimes in, always with the last word.

Just as I'm starting to question why I ever brought Morgan up, my phone starts to hum on the counter. Three sets of eyes pivot to the screen as Morgan's name scrolls along the top.

"Well, speak of the devil," June says.

"Answer it!" Flynn urges, her face animated as they hunker down on the stools with bright eyes. My girls, ready for gossip.

But am *I* ready?

Ghost fingers walk up my spine as I remember Morgan's hooded gaze after we kissed. The way he said *Vandana*, my name soaked with naughty suggestion. How driving home, my entire being felt like one giant erogenous zone.

Forget about all that. Prove to Vaughn you can do this. Prove it to yourself.

Bringing a finger to my lips I whisper, "I'll put him on speaker. But *no* talking."

Chapter Six

MORGAN

I'M LYING IN BED AT THE FAIRMONT, THE CALIFORNIA SUN BEAMING across my naked torso. My earbuds are in, I've dialed her number, and I find myself in the unfamiliar position of having to beg. My balls are swollen and close to bursting at the thought of hearing Mademoiselle Hillman's voice. I'm putting money on her not answering her phone, but she surprises me.

Like she did last night.

"Hello?"

"Good morning, Vandana. It's Morgan." So pretty, her name. Rolling on my tongue like velvety custard.

"How are you?" she asks.

"Very good. Just packing up. Enjoying the view from my suite."

The view across the room *is* impressive: the full and straining length of my cock in the mirror. I'm not usually one to watch myself in the act of self-love, but Vandana is the kind of woman to push a man beyond his comfort zone. All morning, I've dreamed of tongue-fucking her, her helpless body a melting puddle, all the neighbors knowing my name. Now that she's on the line, I start to stroke myself, imagining her generous mouth taking all of me.

"Where we ended last night," I continue. "I didn't want there to be any lingering confusion. I'm very interested in working together." I hope my sincerity rings true. It's not my best quality, and often in short supply.

"Yes, well, we're—I'm," she corrects to my amusement, "interested too."

"Fantastic. I don't suppose you're free for lunch today. I can sign whatever you need me to."

In the background, someone does a poor job of muting a whisper. "Unfortunately not," she says. "I'm busy today. But my assistant can draft the contract and send it so you have it first thing Monday morning, your time."

Dammit. Even while denying me she's smooth as butter. It fires me up so much, a warm ooze of pre-cum trickles out. "Do you need a deposit? I can have that wired over immediately."

She hesitates. "You should look over the contract first. We never discussed figures."

"Sure, send everything to my attention. My accounts person will review it. Schedule-wise, we need to be in Genoa on Friday. I'll arrange for my jet to pick you up Wednesday, for a Thursday morning arrival in Monaco. That gives you a day to overcome the jet lag."

Silence.

Usually I love it, crave it. Nothing but waves lapping on the side of my boat, land nowhere in sight. But Papa taught me to never allow the opportunity for a *no*. If money prevents her from coming to Monaco, I'll never forgive myself.

"It's all-expenses paid," I add. "My company will cover everything."

There it is again, another background whisper. A silent coaching committee?

"Can you give me until Monday to finalize a day and time?" she asks. "I need to sort out a few things on my end."

With her unequivocal *yes*, my cock spasms in glorious anticipation. I close my eyes and increase my tempo. "Let me know if I can do anything to speed things along."

My active imagination is a blessing and a curse, and the danger of jerking off on the phone is that I might momentarily drift off. Sure enough, visions of sweet Vandana spool through my mind and off I go, fantasizing about my hands fisted in her lustrous hair. Vandana heat-slicked and begging for mercy, her ripe, swelling body arching against mine. My dark, corrupted soul insatiable with need.

"Are you still there?" she asks.

My eyes flash open and an inarticulate gurgle spills out before I can stop it. "Yes, I'm here."

"It sounds like you're running."

I back off, biting my lip in agony. I'm so hard, it aches. "Ah … yes. No. Just heading outside for a walk."

Another silence. I've been involved in many awkward pauses, but none quite as embarrassing as this.

"I have to get going," she finally says. "But thank you for the follow-up. Travel back safely, and I'll make sure Timothy sends you everything by tomorrow."

"Very good," I manage. "Until next week."

I thumb the phone off, my cock pulsing angrily between my fingers. That was a close call. It's rare for me to feel anything this intense, but I sense the magnitude of my pending explosion in the way a jockey perched on his thoroughbred feels the trembling power between his legs. This runaway train is on the verge of veering out of control. The last thing I see in the mirror is a man holding on for dear life before my guttural howl shatters the silence and a million little Morgans spurt hot and furious onto my chest.

In the swirling aftermath, my brain is empty but screaming loud. With the room spinning and my heart pounding, the combined sensations are not unlike steering Papa's sailboat safely out of my first storm. That lurching moment when I rode the edge of danger and thrill and came out on the other side, intact.

Merde.

That was downright savage.

Fingers on autopilot, I gently milk out the remains and dab myself clean with the sheet. My eyelids drooping and heavy, I feel a monster slumber coming on. The best thing about owning a jet is the freedom to fly whenever I want. And I've got plenty of time with a late checkout. I drag the sheet over me, and a flash of red suddenly appears, crumpled and wrong, like my unprincipled behavior. Panties. The ones Dakota kept hunting around for late last night. She wasn't thrilled to get kicked out of my room, whining about not wanting to drive home so late. But I couldn't imagine waking up to all that metal on her face staring back at me. Or hearing another story about casting cattle calls and how demoralizing they are. And who has a rat as a pet? With a shudder, I fling her underwear toward the trash can across the room and count my blessings. What was I thinking? The clingy ones are always the worst.

Especially when they're stand-ins.

Vandana is a genuine star. The real goddamned deal. No woman has ever looked me in the eye and asked me what was in my heart. What makes me fucking tick as a man. It took me by surprise, and she had no clue my response was total shit. All I could think about were her curves under that deceptively simple dress. I know the only way to strip her bare will involve wrangling. And that's where the complexity comes in.

The challenge.

Vandana's going to make me work for it, of that I am sure. Her natural inclination is to resist. She's not used to be being tamed. She's an equal; she'll want to take charge.

Maybe I'll let her.

Nothing is sexier than ambition.

"Your drink, sir."

A gin and tonic lands with a slam on the table in front of me. I raise an eyebrow at Gabby, a former Miss Budapest, or so she claimed.

"Thank you," I say, regretting my decision to fuck her and glad I didn't risk putting my head between her muscled Hungarian thighs. Her flight-attendant professionalism is nowhere near the blatant fawning she displayed two weeks ago on my trip to Fort Lauderdale, and she marches back to the galley with her attitude and ample breasts. Beyond her, the captain and co-pilot are in the cockpit completing last-minute communications before we take off. They're my usual crew; only Gabby is a newcomer. I suppose she'll find a new crew if I don't fire her first. Sleeping with the hired help isn't recommended, but what else is there to do, bored and drunk on an eight-hour flight? Unfortunately, I wasn't wasted enough to block out her squealing. Good lord. With visions of a traumatized piglet running around in my head, it took forever to climax. My rebuff on this trip has stung her, but as the saying goes, once bitten, twice shy.

Calling me a dangerous beast earlier was a little over the top, and hypocritical, considering *she* stalked *me* in the airport terminal bathroom. I politely told her no, and then she accused me of being heartless, which is the furthest thing from the truth.

My heart beats ferociously.

It's like a shark, always moving, always on the lookout. The trouble is, I'm swimming in an ocean of sameness. I'm restless. Bored and endlessly seeking. It's useless to try and explain it to the likes of Gabby; there's no way she can grasp the inner workings of me. She sees what all of them see: money, yachts, my looks. A life of leisure. No effort. I need a woman who can match my drive, in and out of bed; a woman who adores and covets *me*, not all the exterior trappings. But the hunt for *the one* drags on longer than a snail trying to cross the Saharan sands.

What a surprise the lovely Vandana has turned out to be.

Tall, slender, and brilliant as well as ravishing, and unwilling to be pushed around.

I can't get her out of my mind.

I must thank Olivier, my right-hand man at Royal Morgan Yachts, for sending me on this mission despite my reluctance. I rarely take his advice, as it has often proven dubious, half-baked, or more beneficial to him than me. But this time he might finally be right.

And his ears must be burning because lo and behold, here he is calling. We're beyond the need for salutations, so I answer with what I know he wants to hear.

"All is well," I assure him.

"With your radio silence last night and delayed flight, I hoped that was the case," he grumbles. "There is a thing called texting. You might want to try it. Details, please."

Dear, dry, dull Olivier Lepage. Always cutting to the chase. And he thinks *I'm* a social outcast.

"She's clever, very spirited, and even more breathtaking in person."

"Did you behave yourself?" he asks warily.

"More or less."

"If she's still talking to you, we can consider it a success. Remember," he warns, "no funny business. She's married."

Gabby is at the front of the cabin, laughing too hard at one of the captain's jokes. Making a big production of forced gaiety. Poor thing. I'm nowhere near jealous.

"Remind me again who told you that?" I ask.

"It doesn't—"

"Answer the question."

He sucks hard on his cigarette. Smoking's a filthy habit he refuses to curtail, although his greater crime is wearing turtlenecks with plaid suits. "Her business partner," he says. "I initially suggested Vandana's husband join her on the trip. You know, sweeten the pot. Apparently, he travels for work all the time and Vaughn said he'd likely not come along. Which means that unless she's miraculously divorced him in the past week, hands off."

"I *said* all went fine." Olivier's getting under my skin too easily these days. "She's sending me the contract Sunday night. I'll forward it, and you need to wire funds first thing Monday morning."

"How much?" Olivier the bean counter asks.

"Who cares? Have the jet pick her up on Wednesday afternoon. Call Mirielle at The Bay and book the best suite for a week. And call Marco at the Meliá in Genoa. She needs a room there Friday through Sunday."

"The Bay? Why not the Hotel de Paris?"

"Because it'll be crawling with Russians, and The Bay has a more American feel. Just do as I say."

"Fine," he mutters, none too pleased with my dress-down. "On it."

I tip back my drink, draining half of it. "What's the latest on Prince Khaled?"

Olivier clears his throat. "I'm arranging a dinner for the two of you during the Monaco show. You're still one of three contenders."

"Along with Renan?"

Renan Sadik is another childhood friend. Or, should I say, was a friend before familial differences got in the way. Archenemy sounds a bit dramatic, but let's just say things aren't gentlemanly between us. He'll stop at nothing to snag what should be mine.

"If you keep it together," Olivier cautions, "you have a fighting chance."

"A chance?" I lash out. "Why the hell am I even doing the dance with the likes of Renan? My work is superior. The prince must see that."

"Maybe you can try not fucking everything that moves," Olivier flips back. "Bear some responsibility for your reputation. Your work still has you in the mix, but you've made plenty of enemies with your shenanigans. Khaled is ultra conservative. You know that. The rumors after the Cannes show didn't help."

"That woman was relentless," I argue, which isn't a great excuse but it's the only one I have. "If I didn't know any better, I might think someone paid her to chase me."

Olivier slurps his coffee—always dark roast, black, and cold. "That's your excuse?"

"Can I help it if they throw themselves at me?"

"Yes, well, I feel your pain, friend. Ladies clinging to your ankles, begging to be fucked. However do you cope?"

He stubs out his cigarette with aggressive, staccato taps. Olivier's never been thrilled to live in my shadow, and more often than not our communication resembles two stubborn teenagers squaring off against each other at boarding school. Once a decent yacht broker—his connections are why I hired him—I believe his loyalty to me is greater than his hatred, although lately the percentages seem to be skewing in favor of the latter. If anything, *he* needs to get laid. Except there isn't much demand on the Riviera for a squat, balding Harry Potter.

"Must you be so vulgar?" I ask.

"For once," he pleads, "can you not let your dick get in the way of things? Khaled doesn't want to be associated with any scandals or bad behavior. I told his people we're hiring the best PR money can buy, and that he'll be in good hands moving forward. Promise me you will not screw this up."

The Falcon's engines begin to whine and I quietly seethe. If he had sewed up this deal ahead of the Cannes show, we wouldn't be in this predicament.

"From someone who has failed to keep their own promises," I remind him, "asking me for one is absurd."

I hang up without saying goodbye. The plane pivots, heading for the runway. Gabby signals me that we're ready to take off with a smug smile, pleased to see me agitated.

Like she's not part of the problem.

While we taxi, I stare gloomily out the window. Heat floats up from the tarmac, turning the horizon into rippling abstraction. Soon we're soaring over the crystal-blue Pacific, banking right for the long journey east. As the jet crosses back over the spaghetti network of Los Angeles freeways, I think of Vandana and my frustration seeps away.

The married thing is a definite question mark in my mind. In my experience, married women don't take off wedding rings with the same intentions as men, so why was hers off last night? And she didn't play the married card when I invited her to my room. (Admittedly, that whole scene played out to perfection. Signing the contract was the last thing on my mind, and I deliberately constructed the inquiry to be misleading, giving myself an out, just in case. Far better for her to think *she* went there.)

I nestle into my seat, drag a blanket over me and dare to dream. Nothing is ever simple when it comes to women and me, and the next two weeks will be very, very interesting.

I'm so sorry, Olivier, but I can't promise you shit.

Chapter Seven

VANDANA

SO MUCH FOR A RELAXING SUNDAY.

I slept poorly, and a three-car pileup turns a no-brainer commute to Laguna Bach into gridlock. Inching along Pacific Coast Highway, multiple espressos churn in my empty stomach. Today isn't just another torturous visit with my mother. It's time to drop the Derek bomb. Mom would sooner feed the homeless than find a speck of compassion for the man she warned me not to marry, and I'm depressingly aware this news will be the bright spot of her day.

There's a reason why I rarely come home.

But I'm overdue, and my father wants a family photo for his campaign—he's the mayor of Laguna Beach and is running for a second term. The race is tight, and with a few weeks left to go, it's all about presenting the perfect picture. When Morgan asked if I cared what people thought about me, it hit too close to home. I care because in the Hillman universe, not caring lives in a galaxy, far, far away. To the public, we're a family of bright smiles and accomplishments. We aren't a dysfunctional mess including a cheating father, neurotic mother, and an only daughter raised to suck it up no matter what.

In my youth, bearing the weight of perfection was a challenge. As a teenager, I rebelled hard against it. Somewhere down the line it settled on my shoulders, and I've accepted it ever since.

Turning off the highway to wind up the hillside slope to Coronado Drive, I detour down a side street and park. With a view of Laguna Beach High's faded football bleachers, I let a rush of emotions flutter through me. On a windy, moonless night, Stryker Talone and I consummated our teenage lust underneath those bleachers, and shortly thereafter he broke my heart, just like my mother said he would. She tried valiantly to set me up with suitable boyfriends after the fact, but her match-making advice always fell on deaf ears. The only thing I could look forward to on a date night with one of her Republican groaners was drinking myself into a coma. So I blazed off to Stanford, a filly hell-bent on finding another wild cowboy. One pregnancy scare reined me in for a while, but after graduation, I moved back to LA and worked my way through the dating pool, eventually landing on my mother's worst nightmare—Derek, a man without a trust fund. She went ballistic. The only logical choice was to marry him.

Much has changed since then, but in a way, many things haven't.

I'm still fighting my mother.

Still attracted to maverick men.

And Morgan's catnip for my deprived soul. It's why his contract is still sitting with TQ. It's why TQ texts me again, the second time today.

TQ: Can I send?

VH: Still thinking about it. Gimme a couple hours

TQ: U gonna last that long???

When it comes to visiting my parents, two hours is the equivalent of a life sentence. TQ's been there, done the time. The sooner I get there, the sooner it's over with and minutes later, I pull into the secluded driveway of their mansion. After my dad, Lorne, sold his network of car dealerships and eased into politics, my mother spent buckets of money endlessly renovating. The front door is now an immense pivoting piece of metal and as I slide past the riveted mass, it reminds me of the gates of Alcatraz.

Ironic, since I already escaped once from this place.

"Hey," I call out from the foyer. "I'm here."

In the vaulted interior of their glass palace, my voice echoes back to me like I'm in a canyon. An impractical white sectional dominates the living room and looks like it's never been sat on.

"I'm on the deck," Mom yells, her voice traveling down from the top floor.

I trudge upstairs into the kitchen, a masterclass in beige minimalism. (Mom's idea of mixing it up is using colored napkins.) Helping myself to a glass of water, I take a deep breath and step outside. In a Gucci power suit and stilettos, Mom lounges on a sun chair enjoying her usual breakfast of caffeine, nicotine, and high-brow celebrity gossip. Not a hair is out of place on her blonde bob, a shellacked helmet that's harder to move than her emotions.

Without looking up from her *Vanity Fair* she asks, "How was the drive, darling?"

"A nightmare. There was an accident. Everyone stopped to rubberneck."

"Hmm," she says absently, taking a drag off her Marlboro. "Your father's still at the campaign office. I told him noon, but you know what he's like."

"I can't stay long today. Lots going on."

"You sound stressed. There's a bowl of Ativan in the kitchen if you need one."

"How many have you taken?"

Behind the bumblebee Prada shades, I can feel her death stare. "I don't see the purpose in making my life more difficult. You might want to consider doing the same."

Here we go. The first step in the downward spiral. I wander to the deck railing, taking in a million-dollar vista I can't even enjoy. Half a mile away, waves break in a frothy mess on the shoreline dotted with families and sun worshipers. We lived closer to the beach until I was ten. I splashed in the surf until dusk every night, coming home happy and red-faced, trailing sand into the house, which drove mom bananas. It feels like a lifetime ago, being that carefree.

"Derek too busy on his time off to join you today?" Mom throws out one of her classic passive-aggressive openers, the kind of needling comment I'd claim on a witness stand was the last straw.

"Actually…" I turn around to face her, arms crossed. "I have some bad news."

She lowers her sunglasses, eyes raking over my wrap dress. "Oh, no. Are you pregnant?"

"No. But if I was, thanks for the support."

"Darling," she sighs. "I told you motherhood is overrated. The last thing you need is to lose your figure at thirty-three. The boobs your father bought you will always hold up, but the rest of it? You can kiss it all goodbye. You'll never bounce back."

The only thing I wished I'd inherited from mom was her cleavage. Instead, I got her size ten feet, aversion to cilantro, and high metabolism. At sixteen, I barely had bumps on my chest and couldn't bear a life of inserts. Maybe it was shallow, but I felt deprived. Mom didn't help, always flaunting what she had in my face. When she found out dad and I had secretly scheduled the surgery, she'd been livid. She liked me unhappy.

"Is that your way of blaming me for the five pounds you can never lose?"

Her cigarette butt sizzles, extinguished in the coffee mug. "This news of yours must be bad given how snippy you're being. Everything okay at home?"

With that simple question, my throat closes in.

Do it fast. Like ripping off a band-aid.

"No, it's not. Derek and I are splitting up."

Mom stills. In the long, eerie gap, a squawking seagull passes over-head. "It's him, right?" she asks. "He had an affair?"

"Yeah."

She hurls the *Vanity Fair* halfway across the deck. "I knew it! I knew it all along. I told you that industry is drowning in loose morals," she gloats. "So self-important. All these little films they make. Let me guess, some floozy actress?"

"Not exactly."

"It's not someone you know, is it?"

I squirm, suddenly interested in my espadrilles. Mom's dim view of Hollywood is about to turn blacker than oil. "It's someone he works with. A grip." And because she has no idea what a grip is, she forces me to say the hardest thing I've ever had to say to her, and I've said plenty. "A guy who works on set."

"What?" She whips off her sunglasses with reckless rage. "A *man*?" When I don't deny it, her hand covers her mouth, like she might upchuck on the spot. "Sweet mother of Christ. I told you, you can *never* trust a Democrat."

"I'm a Democrat."

"You wouldn't be if you hadn't landed in his clutches. Oh, God. This is a disaster." She starts to massage her temples. "Your father's campaign is in the final stretch. This isn't the time for our daughter's husband to come out as a homosexual."

"Jesus, mom. My marriage is over. Can we talk about that?"

"You have to keep this under wraps," she says, furtively glancing around for no reason—both neighbors are foreign owners, never around. "Any whiff of a scandal, and these traitors fly it up the flagpole for the world to see. It's a tight race this year."

She's off in her world, one where the catty, coffee shop whispers can't ever be about her. My heart pounds so hard I'm afraid it might blow up. "I cannot believe this. You are incapable of being a mom for me. Not even just once."

I storm into the kitchen, trapped as she trails after me, stiletto heels cracking like machine gun fire on the imported tiles. The kitchen island becomes our battlefield and we each claim a stake on either side of the Corian. Her blue-eyed Valkyrie to my dark-eyed upstart.

"How dare you say that?" she accuses. "Who managed all the details of your wedding?"

"You managed them because you didn't want Derek's family involved."

"And it's a good thing I did," she huffs. "No daughter of mine was going to get married at an Elks Lodge in Minneapolis with a Costco wedding cake." She levels a warning finger at me, her version of a sword. "And don't tell me you wanted that, because I'll know you're lying."

I'm clutching the countertop so hard, my fingers turn white. Derek was everything my mother hated. He was a free spirit in G-Star Raw jeans who whisked her only daughter away from the joys of social climbing, ladies who lunch, and the kind of moneyed housewife ennui that requires pills before bedtime. She's right about my wedding, but damn if I'm giving this one to her. "Can't ever be less than perfect, right, mom?"

She takes that in, and all the bile that comes with it. In her spotless, shiny Poggenpohl kitchen, in a house where her maid works forty hours a week to make it look unlived in, in a life where every decision is calculated for optimum presentation, her feral daughter not understanding the very basics of her existence deflates her. "What have I said your whole life, Vandana? Image is everything. I'm sorry, but Derek was never your equal. I'm surprised he lasted this long."

"Gee, thanks. That makes me feel a whole lot better."

"Darling," she says, her voice a touch softer. "You've always been naive about men. Going after the bad boys, thinking they'll have your back. Stryker never committed despite you practically throwing yourself at his feet. And Derek. We both know you started to date him just to piss me off."

"Wow. I actually got an emotional reaction out of you?"

"Don't be petty," she says. "The facts are, you have a successful business and you make more money than him. You made his career by foisting him onto Stryker. Of course he's decided to shack up with…" She shivers, unable to say it. "He probably feels better about himself."

No matter how bulletproof I think I am, mom finds the cracks. In this case, her barrage is bang on and all the more hurtful because of it. But it's one thing to find fault in someone else's affairs, and entirely another not to address your own shortcomings.

"What's your suggestion?" I ask. "Find a new, rich husband? Live the life of leisure, à la you?"

Her flat-handed slap cracks loudly on the countertop and stings just like it used to on my bare bottom. "Vandana Georgia Hillman. I've tried and tried to help. Suggesting boyfriends. Setting you up with Vaughn. I advised you not to take Derek's last name, and thank god for that moment of clarity." Derek was pissed when I took Mom's advice, but in retrospect, Vandana Slaughter did not pair well with managing luxury brands. I don't know if he ever forgave me that one. "Despite our differences," she continues, "I've always admired your drive. That you're the breed of woman who likes to do it all. But everyone needs a backup plan. If you marry well, you're set."

Adrenaline coats my tongue and is the sour, metallic reminder of similar wars we've waged. I never met my grandmother Pauline, but she obviously had a sixth sense about her only child. It takes a certain kind of foresight to understand that by naming your daughter Ivy, she will sprawl unchecked and eventually strangle everything.

"If marrying well means turning into you, forget it. I'm not going to live a lie."

It's not the first time I've thrown it into her face. How she's over-looked my father's behavior all these years, I'll never understand. I promised myself never to have a marriage like theirs. A power union. Love is somewhere in the picture but never in the forefront.

Her mouth quivers with a response, but the familiar purr of dad's Mercedes pulling into the driveway signals a much-needed break in the drama.

Mom straightens her blazer. "At least I'm not a divorcée," she says. Then, with my new, horrifying life status confirmed, she swans past me, triumphant. "We'll see what your father has to say about all this."

Dad is a successful businessman turned politician, and it's not surprising he's gregarious, a good listener, and possesses the ability to see both sides of the story without committing to either. But after twenty minutes of gale-force winds from Hurricane Ivy and me contradicting everything she says, we're all exhausted. Dad suggests we take a time-out to snap the family photo, our brittle smiles passing as real. He encourages us to regroup over dinner, but I beg off, foolishly mentioning the trip to Monaco. Upon hearing that, Mom immediately shuts the idea down. I can't manage the narrative from overseas, she claims. If Derek struts around in public with his new lover, questions will fly fast and furious. Dad agrees, suggesting I stay put until the election is over. We dissolve into another heated argument and I flee their house, tears stinging in my eyes.

I roar down my childhood streets back to PCH, speeding all the way to Newport Beach. My lungs ache from all the shallow, anxious breathing. Goddamn my mother and her attempts to micromanage my life. And she wonders why I rebel. Try living life with endless meddling. It builds up into a familiar sensation bubbling just under my skin.

Fight or flight.

I tell Siri to dial TQ.

"Good afternoon," he chirps. "This is your captain speaking. Buckle up, you're in for the trip of a lifetime."

I burst out laughing. Thank god for small miracles like him. "How did you know?"

"Oh, honey," he consoles. "Your mother is the equivalent of a bad hair day, a migraine, and a flat tire in the middle of nowhere all rolled into one. If you don't want to run away screaming after seeing her, then something is very wrong in the world."

"You have no idea," I say, my voice a degree darker.

"Trust me, I do. I've met your mother."

"No surprise, she doesn't think Monaco is a good idea."

"Sunshine," he says, with softness. "Don't let her mind-meld you. What do *you* think?"

I think about my kiss with Morgan. How we lost our way for those few seconds, swallowed up in a purple twilight hush. The distinct revving of my libido that had been stuck in idle for way too long.

"I think Morgan and Monaco are the perfect distractions," I say, before realizing TQ has no clue I need a distraction.

"Ha!" he says, not picking up on my slip. "That is excellent news. And you can't change your mind because I just hit send."

Chapter Eight

TALK ABOUT A WHIRLWIND.

Stranger things have happened, but never this fast.

On Monday, Morgan signed the agreement and wired fifty thousand dollars. He sent travel details and our itinerary on Tuesday. Now it's Wednesday afternoon and the car Morgan ordered for me glides to a stop at Atlantic Aviation, a private jet facility south of LAX. I'll land in Nice tomorrow morning and helicopter to Monaco, then it's off to the races. We'll split our time between Monaco and Genoa, attending the final events of the European yacht show season. If I'm interested, Morgan suggested we take a day off in between to relax on his yacht.

I'm rereading that last sentence on my phone with an amused smile.

If I'm interested?

It would be like saying no to a prime seat at the Oscars.

"End of the line, Ms. Hillman," says Big Daddy. The silver-haired wildebeest of a limo driver talked nonstop on the drive here about a rock and roll band he used to drive for, and I did my best to feign interest. He cracks open his door and lays a big ole Southern smile on me. "I'll meet you inside with your luggage."

Flying private is a perk of having wealthy clients, and I've flown on

Cessnas before—short flights to Vegas or San Francisco for events. But Morgan's Falcon jet, sleek and sexy on the tarmac, is next level. It's big enough to whisk ten people across continents, but I'm the only passenger according to Carlie, the attendant checking my bags. She's breezy and comfortable with small talk, like every Aussie I meet.

"Fifteen minutes until departure," she says, handing my passport back. "Please have a seat in the lounge, and I'll escort you on when they're ready for you."

I take a seat by the window, away from a cluster of Asian businessmen halfway through a bottle of cognac and talk-shouting at each other. I try June again, hoping to catch her before I'm in the air. She's up to her eyeballs navigating a crucial tranche of financing for her latest start-up and tends to forget about the outside world when duty beckons. When she answers the phone, I hear it in her voice—the adrenaline she thrives on.

"Thank God you called," she says. "I'm so deep into this, I forget about time. How are you? And more importantly, how amazing do you look?"

I'm casual elegance today. Dark jeans, camisole with white blazer. Tod's. That I managed to squeeze in a mani-pedi, a blow-out and a massage before today was a miracle in scheduling. But worth it, according to my new target market. "My limo driver approves. 'Hot damn' were his exact words."

June laughs. In the background, the sound of her fingers flying over her laptop keyboard is like the chatter of monkeys on amphetamines. "Sorry I couldn't make an appearance last night," she says. "Flynn killed it?"

Putting together outfits is one of my specialties, but another opinion is crucial for big events. Flynn, with her impeccable critical eye, helped me sift through gowns, dresses, suits, and a lifetime's worth of accessories.

"She could be a stylist. So good with the details. Our resident hippie knows about more than beaded headbands and flip-flops."

"Speaking of hippies," June warns, "she brought up Burning Man again. For next year. Cleanse-our-souls type of dodginess."

I groan at the thought. "I don't think Burning Man and cleanse belong in the same sentence."

"Exactamundo," June agrees. "I don't know about you, but I *love* sucking on dusty dicks."

Flynn tirelessly campaigns for us to attend a burn, but as I've told her a million times, flying in on a private jet and five-star glamping still means sleeping in an RV. And don't get me started on sex with a filthy stranger, even if he owns half of Silicon Valley.

"Maybe you should show up in Monaco wearing a fishnet onesie with electrical tape covering your nipples," June adds, poking fun at Burner Girl regalia. "Give your lad a heart attack."

"I don't know. Morgan strikes me as the kind of guy who might embrace that kind of outfit."

June stops typing. Concern leaks into her voice. "On that note, I know you're smart, strong, and capable, all that crap... But do me a favor and keep your wits about you. He seems legit, but you don't really know him. And he sounds a little full of himself. Even on the phone, he was telling you what and where and how. Not asking you."

She has a point, although Morgan's arrogance is part of his allure ... among other things. While June and Flynn pissed themselves laughing over his audaciousness after their Saturday phone call listen-in, I didn't comment about what I think was going down. Didn't dare. During his many stretches away from home, Derek and I had enough phone sex for me to recognize the tight clip in Morgan's voice. The stop-and-start breathing. The other sounds. The idea of him getting off while talking to me? Huge, flipping turn-on.

Kind of dirty. My kind of dirty. Sorry, Burning Man.

"I have my own hotel rooms," I say, like this means something.

"You see where your mind automatically went?" June asks. "I'm just saying be careful. You're in a weakened state and we know what that means. I slept next door to you for four years and still can't look at ear plugs to this day without thinking of you."

"You're never going to let me live that down, are you?"

"Noise complaints aside, Flynn and I did learn the basics of giving head from you. The downside is, every time I see one of those jumbo carrots, I think dirty thoughts."

We both snicker at the memory, me in my Juicy Couture sweats, the consummate instructor giving up her trade secrets by demonstrating on various root vegetables.

"It's not like I'm going there to sleep with him," I say, telling her the same thing I've told myself for the past three days with varying degrees of success. Not sure if reverse manifestation works. Or if I want it to.

"I know you'll do the right thing. Just wanted to put it out there. Now, how are things playing out with Derek?" Never one to shy away from the tough questions, June is the ultimate mirror reflecting both the good and bad back to me. If she was a man, I would've married her.

"I don't think it's going to get ugly, but—"

"Bank on it getting ugly," she interrupts. "Especially with this kind of situation."

What she means is, Derek is facing a world that, on the surface, supports individual rights and freedoms, but can turn cruel very quickly. Something he and I haven't had time to discuss.

The fallout.

"Flynn's staying at the house while I'm gone," I say. "Just to keep an eye on things."

"Smart move," June replies. "Don't need a repeat of my misery."

Her ex, Russ, attempted to squirrel half of her belongings onto a moving truck one morning. The only saving grace was June returning back home to collect her forgotten phone. I don't think it will come to that with Derek, but while Flynn and I played stylist and starlet last night, I noticed the empty spaces in our walk-in closet. Derek had smuggled out one of our paintings and some clothes while I was at work yesterday. I didn't mind the art so much, but seeing the empty pegs where his beloved collection of baseball hats once hung was another story. For years, I'd griped how ugly they were, but he refused to get rid of them.

Just like I refused to take his last name.

Our of the corner of my eye, Carlie signals to me that it's time. I wave back and wrap it up with June. "Babes, I have to jet. Literally. Text you every day with updates."

She sighs. "I'm mad with jealousy. Good luck, be safe, and please enjoy yourself."

I hang up and follow Carlie onto the tarmac. A small riser of stairs leads me into the Falcon's interior, a sumptuous cocoon of high-gloss wood and buttery leather chairs with Royal Morgan Yachts monogrammed blankets draped over the armrests. The only unwelcoming thing is the pinched face of the flight attendant. Icily pretty and sturdy in a Russian gymnast way, she sports a run in her stocking and last year's trendy manicure.

"Good afternoon Ms. Hillman," she says, eyeing me with reserve. "I'm Gabby, your flight concierge. Can I offer you a beverage?"

"I'd love a Pellegrino," I reply, unsure why she radiates all the warmth of a slug. "And what the hell, a glass of champagne."

She nods coolly, heads into the galley. I settle into one of the plush cabin chairs, organizing my laptop and headphones for the flight. I need to text Morgan as well. He wants a courtesy message before departure.

I message him and he replies immediately.

MdRC: Thank you for the update. Enjoy the flight. I'll meet you at the hotel in Monaco and we'll go for lunch.

VH: Sounds great. Nice plane BTW.

MdRC: The bed is very comfortable. Memory foam. It's my favorite.

Not even in the air and we're on the discussion of beds? I haven't properly joined the mile-high club, and I can only imagine what's gone down on that mattress. I'm sure Gabby has a hundred stories, if I dare ask. She keeps glancing at me sideways with an intense glare of what I think might be jealousy. Mind you, she did take in my Cartier watch and Bulgari necklace with a thieving glance.

VH: I better run. The stewardess is giving me the stink eye.

MdRC: Who is it?

VH: A lovely young woman named Gabby.

A pause.

MdRC: I find her service lackluster. If you experience the same, please let me know.

As if her ears were burning, Gabby appears magically at my side. Setting down both drinks, she asks, "What takes you to Monaco?"

"I handle public relations for luxury brands. Mr. de Rohan-Chabot hired me."

Finally, a smile. "Ah, a work trip. Well, if you need anything, just let me know."

With a jaunty toss of her braid, she heads back to the galley, securing the space for takeoff. I'm not sure what to make of her hot and cold personality or her winged eyeliner. Everyone gripes about us millennials being flighty and unpredictable, but Gen Z are a different breed altogether. She reminds me of the hostess at the Fairmont the other night; she's got the same cool assessment. I chuckle to myself, tipping a healthy pour of Cristal down my throat. I wonder if Dakota's still dreaming about Morgan.

MdRC: I look forward to seeing you.

The bubbles catch in my throat, a shimmering rise of effervescence that takes my breath away. I had a fresh batch of second thoughts while waiting for the car service earlier. But now that the trip is happening, I'm excited. Morgan's a rising star. His personality needs finessing, but he has solid basics. He's the ultimate PR challenge. And yes, I'm looking forward to seeing him, too. As far as anything else goes—like handling myself around a client who is walking sex—I'm a pro. I know the deal.

Keep my head down, do the work.

Ten days in and out?

No biggie.

What can possibly go wrong?

Chapter Nine

THE HELICOPTER RIDE FROM THE NICE AIRPORT TAKES FIFTEEN minutes, long enough to be awed by the villas dotting the Cote D'Azur coastline, the craggy mountains, and the cobalt carpet of the Mediterranean stretching southward. But this. We bank left in a cloudless sky, and there she is—The Hope Diamond of countries. If Los Angeles is unforgiving high definition, Monaco is awash in seductive 35 mm glory. A glittering crescent of opportunity and ridiculous wealth.

As the pilot lowers onto the oceanside helipad, I get a birds-eye view of The Monte Carlo Bay Hotel. A sprawling property hugging the shoreline, it's a tranquil world of light pinks and tawny creams, with bright green pops of lush landscaping. After the pilot secures the rotors and helps me outside, I inhale deeply, the warm air fragrant with the sea. I didn't sleep, never can on planes, and even though it's bedtime back in LA, there's something about arriving in a foreign country that sweeps away all thoughts of rest.

I'm fully reenergized.

"Bonjour, Mademoiselle Hillman." An older bellman in a spotless uniform pushes his luggage cart forward and hands me an envelope with an easy smile. "Your room keys for your suite. Please see Mirielle at the front desk for a message."

"Thank you," I say. "I mean, merci."

After two failed attempts at Rosetta Stone Spanish, Derek suggested I try meat if I really wanted to butcher something. But my meager attempt at this man's local tongue nets me a bigger smile. I'll have to make more of an effort.

"Straight along the walkway, mademoiselle," he instructs, his finger indicating the route. "Your bags will be up shortly."

I wander alongside a massive pool, the ocean only a few yards away and a similar shade of ultramarine. The raised walkways and swaying palm trees on the pool deck remind me of The Venetian in Vegas, Derek's favorite getaway. He was never keen on the real Europe, and I never cared for fake gondoliers and gauche crowds. This is more my speed. Tasteful luxury with a dash of international flair, judging from the two hijab-wearing women sipping coffees under a sun umbrella and a group of Slavic-looking babes lounging poolside with matching Birkin bags and jeweled bracelets.

In the posh, inner sanctum of the hotel, a smartly put-together brunette introduces herself as Mireille, the hotel manager, and a friend of Morgan's. She insists I take her cell phone number and to call anytime, for anything. I thank her as I scan her digital business card, but after twelve hours of travel, the only thing on my mind is chilling in a hotel room.

Or should I say, my oasis of European glamour.

Seriously.

I don't care who you are, a fabulous hotel room is a fabulous hotel room. I drop my purse and head straight for the balcony overlooking the endless Mediterranean. The view deserves a classic Rose *Titanic* pose, and with arms stretched wide, I breathe in my new surroundings. Wow. Not even in Monaco proper for twenty minutes, and my mind is already made up. A-list, all the way.

I take a snap and send it to the girls with the caption, *Eat your hearts out!* Morgan texts me seconds later. He feels bad that he wasn't at the hotel to greet me when I arrived. He's putting out a last-minute fire but is on time to pick me up at 11:30. I text back:

VH: No rush. Just settling in. Love the hotel!

MdRC: Don't eat all the chocolate before lunch.

Chocolate?

What?

I step back into the room, not sure how I missed the enormous gift basket swathed in iridescent cellophane. Nestled inside is a bottle of Dom Perignon, cheese and crackers, and a box of truffles with a note-card tucked under a red ribbon. I crack open the box, and with a truffle in my mouth, read the note embossed with the Royal Morgan Yachts logo.

To our success, Morgan.

His handwriting reminds me of an EKG reading: confident lines swooping up and down like severe heart palpitations. I trace the ink with my finger, the fine linen of the stationery as luxurious as the dark cocoa melting in the heat of my mouth. An ocean breeze flutters the curtains, bringing with it a taste of salt and sun.

I smile a private smile.

Morgan sure knows how to make an impression.

A girl could get used to this.

At 11:25 I find Morgan in the lobby, rapid fire texting and oblivious to my approach.

"Good morning."

Startled, he lifts his head. His eyes scrape over me in a very obvious head to toe. I changed into a white and navy linen shift and tied my hair back into a chignon. With pearl earrings and a bright red handbag and heels, it's a classic look and one I wear well. The over-stuffed chair seems to trap him momentarily before he stands.

"Bonjour, welcome to Monaco. Everything went well with the flights?" His kisses land chaste and quick, unlike the hot and wine-soaked ones I've played over and over in my mind. But they still send a shiver up my spine.

"The trip was perfect, thank you. I felt like a movie star jetting to a premiere."

He's pretty much perfect, all symmetry and angles that defy the natural world. Windswept bangs Harry Styles no longer has the market cornered on. And he smells better than any man has a right to. I thought I was prepared to see him again, but he's too much hotness in one man. The best of Europe funnelled into a single human.

Sensory overload.

I smile, just to do something.

"My car's out front," he says. "Shall we?"

As we cross the lobby, I can feel the eyes of staff and hotel guests following us. This is Morgan's world and damn, he looks good in it. He's effortlessly stylish in dove-grey dress pants and a soft white dress shirt, links of rubies and diamonds glittering on the French cuffs. "We're doing lunch at the Yacht Club. I'll give you an overview of what to expect," Morgan says. "Bring you up to speed on the company, our expansion plans."

"That's a great idea. I should be familiar with you and your story."

In the hotel roundabout, Morgan pops open the passenger door of a gleaming, midnight blue vehicle. Flashy cars are a dime a dozen in LA, but the description of *car* doesn't do this thing justice. Part fantasy creature, part racing machine, part carbon fiber work of art, it's the stuff of Elon Musk's dreams. I slip into a divine sanctuary of fine leather and impossible curves. A cockpit, really.

"I've never seen one of these before," I say, admiring the craftsmanship.

He slides into the driver's seat and tugs on thin, leather driving gloves. "It's a Bugatti Chiron. Limited production. Less than three hundred in the world."

He fires up the engine, and a beastly growl vibrates into the warmth of my throat. June's the car nut—she can't get enough of all the power and design specs. What I like about cars has nothing to do with speed. This interior is tricky, though.

I wonder if he's done it in here.

"You okay with a bit of speed?" Morgan clocks the look on my face, the one that has no business being there, but interprets it differently.

No, I'm not fantasizing about you. Carry on.

"Go for it," I say.

Gunning the engine, he takes off with tires squealing. The Chiron blisters along every curve in the road, but I don't feel unsafe. He's a skilled driver. Aggressive, like June. We're heading west, judging from the towering peaks of rock to my right. Monaco is built into the mountainside, a city stacked like Asian rice paddies tiered with apartment towers instead of grain. I like how close the mountains are. Blush-pink rock I can almost reach out and touch.

"Have you lived in Monaco your whole life?" I ask.

"Close enough," he says. "I grew up outside of Nice but moved to Monaco when I started my company."

"You mentioned in LA you were born on a boat. That must have been quite the experience for your parents."

"My father is like me, a lover of the water. He insisted his son be born at sea."

"Your mother had no say?" I ask in disbelief.

He flashes a winning smile. "The de Rohan-Chabot men can be very persuasive. She loved the idea, in all honesty. Boats are in our blood."

A pang of jealousy hits me harder than expected. I can't compare myself in any way to my parents. The only shared thing in our blood is platelets.

But it reminds me to share a detail of my own.

"I probably should have mentioned this, but I've never set foot on a yacht before."

"Really?" He looks over in shock. "How do you feel about the ocean, boats in general?"

"I love the water. Don't spend nearly as much time at the beach as I used to though. Yachts … I don't know anyone who owns one, but to me, they seem to say adventure. The ability to get away from it all."

An amber traffic light switches to red and Morgan downshifts to stop. "I spend weeks at a time on the water. I couldn't imagine life any other way."

"Weeks? You don't get lonely by yourself?"

"I'm not always by myself."

Morgan turns to watch me quietly die of embarrassment in the passenger seat. Oh, god. Derek used to laugh at the stuff that flew out of my mouth. *Think before you talk, V*, he'd joke—sort of.

"That wasn't meant to be a personal question."

"I'm not married," he says, "if that's what you're wondering."

The flush on my cheeks deepens. "What's the name of your yacht?"

A smile curls up one side of his mouth. "*Liberté*. Freedom," he translates. "We can take her for a spin on Wednesday, if your husband won't mind you being on another man's boat."

Very sneaky. Or clever, depending on how you look at it. It's also an odd comment, given that I'm not wearing my wedding ring. What-ever the case, I'm not steering back into that conversational dead end. No way I'm letting Derek, in absentia, black cloud my trip. It's hard enough not thinking about us; how we were supposed to be here together. "I'd like that," I say. "Seems fitting to have my inaugural yacht voyage in Monaco."

The traffic light turns green and he wastes no time roaring fast and hard into fourth. We whiz past grand apartment towers and cute store-fronts, well-dressed citizens out for the day. Through every crack between buildings, blue snippets of the Mediterranean peek through. It's addictive, those slivers of ocean and…

Oh my.

My gaze travels back from the view outside his window and makes a quick pit stop. Morgan's dress pants are so fitted, they qualify as body-con. Between his legs, the fabric stretches tight over a sizeable mound.

Wish I could whip out my phone and take a photo.

TQ's just gonna have to take my word for it.

Monaco is one of those places with no shortage of beautiful sights.

Chapter Ten

CURBSIDE, THE MONACO YACHT CLUB IS UNASSUMING. MINIMALIST entrance, a major thoroughfare just outside, cars roaring past. Nothing to suggest yachts worth billions bob in the marina behind it. But inside, one of the world's most famous marine clubs lives up to its lofty reputation. Airy and chic with travertine floors so pristine, I almost check my shoes in case I carry in a speck of dirt.

Lunch is on the third floor, on a covered outdoor deck with a prime view of the harbor. A waiter leads us past tables full of middle-aged men, well-groomed with expensive watches. Their conversations are quiet with the hush of serious money. One or two nod in cool acknowledgment at Morgan; another gives the French version of a stink eye. None stand to shake hands or engage in pleasantries. They have no trouble staring at me though.

Our table is in a cozy corner, no one at the tables next to us. "Will you be dining from the buffet or á la carte?" our waiter inquires.

"Two buffets," says Morgan. "And a bottle of the Domaine Vacheron Sancerre." The waiter nods and pulls my chair out, but Morgan advises him we'll seat ourselves. "I want to show you something before we eat," he explains.

As he steers me to the deck railing, his hand on the small of my back feels territorial, a response to the hard, unfriendly looks following us.

"This is Port Hercules. Home base for the Monaco show," he says. "And that's one of my designs." He points to a dramatic, grey-hulled yacht in a nearby berth. "*Le Debut.*"

The sinuous lines are, for lack of a better word, sexy. She's also massive, dominating every other vessel, which is no small feat in a harbor filled with boats of staggering sizes.

"They're all gigantic," I marvel. "Is yours that big?"

At that exact moment, all other sounds cease, and my voice carries to the farthest reaches of the deck. A few titters rise from the lunch crowd and Morgan, mercifully, says nothing. But he's smiling a little as he draws my attention to a yacht of less exotic design.

"You see that one with the helicopter on the deck? That's eighty meters. Boat sizes are measured in meters," he explains. "Mine is fifty meters. A baby in comparison."

"What is that in feet?"

"It's about half the size of an American football field. Big enough, no?"

His smile opens up, a man comfortable enough in his own skin to drop penis jokes on day one. Technically I started it, and at this rate my foot will be firmly lodged down my throat by the end of the trip.

"Ma cheri! Long time no seeing."

The bemused twinkle in Morgan's eyes dims as he looks past me. I glance over my shoulder at the mini-me version of Gigi Hadid strutting over. She drapes a bracelet-laden, chummy arm around Morgan, and I can smell the Chanel No. 5 coming off her in waves. I own the same Hervé Léger bandage dress, although she fills it in with boobs two bra sizes bigger than mine. Like those who-wore-it-better pictures in *US Weekly,* I concede defeat.

By the slimmest margin.

Morgan ducks the woman's pouty-lipped kisses, simultaneously shrugging off her arm. "What are you doing here?"

"Same as you," she coos. "Living la dolce vita."

Morgan rolls his eyes. "Vandana, this is Perla. She's Monaco's local gossip queen."

Perla swats him with her YSL clutch. "I am not. I just know everyone and everythings."

"Nice to meet you," I say, certain her mane of blonde locks owes a debt to the extension industry.

Perla sizes me up in similar fashion. "You the American. The PR agent."

"Co-president of a PR company," I correct her, wondering if, and why, Morgan told her about me. I can't place her accent, but her look is Eastern Bloc bedazzled.

"We're about to have lunch, but Gregoire is over there if you're on your usual prowl." Morgan dismisses her, pointing at some indeterminate table across the deck.

"Prowl? I seem to recall I provide comfort?" Her heavily lined eyes land squarely on Morgan, and never have I seen such a reductive stare. There's obviously some history between them, judging from Morgan's sudden interest in the teak flooring. One down, Perla's gaze sharpens on me next. "I don't understand fascination with American women. So … in your face."

Wow. There's nothing I despise more than women who treat other women with disrespect. But if she's going for full bitch mode, challenge accepted. "Perhaps being capable, strong, and successful is out of your wheelhouse," I say, sweetly. "People fear what they can't understand."

I indulge in Perla's reassessment of me while Morgan's slack jaw does a bad job of hiding his surprise.

"I understand fine," she says with a flip of her hair. "You're on learning curve. Have fun. And don't be disappointed." She pats Morgan's shoulder consolingly. "Maybe hope she's miracle worker. Khaled commission is anyone's game."

She flounces off and loudly pronounces, *"Ciao, Gregoire,"* before plunking herself down in front of a bearded man nibbling on lobster.

Morgan, mouth in a joyless line, grumbles, "Let's get our lunch."

We wander through the buffet and, once our plates are filled, seat ourselves. The waiter materializes at the right time with San Pellegrino, a bottle of Sancerre, and two wineglasses. We silently watch him serve our water and wine and when he moves on, Morgan focuses on his food, stabbing at some asparagus. I chalk it up to Perla. She's a couple tables away, deep in a one-way conversation with Gregoire. But she can't resist scoping us out and has clearly gotten under Morgan's skin.

"Can you tell me more about the Khaled commission?" I ask, breaking the silence. "From what you've mentioned, it's a big deal and something I should focus on."

Morgan finishes his mouthful and wipes a napkin across his lips. "Prince Khaled is a Saudi prince. He's commissioning three boats. One for himself and one for each of his two sons. It's a spare-no-expense project. A designer's dream."

"Are you the recommend?"

"More or less."

"Which is it?" I press. "More or less?"

He clears his throat, takes a long sip of wine. "That's one of the reasons why I wanted you here. To help put me in the best position. To win the game."

"I'm not clear on how the process works. Wouldn't he make a decision based on your design ideas and cost, things like that?"

"Those are definitely factors," he answers cagily.

I set down my cutlery. I've done the dance with enough clients to know when someone's sidestepping. "I can't help you if you're not upfront with me, Morgan. This is a team effort. I'm only as good as the information I have."

Under the full weight of my gaze, he shifts in his chair. "I can design circles around anyone. On that basis alone, I should land the commission. The prince, however, is a private and conservative man. He isn't a fan of … excess."

Unconsciously, or maybe not, his eyes dart over to Perla.

"I see." I digest that and all its ramifications. "If I'm understanding you correctly, your personal life might be called into question?"

He scratches the back of his neck. "More or less."

Like monkeys on a tree.

"It's not like I've killed anyone," he adds, quick to run defense. "If anything, I'm being judged by jealousy."

I take in the surrounding tables again, this time with a different understanding. The cool stares. No one coming to say hello. As a hotshot designer, Morgan should be the talk of the town. Instead, he's a pariah who slayed the wrong conquests and is now paying the price.

"There's no judgment here," I assure him. "What you do with your personal life isn't my business. But when it comes to managing your story, in the public's eye, it's impossible to separate the man from the business. Keep that in mind."

"Right," he says, flatly. "The public."

We reach for our wineglasses at the same time. I sip mine, let the air settle without looking at him. But the longer we say nothing, the harder it is to know what to say.

Out of the blue he leans across the table. "Perla," he says, in a quiet voice. "It was nothing."

"Like I said, it's—"

"I know it's none of your business." He drains his wine, and the glass lands hard back on the table. "I just wanted you to know."

"Okay."

What else can I say to a man explaining away his sexual history? Although it makes me wonder. One hundred percent he's a player, but he doesn't wear it like one might expect. Sure, the clothes, the car. I know all about how to look successful. It's easy to present a facade if no one ever sees behind it. There's something else with him, though. It all goes back to his eyes. That restlessness.

Unfulfilled.

Seeking.

All that swirling burnt caramel, staring right into my soul.

"Our focus should be on what we can spin into an advantage," I say diplomatically. "Fill me in on your expansion plans, the award, Khaled." I reach into my handbag for my iPad. "Tell me what to expect. All of it."

Chapter Eleven

THE UNGODLY HOUR OF SEVEN A.M. IS NEW TO ME, BUT AFTER PASSING out early last night and sleeping hard, I'm rested and ready. I think. Yesterday's lunch was quite the exposé session. Morgan's ambitious, with plans to expand his design services to include homes and private jets. He's one of a handful of designers under age thirty-five who are up for a prestigious award at the Genoa yacht show. He also wants Khaled's deal badly. It would be game changing, a career break-through. After surfing on my iPad last night and scoping out the other two designers he said are in contention, it's clear to me that his work is head and shoulders above both. The commission should be his for the taking. But he's obviously docked in a few too many ports and ruffled some feathers. Like most industries, the yacht business is small once you get inside it. Morgan makes no apologies for who he is—and on the surface, I admire that. When it comes to PR though, being the Larry Flynt of the yacht world is problematic.

I have my work cut out for me.

On the drive to Genoa today, I plan to dive deeper into strategy. Morgan's picking me up at eight, so I order a cappuccino and croissant —when in Rome and all that—jump into the shower, and catch up with TQ via Facetime, applying makeup as we talk.

"Twenty euros for a coffee and pastry?" TQ's shocked when he hears the room service rates. "I hope that comes with a lap dance."

"Welcome to Monaco," I say.

"Yeah, yeah. I'm in my jammies eating yesterday's chow mein, watching *Dancing with the Stars* reruns. *Trés d*epressing." He holds up two chopsticks with limp noodles dangling off the ends, and I notice his glitter eyeshadow is smudged from a night of clubbing.

I flick on another coat of mascara. "What happened to that guy you were seeing?"

"What happens to any of them? One new twink on the block, and off they go."

"You'll be happy to know I did your recon."

He gasps. "Already? Did you get a photo?"

"Just a visual."

"And?"

"Sorry to be the bearer of bad news. Full package."

"Fuck!" he yells. In a miserable voice he adds, "I hate you. I hate you and Vaughn, leaving me alone to wither and die in LA."

"That reminds me. Have you heard from Vaughn? I emailed him on Monday about this whole deal and not a peep. He threatened to be in touch every day."

"Nope," TQ says, shoveling more noodles into his mouth, apparently stress eating after my news. "I hope he's not lion carnage somewhere."

"Don't say that. I'm concerned."

"Maybe he's actually enjoying himself."

I make a cringey face. "Don't tell him this, but I never even considered that."

"Of course you didn't, it's Vaughn. Work is the only thing he enjoys." He chuckles morbidly. "By the way, your bathroom is making me cry. It's bigger—"

"Bonjour," a muted voice calls out from the door of the suite. "Service de chambre."

I pause mid-bronzer application. "Can you hold on a sec? Room service is here."

"Eat your gold-filled croissant and we'll talk later," he mutters. "I need to go to bed and lament what's become of my life."

We say our goodbyes and I approach the door, tightening the towel around me. After a creepy experience in Vegas once, I don't let strangers in my room anymore. "Hello. Bonjour," I say, raising my voice to be heard through the door. "Do I need to sign anything, or can you leave the tray outside?"

"Nothing to sign, madame," the attendant replies. "Everything is paid for. Au revoir."

I wait a few minutes, then open the door. Wrapped in a towel, it's sufficient coverage for a quick in and out. But as I reach down for breakfast, the phone spills out of my hand, slick from my body lotion. It bounces off the tray and lands on the other side of the hallway. In my knee-jerk reaction to rescue it, I rush forward, both hands reaching for my lifeline.

After that, it all moves in slow-motion.

The towel snags on the European-style hook door handle. Off balance, I stumble over the tray. The towel slips off inside the suite and *whoosh,* the pneumatic door slams shut.

In a frozen, deer-in-headlights moment, my lungs close in. Blood stops pumping. Sounds disappear. Funny how quiet a hotel hallway is when you're alone in it.

Wearing nothing but a thong.

Oh, God.

I rattle the door handle up and down. Shoulder-bump it, a sick sense of completion settling on my skin.

It's locked.

"Shit!" I hiss under my breath. "Shitty shit shit shit!"

Fighting the urge to cry, I snatch my phone off the floor. Damn thing. Fifteen minutes until Morgan arrives. How do I get a new room key up here?

Think, Vandana. Think.

The maids! Maybe they're at work already. Eyes peeled, I creep down the hall to the service door. Locked. Not a peep. Damn the French and their normal work hours.

Now what?

I gnaw on my lip, mind flipping through increasingly dreadful solutions. I cannot go downstairs. In no world will Vandana Hillman strut through a Monaco hotel lobby in her underwear. Then it dawns on me. Mirielle. The manager. I put her number in my phone. It's early, but if anything qualifies as an emergency…

I count the rings.

Please answer.

"Bonjour."

"Bonjour, Mirielle," I say, gushing with relief. "I'm sorry to bother you so early. It's Vandana Hillman. We met yesterday."

"Ah, oui. I'm at the hotel. Everything okay?"

I explain the situation, minus me in my underwear. She tells me a bellman will be up shortly.

"Actually," I say, "Can you bring it? I—"

I hear a loud crash, and someone swears. "Pardonne-moi, Mademoiselle Hillman," Mirielle says. "We have a situation here. Five minutes please, for the card."

"No, wait—"

But she's gone.

And I'm right back where I started—in need of cover. But where? My brain hurts with all this desperate thinking before it finally latches onto a solution. Near the elevators is a picture window overlooking the hotel entrance. Sheer curtains hang on either side. I sprint over, praying none of the people I ran into on this floor yesterday are early risers.

The sheers are just that, skimpy and translucent, but better than nothing. Draping fabric around me, I think this is not how Karl Lagerfeld got his start. One day, maybe, I'll look back at this and laugh. Right now, the longest ten minutes of my life comes and goes and still nothing. I text Morgan, telling him I might be a few minutes late. He doesn't reply. Hopefully, he's stuck in traffic. Or…

One of the elevators begins to hum and comes to a stop on my floor.

The doors slide open.

Great. Just my luck.

Morgan jerks to a halt, eyes ballooning at the sight of me. Between him and a full view of my womanhood is three square inches of fabric and one sheer curtain. Whatever shade of red my face is, I'm sure there's a tomato out there that will claim me as family.

Of all things, he starts laughing. "What are you doing?"

"Don't look," I plead, pulling one arm tighter over my boobs.

"It's kind of hard *not* to look."

"Can you turn around, please? I locked myself out by accident," I explain. "I'm waiting for a key."

"I know," he says, facing the other way. "I ran into Mirielle in the lobby. She asked me to bring it up."

"You have it? Oh, thank god. Can you give it to me? Without turning around. My room is at the end of the hall. I'll be quick. I'm mostly packed."

"No, no, no," he insists. "Wait." In one smooth tug, he untucks his shirt from his dress pants. His elbows flare out as he unbuttons it, and he hands it to me over his shoulder. "Put this on first."

The functioning universe, the one where I'm supposed to take his shirt and put it on, disappears. I'm now in the alternate universe, the one where I forget I'm nearly naked in a public place and all I can do is stare.

His body.

Wow. Just wow.

Not just fit, he's astonishingly fit.

No gym creates muscles like that. Tanned and rippled, his strength comes from hauling anchors off of seabeds and piling heavy chain link neatly in a circle. His powerful arms can control a rogue mast in gale force winds. I don't know if he does any of these things, but he isn't sculpted by anything done on land. His is a body chiseled by the sea.

"Are you going to take it?" he asks, shaking the shirt.

My attention snaps back. "Uh, yeah, thanks."

Warm from his body heat, the brushed cotton drapes on my skin like a layer of gossamer. It smells delicious. My trembling fingers fumble with the pearlescent buttons, like I've never buttoned a shirt before in my life. When what's left of my dignity is covered, I tell him I'm done.

He turns around, plunging me back into the alternate universe, the one where my fantasies are not only alive and well, but raging. As my mother would say, sweet mother of Christ. How is it possible for one man to be so genetically blessed? Hard obliques carve into a slim waist. Two copper nipples stand at attention from the sudden shock of AC. The only hair on his ripped body is a trim line of dark blond fuzz disappearing under an Hermès belt buckle.

Handing over the key card, he watches me watch him with a bemused expression. He's enjoying this far more than I'd like him to be. "What happened?" he asks.

"I was trying to…" My face flushes with deep embarrassment. "Um, never mind."

I brush past him and can feel his eyes on me all the way down the hall. The key card of course is fiddly, denying me twice but finally the lock clicks open.

"I'll be right back," I say.

Once I'm inside, my heart rate dips but the fog of embarrassment doesn't dissipate as quickly. Never again will I multitask wrapped only in a towel. And I need a minute to digest what I just saw. Oh my god, he is hot, hot, hot. Smooth and muscled and so cavalier about it. Maybe it's a French thing, being comfortable with nudity. Or, as I strip out of the warm finery of his shirt and into my Lanvin dress, maybe it's a Morgan thing.

Whatever.

I'll survive this.

I touch up my hair and with my game face back on, open the door.

I guess it's not enough that he's hypnotically handsome and built for serious debauchery. Why not be as cool as James Dean too? Morgan leans against the opposite wall, arms crossed, prominent biceps flexed. He gazes at me nonchalantly, just another shirtless hunk loitering in the hallway of a five-star hotel. His belt buckle is awfully hard not to look at.

I hand his shirt off, sad to see it go. "Thanks for the donation. I'll be down in fifteen?"

"Don't forget this room is booked until the following Sunday," he says. "Just pack what you need for Genoa."

"Right. Thanks for the reminder."

He buttons himself up like it's no biggie, dressing in front of a woman he barely knows. Sapphire *M* cufflinks sparkle as he adjusts them, and he's unafraid not only to match my stare but also make me feel naked all over again. "No offense to your dress," he says, "but you look better in my shirt."

His daredevil wink is pure scamp and before he decides to unzip his pants and tuck his shirt back in, I mumble something incoherent and escape back into my room.

Falling back against the closed door, I drop my head in my hands and laugh.

Jesus.

What a way to kick off the morning.

Chapter Twelve

MORGAN

I DUCK OUT OF THE MEN'S ROOM AND SHE'S THERE, SCANNING THE lobby for me. A geometry lesson in proportioned curves. Hair down and cascading onto the swell of her breasts that took me over the finish line moments ago. Blood rages hot through my veins and I run both hands over my hair, as if that might contain my hammering heart.

"Sorry to keep you waiting." I reach for the handle of her suitcase. "Is this all your luggage?"

"I downsized for the four days," she replies. Upon closer inspection of my face, her expressive eyebrows knit together. "Are you okay? You look flushed."

"Ah. It's warm in here, no?"

Her head tilts, unsure if I'm joking. The air conditioner is blasting full tilt and granted, I've told better lies. But how can a man think straight after witnessing Vandana in a thong? I had to brace myself with one arm in the bathroom stall, my orgasm so damaging, the poor fellow who walked in to use the urinal must've thought an animal was dying. And now here I am, forced to play it cool, my cock half-stiff and ready for more. Hats off to her. Not a stitch of self-consciousness.

Not for someone who was tangled in hotel curtains minutes ago.

"How long is the drive to Genoa?" she asks, matching my stride across the lobby.

"Two and a half to three hours, depending on traffic."

Outside, I pop the trunk to my Bentley Continental, adding her luggage in with mine. Vandana admires the car's glacier-blue finish. "Great color. Custom?"

"How did you know?" I ask.

"One of my best friends in LA is a car nut. We test drove everything before she bought her Aston Martin. I know way more than I should. She was very jealous when I told her about my ride in your Chiron."

A bubbly sensation fills my chest. She's talking to her friends. About me. What else did she say? "Before we go, I need to swing past my apartment. A package I was waiting for just arrived."

"That's fine," she says. "I don't mind another tour."

Like everything in Monaco, my apartment is close by, but I drive slower than usual, preoccupied with the floral undertones of her perfume. Preoccupied with the image of her ass swaying underneath my shirt. She is the most edible fucking woman I've ever met. I need a taste of her sinful, luscious gateau. Jerking off can't sustain me much longer. How and when is all I can think about, and I will beg for it if I have to.

Like she's reading my mind, I feel her bottomless brown eyes assessing me, unnerving me enough to second-guess.

Fuck. Did I zip up properly?

"Sorry to intrude," she says. Her hand comes toward me and plucks a long, white hair from my black Thom Browne shirt. "I can't let a client be seen with hair on his shirt."

"That's a donation from Asterix. Cat hair," I explain.

She cracks the window and lets the hair flutter away onto Boulevard des Moulins. "You have a cat."

"Are you a cat person?"

"I am, although my lifestyle isn't great for pets. How do you balance yours with a cat, given you spend so much time on your yacht?"

"They always come with me."

"They?" She glances at me. "How many do you have?"

"Five."

I brace myself for the usual commentary, something along the lines of *What normal man owns five cats?* Like it's somehow a personality defect to surround myself with unconditional love. Truthfully, I'll take my cats on board with me sooner than I would most women. I often prefer to be alone. It's easier. Always has been.

Instead of going down the predictable line of questioning, Vandana just smiles the way one does when privy to an inside joke. "Why did you name your cat after a punctuation mark?"

"It's Aster*ix,*" I clarify. "He was a character in a comic book series of the same name."

"I've never heard of it."

"It was popular in Europe. It's set in the era of Julius Caesar's reign," I explain. "A group of villagers living in coastal France who drink a special potion for powers to avoid being conquered by Caesar."

She laughs. "That's a comic? It doesn't sound funny in the slightest."

"They are. Far cleverer than your Archie and Veronica."

"I don't know if that's the greatest comparison," she admits. "I always felt the competition between Betty and Veronica wasn't a healthy example for women."

"Archie was a fool for not marrying Veronica," I say. "Betty was a bit of a doormat."

She swivels to face me. "Ouch."

I'm careful not to ogle at the dress hem riding up her buttery thighs. The sight of all that skin sends me spinning like a satellite kicked out of orbit. It took all my restraint not to shove her up against the door of her room and plunder her right there.

"I know what you're thinking about," she warns, catching me when I do in fact, ogle. She primly tugs the hem lower.

"Can you blame me?"

"Do me a favor and forget about what you saw, okay?"

"And how do you propose I do that?" I ask.

Those lush lips of hers press together in a moment of strategic thought-gathering. "I'm sure it's within your power," she says. "And besides, I saw you half-naked, so … we're sort of even."

"Have you already forgotten?"

It's a throwaway question, one I know the answer to. In the hotel hallway, I tracked her eyes all the way down to my belt buckle. But I don't mind a bit of cat and mouse. Especially when I'm the cat.

She gives me a long look. "In America, we have this saying—quit while you're ahead."

I try my best not to smile. Vandana attempting to command the situation is admirable and unnecessary. The morning has already exceeded my expectations. The boat show season is a time of high stress. To feel relaxed, buoyant even, is highly unusual. But as I veer onto Avenue de Costa and catch a glimpse of the crowd on the Casa del Caffe patio, my mood slips a notch. Every morning, Olivier pounds back espressos at an alarming rate at this neighborhood haunt. Very strange not to see him here. I texted him earlier to see if he could grab the package for me, but he never responded. Unusual, since we're both making the trek to Genoa today.

I'm still mulling over his recent absentee behavior when I pull into my apartment roundabout.

"This is where you live?" Vandana cranes her head for a better look at the dramatic white tower that licks the sky. In a municipality where everyone jockeys to outdo each other, Le Simona apartments are a definite statement piece.

"Yes," I say. "I'll only be a minute."

Leaving the engine running, I dash into the lobby. Ricardo, the volatile Cuban concierge, argues with one of the cleaners again. He's a passionate fellow, one of those old-school fascists who believes revolution is romantic and dirt is unbecoming, and takes an autocratic tone with just about everyone.

"Monsieur de-Rohan Chabot," he says, relieved to see someone who doesn't need reprimanding. "Un moment."

He limps back into his booth to fetch my delivery. Depending on his mood, the story behind the limp involves fighting insurgents or a nasty fall while attempting to tango. Either way, I appreciate a good storyteller. It's a skill I don't have. As a child, I preferred drawing or building to speaking.

Olivier is the people person of the company. Or so he claims. Waiting for Ricardo, I slide my phone out of my pocket and try him one more time.

"Hi," he says, coughing loudly.

"Good morning. Are you on the road?"

"No. I've come down with a fever and hanging back. But the team has everything under control."

"What?" I ask, more worried than before. "This is crunch time."

"I'm doing okay, thanks for asking."

Here we go. Always the drama queen, Olivier. "I'm not suggesting you're lying, but—"

"I can still handle things from here," he interrupts.

This is not the plan, but I know better than to argue with him when he's in a mood. Ricardo hands me a FedEx envelope from across the concierge desk. I mouth *merci* in return. "Any updates?" I ask Olivier.

"Not yet. How's it going with her?" he deflects. "Does she have a handle on things?"

From the lobby, I can see Vandana and admittedly, no one has ever looked so good in my Bentley. Leave it to her to add a ray of splendor to a pile of sheet metal. "It's going great. She knows what she's doing."

He sucks hard on a cigarette. "And you're behaving?"

"Yes," I say, annoyed he's asking. Annoyed he knows me well enough that he needs to ask. That scene in Cannes was absolutely ghastly. I shouldn't have fucked that woman, at least not in the coat room. But everywhere I went, there she was—breasts bulging, leering smile. Sometimes you have to do what you have to do to get rid of them. Then I find out she's the wife of some distant business associate of Khaled. In hindsight, it all feels rather suspect. My capabilities are well honed, but she moaned far too loud, as if she wanted someone to find us.

"Speaking of behaving," I say. "You not coming to Genoa. Does that have anything to do with your debts?"

After a long silence Olivier asks, "Excuse me?"

"You heard me."

"What, are you spying on me now?"

"Don't be a child," I grumble. "I suspected. Will your piece of the Khaled deal, *if* we land it, cover you this time?"

Part of me wants to cover Olivier like I have in the past. The trouble is, he hasn't learned. Last month I intercepted a phone call meant for him and I recognized the ominous Russian accent. Had to deal with it a few times myself. I offered Olivier a piece of the Khaled commission for this very reason. He's close with one of the prince's handlers (also a secret gambling addict) and paved the way for me to be a frontrunner for the commission. But the process seems to have stalled out somewhere. While my extracurricular activities may be partially to blame, my instinct tells me something's up.

"And if it doesn't?" Olivier asks harshly. "Am I fired? Is that what this is all about?"

A rush of indignation flares through me. If he was in front of me, I'd slap the glasses right off his curdled nose. "It's my company. I'll hire or fire whoever I want. You included."

"I've never done you wrong. Not once," he snaps back. "I've cleaned up countless messes of yours, and as far as my messes go, I've paid you back. Every cent." He bleats a grim laugh. "Your newly hired set of tits has no idea what loyalty means. Remember that."

He hangs up abruptly, leaving guilt bubbling under my skin. Threatening to fire Olivier was a bullying gesture. He's as devoted as they come. But the stress of debt can eat away at one's soul and spur bad decisions.

One can never trust a gambler.

This black cloud hangs over me when I join Vandana back in the car.

"Everything all right?" she asks, immediately sensing it's not.

I place the FedEx envelope on the back seat. "Just work and such," I say. "Never a dull moment."

"I love your building," she says as I ease back into traffic. "It reminds me of Gaudí."

Her insight softens the irritation sailing through me. Most women wouldn't know Gaudí from Gucci. Every passing minute she becomes more intriguing. "If Gaudí were purely a modernist," I say, with the slightest correction. "In my opinion, he transcends categorization. A true design nihilist."

"Meaning he rejected all design principles or deemed them meaningless?"

I glance at her with frank admiration. "Precisely."

"Do you consider yourself a design nihilist, nautically speaking?" she asks.

"In spirit," I reply. "In practice, there's only so much latitude you can take in yacht design. A ship is ruled by the laws of water, and the laws are stringent. But I do my best to push the limitations."

"It sounds like that's part of the challenge for you. Testing the rules."

Oh, how right she is. Rules are meant to be tested, just like boats and people. And the breaking points of all three can tell you a lot. I'm so curious what hers are. The pearls, I suspect, are a puritanical front. Run-of-the-mill missionary is a waste with that body. A genuine travesty.

"I'm all about pushing the envelope, no?" I say, and perhaps I reveal too much of my true inner self because she lapses into silence. We wind up the mountainside and out of the principality, toward the A8 motorway. In a few minutes we'll cross into Italy. The sky is brilliant today, not a single cloud. More yachts than usual dot the Mediterranean, many of them here for the upcoming show. Vandana takes in the view, and I sneak a look at her creamy thighs pressed tightly together.

It's like a baby's ass, that skin.

How to win her over?

The bigger question is, do I risk it?

My well of flaws runs deep, to the point that I question if there's much hope of a turnaround. But as the saying goes, every cloud has a silver lining. Vandana's curves and astute mind are a riveting combination I haven't had to contend with in a long time. Maybe reformation has its perks. It seems to work for all those born-again Christians.

First things first, Morgan.

Right. No need to go overboard on day one.

Fuck Vandana senseless, get that shit out of my system.

Clear the pipes. Clear the head.

After that, I'll see where I'm at.

Chapter Thirteen

VANDANA

GENOA'S REPUTATION ISN'T AS GLOSSY AS THE LIKES OF ROME OR Venice and attracts fewer tourists. But it's a proud maritime city, Morgan explains, with deep roots stretching back to the 11th century when it established itself as the dominant naval and economic center of Europe. Hurtling along the autostrada, my first impression of the city is authenticity. Modest homes and apartment buildings line the hillsides while massive shipyards pepper the waterfront. Unlike the one-percent fairy tale of Monaco, Genoa is real Europe.

Morgan alludes to this as we exit the freeway and wind though the urban crush. "Most of the superyacht designers only do the Cannes and Monaco circuit and those shows are relatively new. When my father started in the industry, superyachts didn't exist. Not on the scale you see today. The Genoa show started in the sixties and caters to a wide range of clientele, not just billionaires. My father always came to this show and I tagged along as a teenager."

Very interesting.

Morgan hasn't mentioned his father until now, nothing at all about his family or their means. Alix de Rohan-Chabot comes from serious aristocratic wealth and although my nosing around online didn't uncover specific amounts, stinking rich is the general gist. Alix never had to lift a finger or hold a job. Morgan, I imagine, was born into a similar situation. But like his son, Alix followed his passion, building and designing boats up until only a few years ago.

I'm wondering what the story is, why they've never collaborated, when Morgan turns onto a wide boulevard shaded by a canopy of leafy trees. Must be the ritzy part of town, if the tony boutique hotel we park in front of is any indication.

"This show then," I say, picking up where we left off. "It's a slice of family tradition."

"Tradition and opportunity," he replies. "My yacht in contention for the award came from a commission here three years ago. Now the wife wants a bigger boat." He tips his head with a knowing smile. "As mentioned."

On the drive down, Morgan unloaded a crash course in yacht design that left my brain reeling. It takes three to four years to bring a superyacht to life, from design to finished product. The first year involves engineering and technical logistics, all the formative back-end work. During that time, there's monthly client meetings and back and forth with tech crews and interior designers. Year two, actual building starts. During construction, he flies to Germany, Italy, or Holland to visit the shipyards. Each yacht is a massive undertaking with millions of dollars at stake. Nervous and demanding clients (the wives in particular, always aiming for bigger and better) mean every part of the process requires his seal of approval. One oversight can set back a project for weeks.

It's stressful, he admitted in a candid reveal that shined a light on his inner world. In PR, we feel the heat during a crisis. It's intense but short-lived. To have constant high-level pressure simmering under your skin is a different story. No wonder he burned along the autostrada at Mach speed, flying through mountain tunnels like James Bond escaping the bad guys.

But my takeaway is he loves the work.

Passion is what I keep circling back to.

It's inspiring.

After talking intimately together for three hours, I have to admit he's undeniably captivating. Intelligent and creative. Pushing his clients for better, bolder. We share a kinship with a mutual disdain for mediocrity and blandness and a desire to make a difference. TQ said Morgan's known for his élan and from what I can see, his unique style permeates every part of him. And it's not just his mind I find alluring. He cuts a fine figure in his Saint Laurent suit and the afternoon light through the sunroof catches the copper in his hair, creating streaks of fire. When he rolls down the window to greet the approaching bellman, he shifts effortlessly into Italian and the sweet, saucy rhythm sets off butterflies in my stomach.

What else is his tongue capable of?

"Our VIP shuttle to the show will be here in thirty minutes," Morgan says. "Just enough time to freshen up. If you'd like an espresso beforehand, let me know. Otherwise, there's plenty of food and drink on *Catch Me.*"

The setup for this event is different than the typical yacht show. Every boat qualifying for an award must be on display in the harbor to allow for viewings during the show. *Catch Me* is Morgan's yacht in award contention, and he made a deal with the owner to have her here. To make himself available for judge's questions and to streamline our days, Morgan has arranged all of his meetings to take place on the boat. In comparison, at the Monaco show we'll bounce around: entertain clients at the Yacht Club, have off-site meetings or meet suppliers at their booths.

"Why don't you take the penthouse?" Morgan continues, handing over one of the envelopes the bellman delivered. "I've stayed there enough times."

Reaching for the envelope, our fingers graze and the current between us unmistakable.

Okay, fine.

Witnessing my employer half-naked is not so forgettable, after all.

It's Morgan who lets his hand fall away first. "I forgot to mention that we're invited to a yacht party tonight. You packed black tie?"

Did I? Ha. Flynn made sure the first thing in my suitcase was a backless Versace halter dress. The gown fits me like a second skin, complete with floor-length skirt and thigh-high slit. It brought down the house at Stryker's film premiere two years ago. My very own J.Lo jungle dress moment.

I tuck the envelope into my purse, feeling more ready than ever. "I'm always prepared."

"Why doesn't that surprise me?"

He smiles and hops out of the car, a spring in his step.

Salone Nautico (how Italians refer to the boat show) takes place at an outdoor venue on the Mediterranean shoreline. Morgan weaves us through the buzzy crowd, navigating a maze of nautical supplier booths. We leave land for a zigzag of wide docks, where impressive boats of every size are stacked side by side, gleaming in the sun. *Catch Me* is docked at the far end, the largest yacht on display. She's a beauty with a deep-blue hull that shimmers with gold accents.

Standing guard on the dock behind a podium is a stout woman with a mess of dark curls. Very serious in her pantsuit, she and Morgan banter back and forth in Italian.

Morgan explains the protocol to me once they're done. "Fernanda is the gatekeeper—a necessity at these events. Everyone wants to look. We go by appointment only, especially since the owner isn't here."

A shame for the attendees, because who doesn't want to look? I've seen yachts in magazines and movies and never felt even a slight tinge of interest. But it's altogether different when an improbably ginormous and gorgeous work of art bobs before my eyes. I feel the pull of it, a new and intriguing sensation. Morgan helps me on board and despite her size, *Catch Me* rocks gently with the current. I'm glad I wore flats.

Morgan gives me a quick tour of the yacht, sharing anecdotes about various design features and why he chose certain things. From the hull design to maximize mileage to the colour scheme of navy and arctic white to appeal to the Finnish roots of the owners, he considered every detail. The master bath is a knockout with a rare marble soaker tub surrounded by windows. I see myself drinking wine by candlelight while watching the moon. Back in the bedroom, I admire a Damien Hirst painting of cherry blossoms framed in gold. It adds just the right pop of color.

"Stunning all around," I say. "You did the exterior and the interior?"

"Start to finish."

"Your aesthetic is a perfect balance of masculine and feminine. Not easy to accomplish."

"Thank you." Sensing more than generic interest, he adds, "Interiors are challenging. I have to understand the owner, how they live, how they entertain. How they love. The personal details make all the difference."

"I bet." I run my hand along the shimmering bedspread, a masterpiece of woven silk. If any bed screams *take me down*, it's this one. I wonder if that made it into the design brief.

"You're smiling," Morgan says.

"It's very much my taste."

"Wait until you experience the *Liberté*."

My eyes flicker to his. "I imagine she's your most intimate creation."

"Design perfection," he says, mouth curling into that seductive smile. "If there is such a thing."

Is it me, or is it suddenly very warm in here? Like maybe we shouldn't be standing so close together in case I spontaneously combust. At the very least, he should button up his shirt. A slab of golden pecs staring me in the face all day will not make my job any easier. But Morgan isn't a fan of ties or socks, I discovered. When I asked earlier if he had forgotten them, he said they remind him of land and all the constraints that come with it.

"Let's go upstairs," he says. "I'll introduce you to everyone and show you the top deck."

Morgan's team has set up shop in the upper salon, a sophisticated, tasteful space perfect for discussing deals worth millions. A circular dining table large enough to be a dance floor has pens and notepads laid neatly on crisp napkins in front of each of the ten chairs. In the far corner sits a baby grand piano, the white lacquered surface shining like an ice rink in the sun. Bouquets of blush roses scattered about lend a touch of fragrance to the air. Morgan introduces his junior designer team, two young men who arrived yesterday with Fernanda to get things in order. Henri, French and fabulous in a pinstriped suit, and Alessandro, all mussed hair and Italian charm. They take me in with well-mannered curiosity. I get the impression a woman is a rare sighting within the upper echelon of Royal Morgan Yachts. Morgan addresses them in rapid-fire French that sounds more like orders than friendly conversation.

With last-minute preparations underway, Morgan leads me up a curving stairwell. A pool on the top deck with a 360-degree view leaves me laughing at how outrageous it all is.

This isn't luxury. It's super luxury. The best of the best.

"Okay, I'm hooked," I say. "If this was mine, I'd never leave."

"It's freeing, no? Knowing you can take off and leave everything behind."

Standing at the prow, he points out the shipyard across the harbor, two ocean liners docked for repair. Beyond that, to our left, waves roll out to the horizon. The subtle, soothing motion of the ocean beneath me is like sitting in a comfy rocking chair. Not once did I ever consider living on a boat, but against the backdrop of the sea and dazzling sun, I can see it now. Zoom calls in bikini bottoms. No traffic to fight. A glass of champagne at sunset, skin warm and salty.

"Morgan?" Henri's voice calls up from the salon. "Giancarlo's on his way."

I turn to find Morgan studying me. Like he's trying to figure something out. "You'll like Giancarlo," he says. "He's a character."

"How did the relationship start?"

"My VP Olivier knew his cousin and introduced us. You'll meet Olivier in Monaco. He came down with a bug and isn't here this weekend."

We make our way back to the stairwell, me descending first. "Has he been with the company for a while?"

"Five years, although we go way back. We met at boarding school. I lost a few deals in my twenties because of him," he admits. "Yacht brokers are a nefarious sort. They pit designers against each other and act as a go-between with us and the client. I decided to close the gap. Hire the enemy."

"Has that been a good strategy?"

He stops on the bottom stair and something in his face changes. "More or less."

I get the vague notion his reply is layered, although there's no time to unpack details. Back on the salon level, Morgan indicates where he and I will sit at the table for the meetings. I'm a silent observer today, jotting down questions for clarification later. A tanned and pony-tailed female crew member appears from the lower deck, nods politely, and sets heavy crystal glasses and frosty bottles of San Pellegrino on the table. Morgan mentioned earlier the captain and crew remain with the yacht for security reasons while she's docked here. Morgan pours us both a glass of water just as Henri reappears. Strutting beside him is a buff, olive-skinned man with piercing eyes and dark, flowing hair pretty enough to be mine.

Giancarlo Berretti. An Italian Formula 1 racer.

On his third wife. Second boat. The first appointment of the day.

Morgan flashes a megawatt smile although his outstretched hand hangs in space, unshaken. Giancarlo gawks at me like a fat kid lusting after a lollipop.

I smile and introduce myself and Henri settles at my side with his Moleskine notebook. Across the table, he and Alessandro share a look.

Today just got interesting.

Chapter Fourteen

"HOLY HOTNESS, GIRL." FLYNN'S EAR-SPLITTING WOLF WHISTLE blisters out of my iPhone speakers. "I told you that Versace had to make another appearance."

We're FaceTiming in my hotel room before I meet Morgan in the lobby. Half a world away, Flynn sits cross-legged on the floor of her Hollywood home in her usual writing attire of pajamas, messy bun, and tortoiseshell glasses. She claims people take her more seriously with glasses, as if thousands of people hanging on her every piece of advice isn't serious enough.

"I can't believe you're going to a yacht party," she says wistfully. "Sound like it's going great so far. What's the vibe? What's he like?"

"Today I sat in on some meetings and got a sense of how it all comes together. He's a personality, for sure. A little imperious with his staff and even with potential clients. I made a couple of comments."

"How did that go over?" she asks, drinking some kind of ancient healing tea from her thermos.

When Morgan and I regrouped at the end of the day, I explained how Vaughn and I often play the sidekick game in meetings. Good cop, bad cop. Pick up on things the other didn't. Morgan bristled a little at my feedback that one of the meetings might've ended more positively if he'd agreed to a benign client request rather than dismissing it. His argument: *I don't need every client.* My counterargument: *you need some clients*.

"He took it in stride."

"Anything else going on?" she asks, smile widening.

I take a seat on the edge of the bed and chuckle. "You haven't won your bet, if that's what you're asking."

"It's only day one. What about sparks?"

I don't tell her about the hotel fiasco. I'm still processing that myself. "Definitely some of those. Why are you grinning like the cat who ate the canary?"

"Because it will be so good to have the old Vandana back."

I tilt my head. "What do you mean?"

She hesitates, very unlike Flynn. "At Stanford you were this ball of wild, unstoppable fire. You wanted to pursue design, not PR. Then you started with Vaughn, met Derek, and … I know people change, but it's like we lost a little piece of you."

"We? You and June have had a conversation about this?" I ask, more sharply than intended.

"Bella," she says in a soft voice. "It's not like we're having dark, secret discussions about you."

"It sounds like you are."

She undoes her bun and twirls it back into place. This happens at least twenty times a day. "This is kind of what I'm getting at. You never used to worry about people talking about you."

"I manage reputations. At some point I have to care about mine."

"Aren't you fricking bored with all that?" she asks. "Always doing the right thing. Be here, look like that. You railed against your mom for the very same shit."

I don't say anything. Don't know what to say. Other than she's right.

Flynn, apparently with plenty more on her mind, adds, "All I'm saying is, your life is taking a hard left from here. Embrace it. Let your guard down."

"You really want to win that bet, don't you?"

She howls with laughter. "What's the worst thing that can happen if you have a fling with him?"

"Aside from obliterating all my business ethics and morals?"

"See what I mean? Right there. Get out of your little box of do-the-right-thing. Your dirty ex-husband's left you high and dry. Live a little. Have a screamer orgasm, or at least make out with the dude. June said his car is worth, like, three million dollars, so he's obviously loaded. Maybe it all works out with a happily ever after."

Flynn's a best-selling author of inspirational non-fiction, and June and I suspect that underneath all her positivity, inner demons lurk. If someone dishes out relationship advice like no one's business while remaining single for most of her adult life, it's a sign. Try pushing Flynn's buttons, however, and she shuts you out.

And yet, we happily let her push ours.

"Are you writing fiction now?" I joke.

"Speaking of that, I've got another chapter to grind out. For the love of God, have *fun* tonight. Over and out."

Flynn's like that. Boom, call over. Wound tight with discipline. I need to go too, so I finish up my hair and on the elevator ride down to the lobby, I think long and hard on her words. I miss the old me too. It wouldn't kill me to kick up my heels for one night. I'm in Italy, going to a yacht party and…

Oh my.

Morgan sits alone at the lobby bar chatting with a young bartender who stops mid-sentence when he sees me. Morgan swivels on the barstool to see what's caught his attention. I never believe those *our eyes met across the room* stories, but then again, maybe I've just never looked into the right pair.

God, he looks amazing.

A dark-blue velvet suit of a premium fabric, not that tacky velour garbage. Crisp white shirt unbuttoned and flared open. Hair freshly slicked back. Instead of piling my hair into a bun I left it down, and I take the bartender's continued slack jaw as proof it was the right decision.

94

I greet them both and admire Morgan's white lizard brogues. "Great shoes."

He admires me back, top to bottom. "Great everything. So much for me being the main event." He says this without malice, although I'm well aware of today's events—how the clients engaged with me first. To the point that Morgan had to redirect their attention to the business at hand.

"Ugh. Please don't say that. I felt like a major distraction today."

"You were," he admits. "But I like having you here."

"Until I share my notes with you."

Morgan smiles at the challenge in my voice, finishes his whiskey, and leaves a twenty euro note with the bartender who appears to have forgotten his purpose in life. "I've since decided it's good to have another opinion."

"Really," I say. "When did you decide that?"

"In the shower."

I start laughing, and his smile gives way to a chuckle. I'm glad he can find the humor in it and laugh at himself. Maybe a night out will do us both good.

"I believe there's another yacht with your name on it, Mademoiselle Hillman." He crooks out his elbow for me to wind my arm through. "Shall we?"

Let the party begin.

Arms still laced together, Morgan keeps me steady as I navigate the uneven dock in sky-high Jimmy Choos. We were dropped off at a private marina north of the city, and our party home base is a hundred-meter yacht taking up the entire length of a single dock.

"Wow," I say. "Look at that thing."

"There are boats twice her size," he says, "believe it or not."

A white-gloved attendant checks our IDs and we join the festivities, which are already in full swing. The glam crowd is dressed to thrill and it's a perfect night for a yacht party—no wind, sun waning, but it's still warm enough not to wear a wrap and spoil the effect of my dress. Morgan grabs us drinks and introduces me to Dallas Evener, the American venture capitalist hosting tonight's party. His calculating, corporate-raider eyes are at odds with his pretty-boy face and Golden Goose sneakers peeking out from the frayed hems of his designer denim. He draws Morgan and me into a huddle of thick-necked Ivy League-types with white bread privilege written all over them. Upon hearing who Morgan is, they toss one outlandish design question after another at him and ten minutes in, sensing I'm a touch bored, he encourages me to mingle.

"I'll come find you," he says, and squeezes my hand.

I break away to do the rounds and take in the surroundings. Earlier, Morgan explained the difference between European and American clients. Europeans put a premium on style, Americans like big comfort, nothing too avant-garde. Hence the dark wood and boring cream furniture in here. It's a look that's been done a hundred times. The guests, on the other hand, are original. Or at least their stories are. I float from group to group, thrilled not to discuss American politics, LA traffic, or Hollywood scandals for a change. By the time I head to the bar for a champagne refill, I'm happily buzzing along.

"Nice dress."

The dark and heavily accented voice belongs to a hulk of a man hunched over his rocks glass, one boot on the bar rail. I estimate he's close to my age, although acne scars, deeply cratered, add a few more miles to his face. With unruly black hair in need of a cut and all the bug-eyed charm of a pug, he oozes a crude aura.

But at least he has good taste.

"Thank you," I say, preening just a little. "It's Versace."

"I know," he says. "It's also two years old."

My smile deflates. Here I am finally enjoying myself and this jerk pops my balloon. Rudely, to boot. "Your knowledge of women's wear is impressive," I sniff. "For a man."

He snorts a laugh. "Donatella's my client, much to your boyfriend's chagrin."

"The good news is, you must have me confused with someone else," I say, somewhat relieved at the mistaken case of identity. "I don't have a boyfriend."

"Aren't you fucking Morgan?"

He turns to face me in what feels like a menacing gesture. It triggers every warning bell.

"I'm handling his public relations, if that's what you mean."

"Public relations." He scoffs and slams back the copper remains of his drink. "Is that how you describe it?"

I match the weight of his stare, adding some ice for good measure. "Given your manners, *you* might want to consider some PR. If you'll excuse me."

With my champagne topped up, the intention is to march past this lout, but his hand clamps around my wrist. I stagger and feel it like a slick of ice down my spine. Underneath the swagger is a dangerous, boozy vibe of a man unafraid to be violent. I've come across one or two in my lifetime and took a self-defense course because of it.

"Let go of me, please," I say, my voice low and steely. We haven't caused a stir, yet. Only one sideways glance from the bartender.

"I'll pay you triple what he's paying you," he slurs, drunk, but faculties intact.

"I'm sorry, but I'm not taking on new clients."

"I'm not talking PR." With one powerful yank on my wrist, we're belly to belly. He leers at my boobs with an oily smile. "I bet you're an amazing fuck."

I can smell his acrid breath. A cologne that doesn't mix with his pH. In general, I never trust a man who wears more diamonds than I do. Especially one in his nose.

"That's very classy," I say. "I'll keep your offer in mind. Now, please take your hand off me." I make the mistake of scanning over his shoulder for Morgan. A damsel in distress signal he pounces all over.

"He's probably banging some chick in the bathroom. Women are a dime a dozen to him, so don't get so high on yourself, Miss Public Relations."

Normally, I'd let a heckler run off his mouth. Once they're out of steam they've got nothing. But he's particularly insidious, and I've had enough. "Grow up, creep."

I toss my champagne into his face and he sputters in shock. A murmur of surprise rises from the lineup at the bar, the air shifting as everyone takes a step back. I attempt to yank out of his grip, but his meaty hand becomes a band of steel, squeezing tighter as his face contorts with red rage.

"You dumb cunt," he hisses.

I've never been backhanded before, and I'm surprised my neck doesn't do a three-sixty with the force of his hand. Music, chatter, everything skids to a halt. I bring a hand to my face, heat rising from my cheek. I'm not aware Morgan is alert to any of this, until his fist connects with the man's unibrow. The jerk staggers backward, upending a tray of dirty glasses. They explode in a shattering mess and someone gasps, "Oh my god."

Dusting himself off, the man collects his bearings and growls, "Pretentious asshole."

Head down like a bull, he charges at Morgan, who absorbs the hit. They swirl around in a mad hurricane of grunts, flying fists, and *fuck yous.* They're evenly matched, and it seems impossible for anyone to break up the sheer force of their violence. Mortified guests clear the parquet dance floor, skittering to the safety of the sidelines. Cameras come out, flashes lighting up in the dim room like pops of visual noise.

It sets my heart rate flying.

This can't be good.

Morgan finds an advantage and ratchets the man's head into the crook of his elbow. "You're nothing better than a thug," he mutters.

The other guy does his best to stop the chokehold, calling Morgan names a lady shouldn't repeat. They wrestle for control until Morgan finally flings his opponent hard onto the floor. But he's not down for long. He staggers to his feet, crimson droplets falling like rain from his nose.

With the grace of a bad-tempered camel, he spits out a bloody stream of saliva and sneers at Morgan. "We'll see who's the last man standing."

The troll departs, shoving past stunned bystanders, leaving nothing but a damning silence in his wake. More than one woman whispers into the ear of her date, heads tipping discreetly in my direction.

And that's my debut in Genoa.

Day one, and I'm already in damage control mode.

Chapter Fifteen

MORGAN'S HAND CLAMPS HARD ONTO MINE, AND HE WHISKS US AWAY from all the staring faces. Away from my humiliation. I scramble to keep up with him.

"Where are we going?"

He shoulders past a huddle of suited men with stubby cigars and sunburnt faces. "Somewhere private," he says, his voice low.

At the end of the hall, Morgan takes a sharp right onto a staircase rising into darkness. The thick carpet underfoot is like stepping on pillows and with each step, the ambient hum of the stalled-out party fades.

"Are we allowed up here?" I whisper. I've snuck around enough to know when something feels off-limits.

"If anyone complains," he says, "I'll deal with it."

There is only one door on this level, and Morgan guides me through it, shutting it firmly behind us. The evening's last light is fading but still slanting low through a bank of windows, illuminating a bedroom the size of a tennis court. Another man's cologne spikes the air. Next to the fireplace, a stripper pole and mini stage sit dark under show lights. Dry-cleaned shirts draped in plastic hang like ghosts on the closet door handle. Morgan beelines for the ensuite, tugging on my arm like I'm a misbehaving puppy. I'm half-expecting he'll read me the riot act, about protocol at a yacht party full of potential clients and peers. But I've never been talked down to in such a vulgar manner, so he can save the speech.

I reclaim my hand while he searches for the light switch. "Please don't treat me like a child. Remember what we talked about? Communication? And running away makes us look like cowards."

"Coward?" he scoffs. "Is that what you think of me?"

The overhead pot lamps burst on with an assault of brightness. He's breathing heavily, hair and tuxedo in disarray although it's the contained fury in his eyes that puts me on guard.

"That's not what I meant. He should stew in his own behavior. Leaving makes it look like he's in the right."

With a dismissive shake of his head he says, "Life isn't about being right, Vandana. Sometimes you walk away."

From a pyramid of rolled facecloths sitting on the vanity, he grabs one, cranks on a sink tap, and saturates the towel. Light pink rivulets stream off his knuckles down the drain. Truth be told, he makes bloody and disheveled look pretty damn good.

"How's your hand?" I ask.

"Good enough to go another round if need be."

"You didn't strike me as a fighter."

"Only when provoked."

I meet his eyes in the mirror because it feels safer, his anger one step removed. Energy sparks off of him like solar flares. "I'm sorry. I feel like—"

"Why are you apologizing?" he demands. "You did nothing wrong. A man should never strike a woman."

"I know but—"

"Shh," he interrupts, a hand in the air to punctuate his point. "You need something cold on your cheek. The last thing you want is a bruise." He wrings out the towel and hands it to me. "Put pressure on it."

I wince as the cold stings my raw skin. He tidies up in the sink, an opulent basin big enough to bathe a healthy two-year-old. The grandeur of the bathroom décor leans heavily on Baroque, not that eighteenth century nobles had massive fish tanks installed above soaker tubs with baby sharks gliding back and forth in an eerie figure eight.

As Morgan rearranges his hair in the mirror, futzing with bangs no longer held in place with crispy gel, I take ownership of the situation.

"I do need to apologize," I say. "To you. I provoked that man, throwing my champagne in his face. Maybe he took exception to the vintage?"

Morgan glances at me with a wry smile. "Very funny. And highly unlikely. Renan wouldn't know a Brut from a Demi-sec."

I blink, thrown for a loop. "That guy was Renan? The yacht designer?"

"He likes to call himself that."

This news sobers me right up. Derek once explained the hockey rule of offside to me, but I never quite understood it in the context of the word. Watching Morgan and Renan go at each other tonight, their violence felt intimate. Men don't battle like that unless wounded pride is at stake. All of a sudden, a whole new world unfolds, and it smells offside … as I know the word. "He's not just a random designer. You know him on a personal level."

Morgan, arms crossed tightly, says, "We were friends growing up."

"You didn't mention this at the Yacht Club," I say, trying not to sound accusatory. "If the Khaled deal is a sandbox war, that's a whole other tactic."

Briefly silenced, Morgan takes a deep, resigned breath. "I'd prefer not to get into it right now. Not that I don't appreciate your thoroughness."

In other words, something deep-rooted and not easily forgotten is at the crux of this. I wonder if it involves a woman. "Fine if you're not up to it right now, but I asked you for all the details. Don't leave me in the dark."

Beneath us, the dumb throb of eighties disco starts up again, the partygoers keen to move on. Morgan slips out of his broodiness and moves closer to me. "Let me take a look," he says. With the lightest touch, he lifts my jaw, angling the right side of my face into the light.

I lift the cloth so he can see. "Is it bruised?"

"Mmm." His hand brushes lightly against my cheek. "So far so good." Instead of backing away, his thumb slips down to my jawline, running along it like he's reading braille. He's so close, I can see a tiny cluster of hair on his throat, where his razor missed. "You look beautiful tonight," he says, breath warm and dark with whiskey. "Your skin is luminous."

His body is a furnace, licks of heat dancing between us. The stupid, mad thrill of his nakedness this morning thrums in my brain. The wanting.

Embrace it.

"Well…" I swallow past the thickening in my throat. "You have seen all of it."

A faint smile curls his mouth higher. "Almost all of it."

My eyes shift to find his unblinking, all that molten amber swirling like a dangerous whirlpool. His thumb makes its way higher to slide back and forth along the scarlet gloss on my lower lip. For a breathless few seconds, we regard each other in a state of perfect understanding.

The facecloth falls out of my hand and splats onto the floor, my willpower joining it.

And it just … happens.

My lips part and the tip of his thumb slips inside.

Morgan inhales sharply, face alight with shock. Oh, god it's so wrong, nibbling on him, tasting the faint metallic residue of his blood mixed with soap. But it feels so right as my teeth skate across the buff of his nail, the flesh of his thumb pressing into the inner wet parts of me.

Morgan finds his voice and my name quavers out from his lips, hushed and scandalous.

The thing is, there's no turning back. It's not like putting coffee creamer in someone else's shopping cart by mistake. Where you smile and say, *Oops.*

A man's thumb doesn't end up in your mouth by mistake.

Your tongue doesn't spiral around it by mistake.

You don't inhale it, right down to the base, and suck on it like a dick.

Not by mistake.

His deep growl of surprise bleeds into a choked *Fuck.* He shoves me against the vanity, one knee jamming between my legs, forcing them apart. His free hand slides up the slit of my dress, the bare skin of my ass squeezed like clay between his fingers. I can feel adrenaline rocketing through him, smell the fight sweat on his skin as he devours my neck and shoulders with hot carnal kisses, feeds on me like a starved animal. I suck on him greedily and shift my hips to let him fall into the molten fire between my legs. He mutters something that sounds French and utterly foul before freeing his thumb with a squelching *pop.* His mouth crushes against mine and caution, restraint, decency—all of it gets trampled in a crazed stampede as he plunders the dark reaches of my soul, our tongues in an instant duel, frantic with need. Lit up and burning dangerously, blood rushes through my veins, funneling to join the heat throbbing between my legs.

Just as all the details start to fall away, a flutter of remorse dances across my heart. My passion for Derek stalled out long before he found Alistair. But it was like this between us in the beginning: a mad, uncontrollable thunder of desire. Morgan is hard as concrete, raging against me, a man who's seen me almost naked and unable to do a thing about it until now.

I've missed this. Need this. Badly.

In a dizzying demand for more, my hands claw at the back of his shirt.

Then, dim and distant, the sound of a door opening.

"Oh my God, Frankie!" a female voice gasps. "Now *this* is a bedroom."

Morgan's mouth rips off mine and he staggers backward with a groan. Flushed and lightheaded, I smooth down the fabric of my dress. We share a panicky look. There is no place to hide.

"I don't know if we should be snooping around, Dorothy," a male Texan twang responds.

"Let's take a quick peek."

They stop in unison, two startled faces framed in the bathroom doorway. I assume they're husband and wife, because only married couples dress in similar outfits. Dorothy, tall and proud with flame-red hair, stares at us unashamed. Nebbish Frankie, all 5'8 of him, has the decency to blush.

"Oh dear," he says. "Sorry to interrupt."

"Do you mind?" Morgan asks, tucking his shirt back in. A smear of my lip gloss stains his lips. "We're in the middle of a conversation."

"Conversation?" Dorothy cackles, reading the situation for what it is. "I might look young, but I wasn't born yesterday. Besides," she asks with challenge in her tone, "is this your boat?'

"It doesn't matter whose boat it is," Morgan snaps back.

Frankie's quick to wave down potential friction. He has a kind face, a Charlie Chaplin moustache, and a well-practiced air of smoothing over differences. "Sorry. Wife's on a mission these days. She gets a bit feisty." He attempts to commandeer Dorothy out, but she's having none of it.

"I have to look at *everything,* Bubs. That's the whole point of being here." In her assessing sweep of the bathroom, she wrinkles her nose in distaste.

I can tell Morgan thinks these two are party crashers, both of them in jeans, hoodies, and boat shoes. But their soft, well-fattened look is all American blueblood. And I recognize the Van Cleef & Arpels necklace draped on Dorothy's sunbaked chest. If she has the matching earrings, that's close to three million in diamonds.

"Are you two in the market for a yacht?" I ask on a hunch.

"Yes!" Dorothy says, spinning around to face me. "But we're not looking to buy pre-owned," she warns, as if I'm about to hard sell her. "We want something unusual. We want to make a statement." Her arms fling skyward, indicating how grandiose she intends said statement to be. In my peripheral vision, Morgan rolls his eyes.

"You want to one-up Gladys and Melvin," Frankie grumbles, his delivery suggesting a husband well versed with being dragged into boutiques or auction houses and leaving with a much lighter wallet.

"Are you familiar with *Le Debut* by chance?" I ask. "This is the man behind the masterpiece. Morgan de Rohan-Chabot." I blaze my best PR smile and Dorothy scopes out Morgan with a fresh eye.

"You did *Le Debut?* I love that boat." She elbows Frankie. "Remember the cover of Yacht World? Chuck's boat."

Frankie nods. "I remember. It was the talk of the town."

"Give him your card, Bubs."

Frankie digs out a faded nylon wallet, yanking hard on the stubborn Velcro closure. He riffles through business cards that look like they went through a washing machine. "The name's Delmar. Frank Delmar."

"Delmar." Morgan takes the offered card, voice perking up. "Delmar Oil and Gas out of Texas."

"You know us!" Dorothy beams, the way everyone who's not famous in the classic sense is when recognized. But in this case, most of the civilized world knows who they are. A classic American success story, Delmar is one of the few indie companies taking on the big oil players. Privately held. Worth billions.

"What's your schedule like tomorrow?" I ask, snapping open my evening bag to hand Dorothy one of Morgan's cards. "One of Morgan's boats is up for a design award. *Catch Me.* It's in the harbor; we can meet there."

"Chuck Parsons works with me on all his yachts." Morgan steps in, now realizing these two may not be the poseurs he originally thought.

"I swear Chuck reached out on our behalf," Dorothy says, brow furrowing with memory recall. "We've been looking for a designer, but he said you weren't taking on new business?"

"Really?" Morgan looks genuinely mystified. "I always talk to new clients. If we can, we make it work."

"Does tomorrow work for a meeting?" I'm not letting these two out of our sight until I nail them down. They're low hanging fruit.

Frankie turns to his wife. "What time are we looking at that villa?"

"That's in Nice on Sunday. Tomorrow we're looking at the Ferraris." Dorothy pats his arm. "I think someone had a bit too much wine today in Tuscany. Pardon our attire; we came straight from the vineyards." Her very pointed glance lands right on Morgan. She felt the judgment.

"If you're coming to Nice, we can meet in Monaco if that's easier," Morgan suggests. "We're there all next week."

"Can you believe this?" Dorothy marvels. "Here we are looking for a designer, and you of all people to fall right into—"

Before she can finish, a security detail wanders in and politely asks us to rejoin the party downstairs. After promises to connect and chirpy goodbyes, the Delmars get back to mingling. Morgan pulls me aside and suggests we call it a night. I know he feels eyes on us because I feel them too. Renan must have left after the fight and I'm happy not to see him a second time. We thank Dallas for the party, and he seems unconcerned we created a spectacle on his yacht. No doubt he's been in boardroom battles that were bloodier. While we wait on the dock for a taxi to arrive, Morgan's quiet, watching moonlight ripple on the water. I hope he isn't second-guessing hiring a woman who inspires drag-down fights and blows his thumb like he's the last man on earth. But it wasn't one way up there. If Dorothy and Frankie hadn't rolled in, that bathroom would be in serious shambles.

My own thoughts are scattershot and totally uneven. I don't know what to say, but I have to say something. "Um … what just happened. Upstairs. It wasn't very professional."

"I agree," he says, back to starched and formal. "Please accept my apologies."

"It's best not to mix business with pleasure," I prattle on. "Keep things clean."

"Clean," he repeats, like he's trying out a new word.

"You know, not creating a mess."

He searches my face, and it's impossible to stay clear-headed in the depths of his amber pools. They're agitated and swirling, like my insides. I can still feel his dick smashed against me. I still crave that tongue wrestling for control over mine.

"Fair enough," he says and drags his eyes off mine.

His response lands wrong, matching nothing that I feel. Fair? This is so unfair. To have this rush, such a connection and then, *pfft.*

But you said…

Yes, I know what I said. Thanks for the reminder.

The reality is, no matter what lies I tell myself, I can't blip tonight out of existence. Adrenaline still hovers under my skin, not a hint of give. We're like one of those beds that come in a box—packing up our explosion of lust and shipping it back to the sender is an impossible task.

We own it.

And it's never going back to its original state.

Chapter Sixteen

DAY TWO.

So far, running without a hitch.

I make it out of my hotel room fully clothed. Breakfast doesn't involve tossing liquids in the face of disgusting men. On the deck of *Catch Me,* Morgan and I go over the day's appointments while the crew serves rich espresso and pastries. Frankie already emailed Morgan this morning, and they've been going back and forth on some initial ideas.

"That's fantastic," I say, glad to see Morgan back in a positive mood. On the drive home last night, he brought me up to speed on Renan, and it left him in a dark place. Turns out Renan's father Burak used to work for Morgan's father. Morgan and Renan, close in age, were friends until Burak got fired for alcoholism. With no money coming in and a sickly mother who needed in-home care, things disintegrated. Renan asked Morgan for money, which only went straight down Burak's throat. In a horrible twist of fate, he died of alcohol poisoning, suffocating his wife as he slumped on top of her.

Renan never forgave Morgan or his family.

"The trouble is," Morgan explained, "my father gave Burak so many chances. But after a while, you're an enabler. I fell into that trap, offering money every time Renan asked. In a way, I feel partly to blame for the tragedy. I've been his sworn enemy ever since."

Because of this, Renan had tried to undermine several of Morgan's deals. He began running with a suspect crowd of mafiosos, both Russian and Italian, who threw their weight and threats around in equal proportion. Morgan was pissed that Renan finagled his way into the Khaled deal. It prompted me to ask how he got involved, but Morgan's unsure. According to Olivier, the former yacht broker with a deep Rolodex, Morgan was tipped to be the only designer in contention. Somehow Renan and a lesser-known German designer cropped up in the mix.

Nothing can be done about it now.

It all boils down to Khaled.

The story swirls in my head throughout the morning. It has all the juicy elements of a blockbuster: bitter rivals, mafia, the underbelly of a dazzling and prestigious industry. The unexpected side effect of knowing the backstory is feeling better about last night. Gives me some perspective on why Morgan shut down on the dock. A lot to process on his end.

A lot on my end.

If last night didn't doom me to eternal damnation, the immense pleasure of it surely will. Holy smokes, can that man's tongue duel. He found every nook and cranny like there was money to be had in new exploration. And in the mirror this morning, I noticed bruises blooming along the curve of my butt. Territorial markings.

He did not want to let go.

Although we agreed to maintain decorum, all morning Morgan keeps stealing looks, checking out my body language, finding my eyes. It's distracting. By the time mid-afternoon rolls around, my focus is toast.

Morgan's in deep discussion over hull shapes with Mielo, a Ukrainian LNG tycoon, when a flurry of incoming messages sets my phone off. I forgot to silence it after lunch and reach into my handbag to do so now, apologizing. I peek at the screen to see what's up and scroll through Flynn's trademark one text per thought with a heavy heart.

FD: OMG. If I screwed up I'm sorry!
FD: U shoulda told me.
FD: Derek's here. Wanted to know where U were
FD: I told him
FD: He's flipping out
FD: He's calling U
FD: Call me after! Sorry…

Shitty shit.

Right away the phone starts to ring. With a sheepish smile, I stand and excuse myself. "I need to take this."

Morgan clocks the shift in my mood, me not willing to look him in the eyes before I hustle away. Derek is the last person I want to talk to, but now that he knows where I am, he won't stop calling. The tenacity of film people is next level.

I silence the ringer, and once I'm at the far end of the deck, answer. "Hi."

"What the hell is Flynn doing in our house?" he demands.

"House-sitting, obviously."

"Did you think about asking me? And what's this shit about you taking off without saying anything? Or is that how it's going down now? Us, not talking?"

"The trip was last minute. It slipped my mind to tell you," I lie. Derek needs to know everything, all the time, but now he needs to get used to not knowing my whereabouts.

"Nice try," he grumbles. "You live on your phone. One text wouldn't have killed you."

"Why are you being so pissy?" I ask.

"Because Flynn's following me around like I'm trying to steal something!"

"Are you?"

"Really, V?" he scoffs. "I didn't think you'd be this fucking petty." Says the guy who nabs every complimentary toiletry from any hotel room, including the spare roll of toilet paper.

"I'm with my client right now," I say. "What do you want?"

"Have you talked to Stryker lately?"

"No."

"You're sure?"

"Yes, I'm sure. Why?" Then, thinking about it, "Does he know?"

In a moment of taut silence, we digest the indigestible. The only same sex coupling justifiable in Stryker's world is two strippers servicing him simultaneously. If he's on to Derek, it's game over.

"I don't know," Derek finally says. "He sent some cryptic text last night saying an exec at Warner is pushing a new guy onto him for the superhero movie. The timing feels weird."

Crap. The superhero flick is a reboot and they're already talking a three-picture deal. It's Derek's chance to direct second unit, and opportunities like this come around once a millennium. Stryker lobbied hard for Derek at first, but it's his house, his rules. That's how it works in Hollywood when you're making people billions of dollars. Something tells me this is just the beginning for Derek. Career crush.

But he should have thought of that.

"What do you want me to do?" I ask.

"He listens to you. Maybe you can … I don't know. Tell him nothing's changed. I'm still the same guy."

Nothing's changed? Is he a fool? If my mother were here, she'd be foaming at the mouth. "Jesus, Derek. Everything's changed! Didn't you and Alistair talk about this? Please tell you gave some consideration to how coming out might impact your life. And mine."

My rising voice carries and in the salon, Morgan glances over his shoulder. I move to the farthest outpost of the deck, breeze whipping through my hair.

"You don't think I thought about it?" he snaps. "It's all I thought about! Breaking your heart. Your fucking witch of a mother gloating over our breakup. I know my family wasn't good enough for you, but they were at least decent and kind. They embraced you. Tried to, anyway."

Guilt slices through my heart, just like he wants it to. Both his parents divorced and remarried, and we once shuttled between

Bozeman and Bismarck for a week of snowy Christmas hell. It's not like I can't relate to people with miniature spoon collections and vinyl recliners, but when conversation turns to what ammunition works best to take down a moose, I'm sorry, but I got nothing. I do, however, regret catching up on back issues of *Vogue* instead of eating waffles and watching *Home Alone* with them. Derek was fuming, and hauled me and my Uggs into a frigid snowstorm to tear a strip off me. Deeply offended at his *spoiled rich girl* slag, I pointed out we were arguing in a trailer park. That had to count for something. But apparently it did not.

"You know what, V?" Derek's voice turns bitter and beat down. "I knew when I married you that it was going to be all about you. Your mom made damn sure of it. The pauper marrying the princess. But it's pretty shitty of you to be so high and mighty. Like you had nothing to do with this."

It's like he's punched me in the gut. It takes a few seconds to find my voice. "You're saying this is *my* fault?"

"I wasn't the one unhappy with our sex life."

Another knife in my heart.

Eighteen months ago, after some uninspired sex and a few too many glasses of Zinfandel, I threw it out there—a threesome. Derek insisted he wasn't unsatisfied, but I pushed for it. We tried two different girls two different times, and it was awkward. Derek was not so into it. He then suggested we try a guy; equal opportunity was how he put it. It says a lot about a husband if he's willing to offer up what most men would run away screaming from in the name of keeping his wife happy. In retrospect, Derek knew it was all about me. I was bored. With him. Little did I know inviting another man into our bed would turn the tables in ways we never imagined.

And I don't feel like reliving it at this precise moment.

"I have to go," I say, tersely. "We can talk about this when I get back."

"Can you send one text, V? All I'm asking for is one text. Feel him out. Please?"

It's not my job to salvage his career. Not after everything I did for him. And calling me petty is utter ridiculousness. I courier my used clothes to Goodwill. Graciously accept the carnations and baby's breath his family sends on my birthday. "Fine. I'll reach out to him."

"While you're at it, can you call off Flynn? She's on me like a pit bull on a steak. I'm just getting some clothes out of my own fucking house."

The phone goes dead and I'm stewing hard when I notice Morgan has slipped in beside me, unseen.

"Everything all right?" he asks.

"Oh, you scared me! Yes, I'm fine," I say, fake and bright. "That was, uh, my maid calling. She couldn't find the vacuum."

I pump up my smile, but Morgan's not buying the brittle show of teeth. "Why don't you take a break?" he suggests. "It's been a long day. Mielo's about to leave and the last meeting isn't important. The awards show doesn't start until seven."

"I can stay. It's not a problem."

He leans against the railing, not letting go of my eyes. At the best of times, I'm a horrible liar and overcompensate when I do try. I can tell he's working out what to say next, and I start randomly counting the quiet seconds to calm myself. I'm at five when he reaches for my left hand, fisted against my thigh. His touch rattles every nerve and I react with a jolt. All day, I watched his graceful fingers wrapped around a sleek Montblanc as he scribbled notes and sketches. Remembered the violent plunge of them deep into my flesh last night.

"I appreciate your diligence, Vandana," he says. "Among other things."

Slowly, he spreads my fingers apart like he's untying the knot in my heart. A circling storm in my throat makes it difficult to breathe. At this point in my life, I've gotten used to being the comforter, not the comfortee, but deep down there's nothing more I crave than understanding. That it's not easy to prop up neurotic clients and fight the ruthless media and manage my career and Derek's, and do it all with a smile on my face.

I'm not a machine.

"I'm excited for tonight," he continues, massaging my palm with deep strokes of his thumb. "If I win, how will we celebrate?"

"Um …" My brain needs a second to reboot. I'm in a trance from his caresses. "With the best champagne?"

"Sounds like a good start." One by one, he works every finger, turning them into putty. He's highly attuned to my reactions, watching every bat of my lashes, every rise of my throat. "Just be forewarned," he adds. "These events often get messy."

"Messy, huh?" His drug-like effect is like all drugs. I want more. I start to twine my fingers into his, but he lets my relaxed hand fall limply.

"It might require a vacuum."

He smiles and I know he knows my phone call had nothing to do with a vacuum. Why else did he just linger on my ringless finger, rubbing heat on it as if he could darken the white ring of skin? Why else did I crash reckless against him last night, pulled in by the fierce undertow of desire?

Other things.

There are times I know I've won. Times when I know I've lost the game. But to know I'm losing before I even start is entirely foreign.

Like a shark, he senses I'm drowning, flailing in the depths and getting weaker.

He's in the dark water, circling patiently.

Waiting for the right moment to strike.

Chapter Seventeen

With a San Pellegrino in hand, I take a break as Morgan suggested. In a minor funk after Derek's call, I wander aimlessly along the docks. I don't know where or when or how the spark between us fizzled. It just did. The sound of a marriage falling apart is a lot quieter than people think and why I stuck around is the same reason everyone sticks around. Uncoupling, as Gwyneth Paltrow famously coined it, is hard.

I'll get through it. I have to.

Getting through this trip without kissing Morgan again feels like the more impossible task. I'm still buzzing from his hand love, and what is he doing throwing it all back in my face? *Things might get messy.* The push/pull with him drives me crazy. Finding a quiet section of dock far away from *Catch Me,* I lean against a pillar to mull things over.

But so much for solace.

Minutes later, a man stomps into my space, talking aggressively into earbuds. Large and sweaty, with intense piggy eyes and owlish glasses, he could be an extra in a Scorsese movie. I'm partially hidden by the pillar so he doesn't see me at first.

"Why did you engage with her? That's not the plan. Be a fly on the wall. Right now, the buzz is he defended a woman's honor. That won't help, and the asshole also has no idea what honor means. He threatened to fire me." He pauses, takes a drag of his cigarette. Stomps around some more. "Yes, I know. The hot ones are always the biggest bitches. But remember, she's the bait. Not the final catch."

What is up with this guy's suit? Plaid doesn't flatter most people, and even TJ Maxx wouldn't be caught dead selling that highland check.

"He doesn't know I'm here," he continues. "I'm working some other side deals for us. Preparing. Uh-huh. Don't worry, I've got a few things planned. This is…" He turns suddenly and startles at the sight of me. "I've got to run," he says to whomever he's speaking to. "Ciao." Flicking his butt into the ocean, he eyes me suspiciously. "Buongiorno."

"Buongiorno."

Hearing my accent, he clears his throat and continues in English. "I didn't realize you were standing there."

He said *you* with an air of familiarity. "Have we met before?"

"I don't believe so."

If he's twitchy from me overhearing his tirade or it's his general nature, I can't say. Whatever the case, he's itching to get the hell out of here. But something tells me to engage him.

"My name's Vandana," I say, offering my hand.

"Hi." He's quick to end our handshake and I wipe my hand surreptitiously along my skirt, glad to be wearing black. Sweaty hands gross me out. "Having a good show?" he asks.

"Yes, this is my first time here, actually. I've been hired by a Monaco designer to help with public relations. Have you heard of Royal Morgan Yachts?"

"Mmm … no, doesn't sound familiar."

"What about Renan Sadik? Do you know him? He's a designer as well."

In the slight pause, his eyes narrow. "Why are you asking?"

"I'm wrapping my head around all the players, the names I've heard. What do you do in the industry?"

"Uh…" Cuffing sweat off his brow, he says, "I'm a yacht broker."

"Oh. If you don't me asking, I understand yacht brokers often work as intermediaries with designers and clients, is that right?"

"That's right."

"In your estimation, if a client has a choice between one designer or another, and money isn't a factor, what's the tipping point?"

His face twitches, a mouse in the throes of cornered, doomed paralysis. I get the impression he'd rather take a bullet than answer. With a tight, unfriendly smile he says, "Pardon me. I have to run."

And he trudges away, his unathletic stride and weight rocking the dock.

Well, that was something. What an odd man. Morgan said yacht brokers are the ultimate schmoozers, but that guy wouldn't last ten minutes at a mixer. I wonder who it was on the other end of that phone call. Not the first tetchy conversation of the day, that's for sure. But if today has taught me anything, it's that the yacht business is fraught with billionaire drama. No shortage of egos or zeros in bank accounts. Budgets higher than most countries' economies. All day I watched Morgan navigate, and own, the high-intensity meetings. He refuses to fluff up clients. Unless there's a handshake—a gentleman's agreement—the deal isn't his.

Everyone's hustling.

Behind the gilded curtain of the glamorous yacht industry, it's a dog-eat-dog world.

We leave the show at five, with one last stop at a bar in the city. A ship builder Morgan's buddies with wants to connect off-site. Set along the waterfront, the bar patio is packed with boat folks. While Morgan freshens up in the restroom, I'm at our table deciding what to order when a battle cry reverberates over the crowd.

"Vanarama!!!"

I, and all my neighbors, turn toward the colorful intrusion bumping between tables and heading straight for me. On any given day, Stryker Talone turns heads. On a patio full of buttoned-up, stylish Europeans, a St. Patrick's-green fauxhawk is the equivalent of a slasher movie—you can't look away. He descends with all the nuance of a pterodactyl, the fringes of his buckskin jacket catching air as his arms widen to crush me in a hug.

"Hi," I say, embracing him intimately, the way you do with someone who knows your darkest secrets. "What are you doing here?"

Without asking, Stryker grabs a spare chair from a nearby table and two shocked faces watch as he flips it backwards, straddles it, and makes himself at home.

"Fuck me," he says. "Needed a solo debauch after that shitshow film. Was invited to Venice, but you know how it goes in my world." He shrugs. In addition to being an A-list director, he's also famous for losing track of time and himself when he's not on the job. "What are *you* doing here?"

"Work, believe it or not. I just landed a yacht designer as a client. We're here for the boat show."

He slurps water from my glass, adding a cherry Chapstick smear to the rim. "You look fucking incredible, by the way."

"Thanks." It never fails. Ringed with sexy dark lashes, Stryker's tender eyes always laser into my heart. This time, they burrow into the very core.

"So tell it to me straight, then," he says. "What the shitballs is going on with your husband? When did he start fucking dudes?"

It's hard to imagine an entire patio of people grinding to a complete halt. But it happens. As much as I love him, Stryker is the living embodiment of every bad, American stereotype: poorly dressed, loud, and oblivious to it all. My face flushes a deep red and before any reasonable response kicks in, Stryker's eyes flick behind me.

"Hey, buddy. You mind? This table's taken." He shakes his head, muttering to me, "Fucking Euros. Love their wine and cars but they got no sense of personal space. Anyway, back to my point. Tell me you're here because you're divorcing his sorry ass. He's married to you and thinking dicks? Hasta la vista, baby."

Morgan places his leather messenger bag on the tabletop, and a gagging horror lodges in my throat.

No. Please no.

Oh, yes.

"I hope I'm not interrupting," he says.

"Uh … no," I stammer. "Stryker, this is Morgan. My client." *Hint, hint,* is what I attempt to convey through the raising of my eyebrows. *Shut it down.*

Catching my drift, Stryker holds up his fist for a bump. "Dude. How's it going?"

Morgan scans Stryker with bewilderment, the way everyone does when meeting him for the first time. Baby face still holding up after all the years spent partying hard. Wearing acid wash short shorts and displaying the mannerisms of a skate punk, you'd be hard-pressed to guess he's one of Hollywood's most bankable directors.

With the most awkward return bump, Morgan replies, "Very well." And then, genuinely puzzled, he asks, "How do you two know each other?"

"Stryker's an old friend," I explain. "A film director. He was just shooting a project in Cape Town."

"Old friend?" Stryker scoffs. "That doesn't really do us justice, although we do go way back. Back to when she was a wild child. Bit of a princess now, but trust me, there's a tiger inside." He ruffles my hair affectionately and gestures at Morgan. "Take a seat, bro. No clue you were hanging with this hottie. I'm very protective of her."

He lays a flirty wink on me and I can feel Morgan stiffening. Forget the alarm in his face or how ashen it is. I can't even imagine how the conversation will start once he sits down. Thankfully, a moustached man with a beer belly waves at him across the patio. "Why don't you two catch up?" Morgan offers. "I'll join in when I'm done."

Stryker watches him go. "So tell me. You riding that European train?"

I feel my cheeks warm. "No."

"He seems very interested."

"How do you know?"

"I spend my life trying to get authentic emotion out of batshit crazy actors. My radar knows when it's real. I ruffled your hair and everything clamped up in his face."

Morgan's smiling now, clapping the other man on his back. If a smile could alter the course of planets spinning, change an entire universe, it would be his. That raging internal debate starts up again.

"He's very nice," I say.

"Hey. If you settle for nice, I'm dragging you back to my den by your hair. That guy, *any* guy, better be bringing his A-game to the table." Stryker leans back, a skull tattoo grimacing at me from his broad, shirtless chest. I remember the day he started on it, me at his side in the tattoo parlor. How he wanted to get my name inked over his heart and I talked him out of it. "What?" he asks when my eyes drop. "It's the truth."

I fiddle with the salt and pepper shakers, moving them back and forth. "I never wanted to leave your den."

Reading my mind, knowing where it's spiraling to, his smile falters. "You're a good woman, Vandana. The greatest. Don't ever doubt that."

"I have a lot of doubts lately," I say.

Stryker shuffles his chair closer, and I welcome the familiar weight of his arm draping around my shoulders. "I know I caused you a lot of doubt. But believe me when I say, I would've broken your heart a hundred times more. I knew you were going to do great things. I also knew I was going to do great things. Call it selfish, stupid, or just fucking prescient, but I knew I couldn't be with anyone bigger or better than me. That doesn't mean I ever stopped loving you. Not for one minute."

We share a shaky, loaded look. At one point, he was so essential to every ounce of my happiness. Calling this out only compounds my disquiet.

"You're telling me this now?"

"Vanarama, you have no idea," he says. "I hated every minute you were on set, kissy-facing Derek. He didn't deserve you." His arm tightens around me and I imagine it's to comfort the impact of his confession. "And I give zero fucks that you and I screwed around behind his back."

June calls me an oversharer, but I'll go to my grave telling no one that Stryker and I got up to our old ways one coke-fueled night when Derek was out of town. The only way I could live with myself was if something good came out of that tryst. I begged Stryker to hire him. And he did.

"He called me today," I say. "Said he's on the outs for that super-hero movie."

Stryker's flat expression tells me Derek figured right. "Me and you are family," he explains. "Someone fucks with the family, they're out."

"Half of Hollywood is closeted. At least he had the guts to come out." I squeeze his arm, hoping that if my words don't appeal, maybe my touch will. "If you blackball him, everyone will. You know how that town works."

"It works the way I work," he says. Stryker moved to Laguna Beach with his family when he was thirteen, but his staunch Wyoming farm boy morals never changed. "I gave Derek a shot because of you. I admit, he proved himself, but I have a hundred other guys pounding on my door. Dudes that won't fuck up the best thing that ever happened to them."

I nod, knowing full well once he makes up his mind, it's done.

"That being said," he continues, "if it means that much to you, I won't totally crush him. I'll have to smash him just a little, to put him in his place. So as far as working with me ever again, sorry amiga, no bueno. He pulled the wool over your eyes and I'm not letting anyone hurt you again."

His kiss is one of the sweet, slow ones I cried over for months. I've never seen him cry, but when he pulls back, his pupils are wide and haunted and I understand now that somewhere deep in his heart, he and I are still together. After a contemplative silence, he switches gears. We're talking about old Laguna friends when Morgan returns with a bottle of champagne and three flutes.

"I thought we could start the party here," he says, and I admire him for blowing past the awkward intro. This is the stronger move.

"Hells yeah, bro." Stryker slaps the table with his hand. "Never too early for panty remover."

Morgan pops the cork, letting it fly into the distance. More disapproving stares land our way, only this time it rolls off my back. Screw 'em. While Morgan fills our flutes, Stryker regales us with a story of a champagne-fueled night in Miami and how it ended with him at The Breakers, crawling out of some chick's bathtub at noon.

"To this day," he says, chuckling at the memory, "no clue how I made it to Palm Beach."

Morgan's laugh is so unbridled. I forgot Stryker can easily charm anyone; studio executives, surly crew, insecure actors. Me. He's a natural born storyteller. Cheyenne, Wyoming's biggest pride and joy.

Stryker raises his flute for a toast, bubbly sloshing out. "Cheers," he says in his booming, cowboy voice. "To boats, booze, and broads. What else does a man need?"

"You're forgetting box office," I remind him.

"You see?" He turns to Morgan. "That's why they pay her the big bucks. I hope you're spending some bankroll, dude."

Morgan clinks Stryker's flute, lingers on mine. "She's worth every penny."

I catch Stryker's smirk and my eyes flash in return: *Don't push your luck.*

Chapter Eighteen

MORGAN

IMPOSSIBLE ODDS. ALL WORKING IN MY FAVOR. THIS RAVISHING creature, the one sitting beside me charming everyone with her grace, is officially on the market.

Or will be soon.

"You look happy," Vandana says, turning to me, her smile brighter than the stage lights.

"I am."

Because I'm here with you.

Shoulder-to-shoulder in a packed ballroom, the Design Innovation Awards are about to be announced and tonight's veal tumbles dangerously in my stomach. Or it might be due to her. She's a vision in a royal-blue, one-shouldered ensemble, her hair flowing down her back in sexy waves.

Knowing I have a chance, a window, makes me not want to blow it. I haven't brought up what her friend said at the bar. I'm not that much of an idiot. But it all makes sense. The missing ring, how she ransacked my thumb.

If I do things right for a change…

Applause breaks out as tonight's MC strides onto the stage. Carlo Pasolini is the head of Strazzuza, one of Italy's biggest shipyards, and one of the judges for the awards. We bickered long and hard over costs for *Catch Me,* and I threw down some harsh words when the delivery schedule got delayed. But he's all smiles tonight with his three-piece suit and silvery hair, the anticipation of public speaking most likely washed away by copious amounts of wine.

Vandana leans in and whispers, "I am so nervous."

I need to quiet my brain, but her hand is warm and distracting on the hard muscle of my thigh. Carlo drones on with several minutes of pomp and circumstance. Sponsors thanked, volunteers recognized. My body tenses up as he gets closer to the award announcements. I scan the room to loosen up, and my gaze lands on a shadowy figure in the dark recesses of the ballroom. I can't quite make out the face, although something about the body registers in the back of my mind. I squint for a better look, but the figure seeps into darkness and disappears.

"We'll start the evening with the Talent Award," Carlo begins. "But please don't accuse me of ageism." A murmur of laughter drifts up from the crowd, most of them close in age to Carlo's fifty-five. "This years' designers are an exceptional lot, their yachts reflecting quality and craftsmanship that belies their years."

He runs through a bio of every designer, accompanied by a slideshow of the six boats in contention. It's always surreal to look at images of a creation that first existed only in my mind. When it's time for the winner to be announced, Vandana gulps her remaining wine. Henri and Alessandro offer nods of encouragement.

My stomach fills with butterflies.

"And the award goes to …" Carlo milks it, clearly loving the stage time, "Morgan de Rohan-Chabot for *Catch Me,* Royal Morgan Yachts. *"*

Applause thunders so loud, I barely hear Vandana encouraging me to stand. She's on her feet, clapping and laughing, and her joy overwhelms me. Maman likes to remind me boats will never love me back and she's right. But I've worked hard and long for this peer recognition, the one thing money can't buy.

Caught up in the excitement, I wrap Vandana in my arms, and she hugs me back. "Congratulations," she murmurs, her breath warm in my ear.

The thrill of her breasts pressed against me, the pride in her voice. The spike of jealousy that ruined me when Stryker touched her hair… Before I think about what I'm doing, I kiss her.

I mean, really kiss her.

Under the bright lights of a ballroom with 150 people watching.

And she's right there with me, unashamed. Cutlery clanks against glasses, and the liquored-up crowd, ready to cut loose after a formal dinner, shout *woo-hoos*.

"Well," Carlo says, his rich voice popping the microphone, "we can always give you your trophy tomorrow."

We break apart, laughing with the crowd. Vandana gives our table mates an *Oops, got carried away* look that is so adorable I want to kick open the door to one of the hotel rooms, drop her on the bed and eat her out until she's boneless and begging for mercy.

Don't accept your award with an erection.

Right.

I make my way to the stage, colleagues patting my shoulder, offering congratulations. Carlo hands off the trophy with a shine in his eyes. He knew *Catch Me* was special and put up with me because of it. He steps back, giving me full run of the podium.

It's true what they say—how your mind blanks when you win an award. It's the reason why winners unfold tiny scraps of paper with shaking hands. With the heat from the lights and the hush of an expectant crowd, I don't know where to start. Names and companies involved all blend together. The sensation is not unlike being miles offshore, no land in sight and in need of a beacon.

With a hand on my forehead to cut the glare, I find Vandana. She waves and gives me a thumbs up.

C'est ton moment.

I can do this.

And I do.

My head's a mess from the red wine and flowing champagne. Every time I turn around, another glass of something is thrust into my hand. People want a selfie with me. Someone asks who my girlfriend is.

Fuck.

Was it wrong to kiss her?

Olivier's got me so wound up over Khaled, over keeping my nose clean, the battle to control my brute instincts feels like a thousand tiny cuts on my psyche. There's only so much restraint in my reserves. At the yacht party, Vandana tapped the well dry. Fucking hell. Her hot mouth plundering my thumb detonated the last of my civility. I'm wobbling on a dangerous razor's edge of primal need and the consequences are haunting me. And I can't tell her any of it. Not when she's going around the room, telling everyone how great I am.

Or at least she was.

I excuse myself from a conversation with a dull Dutch couple and scan every corner of the ballroom. She's not here. I slip my phone out and text her. Wait. And wait. Nothing. I try calling, but it goes to her voicemail.

Strange.

I shoulder my way through the crowd that spills out in the foyer, the light so much brighter it stings my eyes. The bathrooms are down the hall and I wait outside the ladies' room for several minutes, finally asking a woman to report back if Vandana is inside.

Upon her return, she shakes her head. "I'm sorry. All the stalls are empty."

I check my phone again, still nothing.

An irrational knot of fear grips my chest just as Marco, the hotel manager, comes over to say hello. He's been running the show here for years and is a valued friend. In the middle of our pleasantries, Vandana streaks into the foyer from an outside balcony, running down the stairs to the lobby.

What the fuck?

"Vandana!"

She looks over her shoulder, and I never want to see her beautiful face so fraught with concern again. Frozen in that one moment, uncertainty and dread coalesce in one tight ball in my throat.

And she keeps running.

"Excuse me." I dash past a startled Marco to the top of the stairs, calling her name again. She doesn't stop.

"Anything I can do to help?" Marco asks, coming up beside me.

The sweeping view of the city is likely why she was out on the balcony, but that can't be the cause of her distress. Torn between heading there to check it out and following her to the lobby, I offload the trophy into Marco's arms.

"Can you hold on to this? I'll be right back."

I fly down the stairs and through the lobby, my head swiveling in hopes of catching any sign of her. The revolving door spits me outside into the warm, humid night. There she is. At the taxi stand. The relief surging through me leaves me lightheaded.

"Vandana. What's wrong?"

"Nothing," she says, on edge, not herself. "I, uh, I'm not feeling well. I'm going to head back."

She's lying. Like her story about the maid and the vacuum. But why? "Just tell me this is the case instead of running off. I'll go back with you."

"No, no," she insists. "This is your night. You need to celebrate. I'll be fine."

Devoid of their usual sparkle, her eyes fill with dark caution and beg me to leave it alone.

But I can't.

With my hand on her elbow, I steer us away from the other couples spilling out from the hotel. She's stiff and resisting and I have no idea why. I land only on this afternoon's events. Her personal pain was broadcast so crudely. Is she still in love with her husband? With

Stryker? (God, I hope not.) I want to ask all these questions, even though the answers might kill me.

Instead I ask, "Was it wrong … what I did in there? I apologize. Heat of the moment."

"Oh god, no," she says, with so much true intent, my spirts lift out of the murk. "I think I just…" She touches her forehead as if checking for fever. "I drank too much. That, and the jet lag. All the excitement. It's catching up with me."

Another lie.

"Honestly, I'll be fine. A good night's sleep will help. What time are we leaving tomorrow?"

Tomorrow.

No, I want to say, let's talk about tonight, now. How you feel so right in my arms. How your endless legs need to be wrapped around my face until your clit is raw and nothing else matters because we're both losing our minds.

"I have a meeting at eight, but it's personal," I say. "You can sleep in."

More crowds gather outside and her eyes dart from face to face. Watching for something. Or someone. The thought of her alone tonight in a troubled mindset is enough to foist myself on her, but if I've learned anything, she is American to the core. Strong and independent. And yet, fragile and giving in other ways. This I sense implicitly. The combination is driving me to a frenzy. With nothing vital on the agenda tomorrow, it's time to strike.

"I was thinking we could do a tour tomorrow. There's a beautiful little town I'd love to show you. It's on the way back. We could have lunch, walk around."

Her face brightens. "That sounds great. I'd like that."

"We'll leave at ten. That gives us most of the day."

"Perfect. Meet you in the lobby at ten." She pats the sleeve of my tuxedo, a send-off if there ever was one. "Please enjoy your night, and know I'm thrilled for you."

The edge is coming off, shoulders less tense, hand no longer clutching her evening bag like an eagle with a fish in its talons. But her voice is wavering and she's still hard to read. There's no point waxing on. She'll offer nothing else, of this I am certain. The best I can do is ensure she's safe in a taxi, with strict instructions for the driver to make sure she's in the hotel door before he drives away.

How out of my league it all feels. Unable to pry out a simple rationale for her behavior. This is madness. Back inside, I investigate the balcony and find nothing. Flighty isn't anything I associate her with, and it leaves a strange taste in my mouth. Propping me up for the rest of the night is her goodbye kiss. I was worried the emotional scope of my actions scared her off. But she let me know, without words, that whatever we started has only just begun.

Chapter Nineteen

VANDANA

AFTER A DARK, DREAMLESS SLEEP, IT'S STILL THERE. THE SLIME OF HIS touch. Another hot shower helps, and I scrub until my skin glows pink. With two hours to kill before we leave, the only way to shrug off the remaining creep factor is a jacked-up heart rate. I lace up my Nikes, tuck a few euros into my Lululemon tights, and go off in search of a free mind and killer espresso.

I leave my phone in the room.

I need to be alert.

I'm going to be plenty ready to drive my knee right into the ball sack of Renan again. What a loser, stalking me on the balcony, corralling me into the corner. It probably didn't help that I pissed him off, asking why he was at the award show with no nominations to his name. But there was no excuse for him grabbing my arms and trying to press those cold, vodka lips onto mine. He lay moaning in the fetal position on the concrete after my bull's-eye retaliation. He deserved it, after what he said to me. Repulsed and needing a time out, I couldn't bear another minute in the hotel.

I just wish Morgan didn't see me. Wish I didn't lie to his face.

Woah, girl.

A car horn blasts and I jump off the street, narrowly avoiding a collision. From inside the Fiat a frumpy woman shakes her fist at me and okay, I get the memo. Time to slow down, take a breath. I've sprinted for a good thirty minutes, running with purpose but no plan. Looking left and right, I'm at a loss. No sense of direction or where I am. The winding streets of Genoa are not at all like the grid pattern of Santa Monica. I decide to retrace my steps, but a delicious baked-goods scent wafts on the breeze and tempts me in the other direction. I follow the heavenly aroma down a narrow, shop-filled alley with huge brightly colored umbrellas strung overheard on thin steel cables. Morning commuters bustle past me, not without a few stares in my direction. Grabbing a coffee on Montana Avenue in skimpy exercise wear is so part of the LA landscape that no one ever looks twice. But Genoa isn't so forgiving. I walk quickly into the bakery, a bell on the door jingling my arrival.

At the sight of me, the twenty-something barista behind a display of glittering pastries does a double take. An older, handsome gentleman sitting alone at a table does the same. He's the only patron, wears a dress shirt with the top buttons undone, and when he smiles, there's something familiar about it.

My boobs are sweat-slicked and spilling out of my sports bra. I feel very self-conscious. "Buongiorno. Un espresso macchiato, per favore," I say to the barista, busting out the only Italian I've mastered.

"If you've never had their sfogliatella," the older man says, "I highly suggest you try one. It looks like you can afford the calories."

His accented English also sounds familiar, but it's his playful wink that hits me. I know him somehow. And when Morgan appears, coming out of the darkness of the side hallway, the connection lands.

They're related.

"Hi," I say.

"Hi." He's shocked to see me, for more than one reason. If anything, I'm usually overdressed.

"Um … this is so random. I was out for a run and smelled the pastries…"

"Est-ce que tu la connais?" the man asks Morgan.

"Oui. Papa, c'est Vandana. Elle m'aide les relations publique." Switching to English, he says to me, "This is Alix, my father."

"Pleasure to meet you," Alix says, getting up to kiss me in greeting like his son does. "Will you join us?"

"I didn't mean to interrupt. It's just a fluke that I'm here." I glance at Morgan for some guidance. It's his call.

"Nonsense," Alix overrides. "Please have a seat." He pulls out a chair for me and instructs Morgan to add a pastry to my order and pay for it. Settling at the table, he regards me with great interest. "How lovely to have such a beautiful woman share our table. Morgan never mentioned he was hiring someone for public relations."

Hearing the spit on the comment, Morgan chimes in. "It's barely been a week, Papa."

Alix blows on his espresso before taking a sip. "My son likes to do things his way. Never mind keeping his parents informed."

"You did everything *your* way."

"He's very sensitive about privacy," Alix carries on. "His maman believes it's our fault. Did you know—"

"You could talk about me like I'm actually here." Morgan slides into the chair beside me, and it's funny to see how exasperated he is. Nothing like a parent to bring you back to earth. He sets down my espresso and a delightful-looking treat rippled with layers of crisp pastry. "And Vandana doesn't need to hear about our family dynamics."

"I don't mind family stories," I say, and Morgan shoots me a dark look.

"Where are you from, Vandana?" Alix asks. "Lovely name, by the way."

"Thank you. Los Angeles. I've lived there for years but grew up in Orange County."

"This one," Alix says, tipping his head at Morgan. "We're still waiting for him to grow up."

This pushes the last of Morgan's buttons. He lets fly a burst of annoyed French, my interpretation of it along the lines of *If you don't shut your mouth, we're out of here.*

Alix, unperturbed, continues. "How long are you here for?"

"I leave on Sunday, after the Monaco show."

"Well, you must come over for dinner. Céline, my wife, would be thrilled to meet you. And see her only child." A little ice on that comment, too.

"We're busy with the show," Morgan says firmly.

Alix scoffs. "One is never too busy to eat. And the show doesn't start until Wednesday so you can come tomorrow night."

I turn to Morgan. "We don't have anything planned."

"If Khaled wants to meet tomorrow night, that's the priority," he reminds me, with an air of *Thanks, you're supposed to be on my side.*

"Then it's settled." Alix folds his napkin into a perfect square, pressing hard on the pleat. "Six o'clock. No need to bring anything but yourselves."

Morgan tosses back the last of his espresso, unamused. I know how he feels, being beat up by the parents. But underneath Alix's challenging fist lies a tone of tender love. Big difference from my experiences. Which is why he and I share conspiratorial smiles. I immediately like him. I like how he's showed me a different side of Morgan. That underneath his suave sophistication he's still a little boy, undone by a parent. Maybe that's why they never worked together.

Nothing like fire and ice to create the perfect storm.

Genoa is several miles behind us when Morgan brings it up.

"We don't have to go for dinner," he says, checking over his shoulder before moving into the left lane. The autostrada is less hectic,

Sunday drivers and transport vehicles moseying along in the slow lane. Morgan refuses to stay stuck behind them.

"It sounds like they want to see you."

He glances over. "You haven't figured out this is all about you?"

"What do I have to do with anything?"

"You can ask me that after you meet Maman," he says, with a hint of foreboding. "If it's up to her, she won't let you leave the house."

"Ah," I say, clueing in. "A little bit of a matchmaker? Sounds like my mom."

"So you're used to this? And you're still happy to watch me suffer through the same fate?" Trying for accusatory, the lightness in his voice calls him out.

I laugh just a little. "Honestly, I didn't know. If you want to cancel, no sweat."

His gloved hands grip the steering wheel tighter. "The thing is, if I don't go, there'll be hell to pay."

"I can be on my utmost terrifying behavior, if that helps your cause," I say.

"Are you capable of such a thing?"

"For what it's worth, your dad seems cool. And they must be proud of you."

"They're wonderful parents," he concurs. "They just want the best for me. Like every parent."

It strikes me that I'm more than a little interested in this dinner. Alix proved to be a personality and I'm curious what Morgan's mother is like. If she's got him under her thumb.

"I meant to ask earlier, but was your father in Genoa for the show?"

"He planned to surprise me at the award ceremony, but there was an accident on the motorway that tied up traffic for hours. He texted me just before we headed out to tell me what was going on. We decided on breakfast instead." His mouth flattens into a thin line. Then, "Did you have a good time last night?"

Like I did with the smells of hot bread from the bakery, he's sniffing down a path, looking for the true source. I keep my gaze straight, my voice level. "I did. Sorry for ducking out early. I feel much better."

"I was concerned," he says. "Your fatigue came on so suddenly."

In my peripheral vision, his face betrays no emotion, but I hear it. His disbelief. I want to tell him how thrilled I was with his win. Tell him our kiss in front of a ballroom of strangers was a moment I'll never forget. Tell him I was ready for messy. But if I tell him what happened, I'm not sure how he'll react. I don't want to relive the incident so for now, I keep it under wraps.

The pensive lines around his mouth will eventually go away.

For a few miles we drive in silence, and I watch the road signs whip past. Names of cities I recognize from the drive down—Arenzano, Savona, San Remo. I like that we're not heading straight back to Monaco. I'm not ready to go back. But I also don't know where we're headed.

"So … where are you taking me?" I ask.

His smile warms the car. Warms all of me. "To a fairy tale."

It most certainly is.

Fit for a princess, Dolce Aqua is a picturesque hamlet nestled along the Nervia River. The town is tiny and cobblestoned, with the magnificent ruins of a castle perched high on the hill above the river's east bank. After parking the car, we meander along a narrow street to reach the famous bridge. It arches over the Nervia and morning sun dapples the river underneath, the water clear and slow moving. The sky is pure cobalt, not a cloud to be seen.

"The air," I say, taking it in. "So pure."

"The castle is one of the oldest in Italy. And famously painted by Monet. Here, take a look."

We've crossed to the other side of the bridge where a weather-worn placard of Monet's painting mirrors our identical view of the castle and bridge.

"Wow, 1884," I say, reading aloud. "And it looks the same. So pretty. Do you mind if I snap a photo of us with the castle?"

"Sure." He stands stiffly beside me, and on my screen his smile is forced and uneven.

"You have to at least look like you're enjoying yourself."

"I am," he insists. "I just hate having my photo taken."

"You have great angles. I doubt you ever take a bad photo. Let's try this. On the count of three, we'll both smile." I hold up the phone and tickle his belly after the count of two, getting a laugh out of him just as I snap.

I show him the screen after. "See? Now that's a smile."

He shades the phone with his hand to assess. "Nick trick. You're a natural. Thank you for making me look good."

I study the screen, his mathematician's dream of a face. We both look amazing. Him in a cornflower-blue dress shirt, the cream of my dress a balanced counterpoint. Natural smiles with beauty behind us. It's a perfect capture.

"Can you send it to me?" he asks.

Across the street, a small plaza ringed with mom and pop restaurants starts to hum with locals and tourists on the lookout for a meal. Hard to believe it's already noon.

"Only if I can buy lunch. I'm starved and could use a glass of wine."

"If you prefer," he says, "my friend Jean-Claude has a vacation home in the hills. It's small and cozy but always stocked, and I know where the key is. He won't mind if we drop in. The view is fantastic."

I text him the photo and tuck my phone away. "Sold, as long as there's wine."

"It's Italy," he says. "If there's water, there's wine."

Chapter Twenty

THE ROLLING DRIVE INTO THE MOUNTAINS FEELS LIKE WE ARE SAYING goodbye to the real world. Buildings and village bustle transform into quaint farmhouses, fields full of swaying grasses, and not a soul in sight. We climb higher with each switchback while the enchanted view of the castle becomes smaller. Warm and heavy, the air spilling in through the car window is fragrant with the scent of lavender and freshly cut grass.

"You sure know how to pick the best spots," I say.

Morgan smiles. "I love it up here. My mind can shut off."

My brain could use an off switch too, and this destination feels about perfect. A rustic stone and stucco home snuggled into the hillside. Morgan parks the Bentley alongside a fence smothered with clusters of purple wisteria and leads me up a pathway lined with lemon trees to a brick patio scattered with teak outdoor furniture and planters filled with fat buds of lavender.

"Is that a bathtub?" I point to a barrel-like contraption next to an outdoor shower.

"There are towels," he says, "if you want to try it."

"Maybe later. I need a minute for this view." Across the valley, a mountain range sparkles with every shade of green. Nestled below the hills sits Dolce Aqua in all its medieval glory. I can see the castle, the river.

"And we're in." Morgan smiles, holding up a key that was left, unoriginally, under a shredded coir doormat. I follow him inside, into the kitchen, all twelve modern and efficient square feet of it. Tucked against the wall is a wooden dining table with two stools tucked underneath. Morgan drags a finger through the layer of dust on the table and shrugs. "No maid service, but it does the trick, no? The bathroom is down the hall if you need it," he adds, gesturing to his left.

I drop my purse on the kitchen counter to take it all in. A small flight of stairs leads into the sunken living room, a king bed wedged into the corner where two walls of windows meet. And wow, the view. Just as incredible from in here. I stretch and yawn, suddenly feeling dopey. The cabin's warm from all the pent-up heat, and the effects of last night's patchy sleep are trickling in.

That bed looks very tempting.

"I already feel relaxed," I say.

Morgan opens the kitchen cupboards one by one. "Speaking of relaxing, why don't you take a seat outside? I'll round up some food and wine."

I so enjoy being pampered and leave him to his devices. It's lovely on the patio, shaded by the branches of olive trees. Butterflies dance among the tall grass. I kick off my flats and stretch out on a teak deck chair weathered by rain and sun. I close my eyes and all the tension in my shoulders starts to unkink. With nothing but absolute silence around me, I drift off fast and hard, into one of those luxurious afternoon naps I never have time for.

It's blissful blackness until the soft *pop* of a cork brings me back. I can feel hot air shift with Morgan's movements.

"Mmm," I mumble, sunbaked and drowsy. "I don't think I can move."

"You were out for thirty minutes. Figured you needed the rest." With the *glug, glug* of wine into glasses, I open both eyes. Morgan's set out a tray of cheese and crackers, olives, and sliced apples. "Not as much as food as I'd hoped," he admits. Handing me a filled glass, he slips off his shoes and settles into the lounge chair next to mine. "Á votre santé, sleepyhead."

We slide wine down our throats, the Viognier perfectly chilled and quaffable. "Yum. Any chance we can work the yacht show from here?"

He chuckles. "I thought you'd like it."

It's cute how he wiggles his toes, nails buffed and trimmed neatly from a recent pedicure. There isn't much about him to criticize. After spending a handful of days together, he's proven to be genuine and thoughtful, more warm-hearted than I initially imagined. Yes, at times, he's demanding and difficult, but what entrepreneur isn't? And he really has a body to die for. A dick made for riding hard and long. Maybe the hot sun is warping what's left of my rules, but I can't stop thinking about the bed inside. How wonderful it would be to wake up to that view.

How wonderful something else might be.

"I didn't realize your friend Stryker is so accomplished," Morgan says out of the blue.

I glance over, surprised. "You stalked him?"

"I was curious," he says, shrugging it off. "How did you meet him?"

With an emphasis on *how,* the subtext is clear. "He was my first boyfriend. Way back when."

"It's nice you've kept the friendship intact."

"And that's all it is now," I say, reading between the lines. "But he's a great guy, very talented. My soon to be ex-husband worked with him." I gulp wine, thinking, *Whatever. He heard. Why deny it?*

"I'm sorry … about what's happened," he says with tact.

I let out a breath, all the dark stuff. "It's not public knowledge yet, so please don't say anything. My father's running for mayor of Laguna Beach, and… Yeah, it'll be interesting. Everyone thought we were the golden couple."

He digests that, lets the moment sit. "By everyone, you mean the public?"

A week ago, that nugget, that Morgan-ism, would've cemented his status as loser number one. But now there's some context. "Throwing it right back at me, huh?" I say, although not unkindly.

"I'm sorry. That was uncalled for." He stares into his wineglass, and I believe Morgan de Rohan-Chabot might be learning a lesson or two.

"It's all right. I've gotten used to you."

He looks up. "Is that good or bad?"

"Mostly good." He scans my face, reads the smile, but is on the hunt for something more. It's appallingly easy to fall under the spell of his eyes. They push me closer to the edge I'm fighting against. I feel myself teetering on the lip of a sinkhole. "But I might change my mind if you keep staring at me like that."

"It's hard not to look at you, Vandana," he says.

A nervous laugh spills out. "You're making me blush."

"You didn't blush when you were sucking my thumb."

My eyes dart to his, and dart away just as quickly. "I don't know what I was thinking."

"I'm pretty sure I know what you were thinking. The same thing I was." His finger brushes my bare thigh, tracing an imaginary circle, over and over. I feel my heart lift into my throat.

"I get it. Is that why you brought me here?" I ask.

"Are you suggesting manipulation on my part? Because you did come willingly."

"I can always leave."

"Not without the keys."

I smile back. "It's come to blackmail, has it?"

His full hand comes to a territorial rest on my thigh. "If anything, I wanted to ravage you properly in a worthy setting."

I lick my suddenly dry lips and the word squeaks out. "Ravage?"

Reaching for my wineglass, he threads the stems of both his and mine between his fingers. His other hand flowers open, fingers beckoning mine as he stands.

"Come with me."

He helps me to my feet and the walk across the patio, up the three uneven steps and into the house, is like being in a dissociative state. I feel heavier by a few pounds, the weight of what's about to happen landing squarely on my shoulders.

In the kitchen, he peruses wine bottles in their horizontal perches. "I think this calls for something headier, no?"

"Uh, yes. Sure. But I'm ... I need to use the restroom first."

"I'll be waiting for you."

His lips brush against mine, and we're fools to think that's going to be enough. Instantly our mouths hunger for each other's. He pulls me close, the wineglasses in his hand clinking against my butt. That damn tongue of his works me over and the thought of it invading my lady parts, all the sublime damage it can cause, brings a soft whimper to my lips.

"Okay," I say, pulling back, breathless and feeling slightly dizzy from the sun and wine and lack of food. "I'll be right back."

I grab my purse from the kitchen counter and in the bathroom, try to calm the hell down. At Stanford, I never left home without my 'night out' kit: condoms, blueberry scented lube, baby wipes, and a pair of roll-up flats so the walk of shame could happen quickly and quietly. My updated Ziploc bag, Italian version, only contains wipes and an array of condoms. I take one, debate two, then put the second one back. Can't look like too much of a keener. After tidying myself up, my parting glance in the mirror is one of heroic determination.

It barely prepares me for the tableau in the living room.

Forget about the view behind Morgan.

He *is* the view.

Leaning against the headboard, one knee bent and the other leg straight, both are rippled with muscle and a light dusting of hair. He's got a glass of wine in one hand and his balls in the other. Isn't it just like him to be that confident and totally, utterly naked.

"Perfect," he says, eyeing me with a languorous smile. "I want to undress you."

He sets his glass down on the bedside table, rearranges himself on the edge of the bed. Legs splayed wide, it's impossible not to stare.

Big and nude, softly swollen and impossibly thick.

"I come bearing gifts," I manage to say, handing him the silver square packet. UltraMega, which, in current company, suddenly seems woefully inadequate.

His brow raises. "Only one?"

"I have more. A bagful."

He tosses the condom on the bed and laughs. "Of course you come prepared. And now I get the pleasure of preparing you."

His hands land ever so gently on my waist, his touch sending a rush of heat all the way to my toes. Turning me so that I face the kitchen, my backside is the territory he's interested in. A warm palm explores, curving over each mound, before a gentle fingertip runs down the length of each leg, all the way back up. I'm jelly under his touch, quivering, I need it so badly.

"You're shaking," he says.

"It's good shaking. Trust me."

The heat of his forehead presses into the small of my back. He breathes slow and deep, the calm before the storm. "All I've wanted to do is touch you," he whispers.

Slowly, he unzips my dress, fabric pooling onto the floor. His fingers along the back of my ass sear my skin, but then he witnesses the prior damage and rains kisses onto the fading bruises. "I promise I'll be gentler."

I glance at him over my shoulder. "You shouldn't promise things you can't deliver on."

"I'll let you be the judge on how I deliver," he says, rising to his feet, imposing himself into my backside, heavy and blunt. He nibbles along the trembling line of my shoulder and I sink into his warmth. "Sweet Vandana," he mumbles. "Before I take over, tell me what you want."

I want it all. The exquisite pain before the drowning pleasure. Waking, breathing, euphoria. Spring fever in September. The kind of coming together fables and myths are built on. But how to articulate that? Seeking an answer, his hands start to roam and explore. One breaches my bra, the touch of his skin on my bare breast sending goosebumps shooting along both arms.

"Just … keep doing what you're doing," I mumble.

"Not to worry, I'll get you warm soon enough."

He's beyond stiff behind me, a pulsing brass rod. The rough pads of his fingers coax my nipple into a tight bud. For every tweak, every moan it elicits, he surges against me. I feel powerless, my own desire a thrilling promise tugging me forward. Eventually he unclasps my bra and I shrug out of it. Warm sun fills the room, my bare breasts lit up and adored by Morgan in a love language all his own. Slowly one hand voyages south, down the flat expanse of my belly, under my thong, into the dampness between my legs.

He cups my Brazilian-ed bits, breathing ragged and erratic. "Can I?"

He's asking?

I'm a quaking mess, drunk on Italian mountain air, not enough sleep and a need that threatens to swallow me alive. "Yes. Yes, you can."

His fingers ease past my slick, outer folds and my thigh muscles tighten in response. Expecting a slow, delicious burn, I close my eyes in surrender. Instead, he buries one finger, swift and deep and sudden. I'm so overdue, the shock of it craters my control. A shattering orgasm rips through me, the room going black.

"Jesus, hold on," he grunts, one arm wrapping around my waist as I spasm, shuddering and convulsing around the finger he keeps plugged tight. "You're on fucking fire."

The waves of pleasure constrict my throat, leaving me gasping for air. "Wait, wait," I pant. "Slow down."

"I can't go much slower," he says, laughing.

I shove his hand away, the space inside me suddenly vast and requiring something much more damaging to fill me. His muscled arm holds onto me like a belt around my waist as he offers me a sample from the finger he's licking clean. When I don't partake, he asks in mock offense, "You don't approve of my finger?"

"Oh, I approve. But it's going to be very busy. You need to last longer than me."

"That's not going to be a problem," he says, laughing again.

I shimmy out of his grasp and shove him playfully. He staggers back, landing hard on the bed.

"We're playing rough?" he asks, a hint of question in his voice. His cock is swollen and pulsing, tip slick with pre-cum.

"Maybe."

In a slow, sultry strip tease, I unwind out of my thong. His eyes transfix on my very slick womanhood, and he breathes hard in and out of his nose. His dick strains, the poor thing needing attention. I bend down and with a gentle glide of my lips, he fists the sheet and his words sound agonized. "You're playing a dangerous game, Mademoiselle Hillman."

"Why don't you lie down on your back?" I suggest.

"You're not taking the lead," he counters.

"Let me enjoy the power of being a woman. For thirty seconds."

He shifts onto his back, not entirely trusting me. I arc one leg over him and sit lightly on his upper thighs. I cup my breasts, tease my nipples, taunt him. Let him bite and suck and lick. Grind on him until lust glazes his eyes and his groans take on a dangerous edge.

Finally he calls it. Two hands on my hips. Stop.

"You are so beautiful," he whispers. "Such a shame I have to destroy you." He pats my butt. "Up. And move forward."

On both knees, I inch my way higher until I'm hovering over that luscious mouth of his. He stacks a pillow under his head, readying himself. Hands back on my hips, he positions me and shifts me lower.

A ball of anticipation channels into the pit of my stomach.

As if pre-apologizing for the pending carnal destruction, he plants the sweetest kiss onto my most personal set of lips.

"You better hold on to the bed frame."

Chapter Twenty-One

A ONE-WAY DELIVERY SYSTEM.

Sweet, simple, divine torture.

His tongue sweeps end-to-end before drilling me with one deep, exquisite stab. I gasp, my back arching like the crack of a whip blistered against me. The cool iron rods of the bed frame clenched between my fingers feel sturdy, but if Italian furniture makers don't take a note from their couturiers' page and build stuff that lasts, things might get ugly.

"Okay?" he asks.

Is he kidding? Wine sluices through my veins and I'm a pulsating jumble, ready for more.

"Don't stop. Even if I tell you to."

Allowing Morgan to possess me—his rules, his world—is an endless state of erotic damnation with no beginning or end. He's relentless but times it all perfectly, backing off, going hard, switching fingers for tongue. Fucking me in long, profound stabs. He knows every button and where he needs to be, or I guide him if he doesn't. The pleasure squeezes my screaming muscles into a ball, with only a vague blur of light visible through my crossed eyes. I'm distantly aware of the bed frame clanging against the wall and at some point I beg him to stop, the pinch of blissful pain a knife's edge.

But he doesn't stop.

He's allergic to that responsibility.

He enforces our contract like a brute.

"I'll stop when you can't talk," he mutters.

Settling in like a newborn on a nipple, he latches onto my swollen nub. Already sore from the nonstop tension, my body tightens again as he sucks and sucks, ratcheting my arousal into an apex of surrendering indulgence.

"Oh god, Morgan," I moan.

I can't shake out of his grip, more bruises a given. The soles of my feet start to burn. My womanhood spreads wider, and my fingers cramp from clutching the frame so tightly.

And then I'm falling. Falling back from the cliff I'm this close to tumbling off.

"What are you doing!" I pant. "Jesus Christ. Keep going."

Looking down, a nasty grin spreads within his stubble. "I will," he says. "In due course."

"For fuck's sake, Morgan." I rattle the bed frame against the wall, a prisoner in my own game. "I said, don't stop."

"Someone's testy."

"You…" I bite my tongue. He's divine, is what he is. A human heat-seeking missile. Playing me to perfection. "Please. Keep going."

"Waiting is good for you," he says, his hands cupping my ass. "It builds character."

Chafed and raw from his stubble and voracious pillaging, my inner thighs beg to differ. My reflection in the window is bedraggled chaos. If my clit was any more swollen, I could tee off with it. This is not character building.

My body sags in defeat. "Please."

"Are you in a rush?" he teases.

"When the tables turn, you're going to be very, very sorry."

He laughs and corkscrews a finger deep inside me, sending a tingle all the way to my quivering ass. "Look at me, Vandana." I drag my eyes down to his villainous ones. His pupils are dilated, full of black, full of sin. He pulses his finger up and down, in and out, thumb pad circling on my clit like a plane spiraling to a crash. "Are you threatening me?" he asks, casually.

I bite my lower lip in agony, everything clenching. "Maybe."

He drives his finger deeper, enjoying my cry. I am so turned on, so unused to his rules of play. Cruel, but lovingly administered. I bounce up and down on his digit, trying to rocket my way higher again.

He pulls out, smacking my ass. "You're not in charge."

"I'm not going to be in this position forever," I challenge back.

The twinkle in his eyes turns wicked. "What's your definition of forever?"

My head drops between numb, tired arms. If it wasn't for the bed frame, I'd be stapled to the ceiling, stuck there in permanent ecstasy. "Fine," I relent. "You're in charge."

"That's better," he says. "Now … Just relax."

Relax meaning, hang on for a ride to places I've never been. Where my drenched body no longer exists within physical laws. And like the Morgan of my dreams, he's a cosmic force, hell-bent on wiping my brain clean of any rational thought.

Of any thought.

I'm floating. Skipping high above the clouds, unshackling from the forces of gravity. But there's friction. So much unbearable friction. The delicious sensation thrusts me higher and higher, launching me beyond the moon and stars. I'm shaking uncontrollably and feel the universe cracking and coming apart. Time and space begin to collapse into a crushing pressure. In blackness and nothingness, a shockwave of pleasure shatters me into a million pieces. I'm falling, falling, no resistance, a meteor shower of Vandana plummeting, entry speed back to earth incalculable.

"Well, hello," he says.

Morgan plants a generous kiss on my mouth and reaches across my trembling body for a glass of wine on the bedside table. My vision is muddy, and the bright hot sun creates a prism effect around his head. He's a glowing ball of golden fantasy.

"Jesus," I whisper. My skin seems powdered with stardust, sparkling from adrenaline and dopamine. After being so savagely dominated, every panting breath is a new exercise in survival. Morgan has no intention of letting me regroup. Not all the way, and certainly not on my terms. He takes a drink of wine and plasters our lips together. A gushing shot of Brunello fills my throat like liquid fire. The stream emptied, his tongue lingers, prying my mouth open. I taste him, me, and want it all, hard and deep and reckless. When we break for air, he runs a hand along my naked torso and smiles at my twitching body, a live wire of nerves.

"You are a deviant," I tell him.

"Finally, a compliment." I chuck a pillow at him and he laughs, mimicking me. "*Don't stop.* I was only following orders."

"Until you stopped," I remind him. "At the worst time."

He curls a finger around a sweat-soaked lock of my hair. "Insubordination is part of my appeal."

"You think so, huh?" I sit up, or at least try to. A belated, shuddering spasm curls me forward, eyes squeezing shut with the intensity.

"Or maybe I'm the gift that keeps on giving." He smiles diabolically.

I shake my head, pawing for his wine. "Give me that."

While I guzzle away the effects of his beautiful trauma, he investigates the bed frame. "Still in one piece," he jokes. "I was worried."

"I don't think you were worried in the slightest."

He stuffs a pillow behind him to lean against the headboard with a contented sigh. It's muggy with sin in here, all the tastes and smells I've missed. I pour the last of the wine into the glass, liquid accelerator to stoke the flames. Relaxing beside him, I like the speckles of me trapped in his scruff. For once, looking into the vortex of his eyes, I'm not dragged away. They're still unwavering, shimmering like the sea, but calmer, a storm passed and settled.

Or readying themselves for the next storm.

My attention rivets onto his dick, and he flexes it up, lets it slap down on his corrugated abs.

"Wow," I say, laughing at how pleased he looks with himself. "What other tricks do you have up your sleeve?"

"Funny you should ask. I believe it's your turn to run the show," he says, stealing back his wine. "If you have the energy."

Smiling over the rim of the glass, he's not on the hunt for accolades or applause. The steamed windows, rumpled sheets and my messy coming apart are hallmarks of a job well done.

"You'll do whatever I say?"

"Anything," he replies.

Reaching for his plump, heavy scrotum, he jerks in response, hissing, "Careful."

"Hmm. Someone's testy."

He glares at me darkly. "If I am in charge again, you can forget about mercy."

If Morgan considers anything that just went down merciful, I hate to think what levels of damage truly exist in his realm. I continue to play with him, loving the slip and slide of his testicles between my fingers. Watching him twist and jerk for a change. I'm tempted to blow him within an inch of his life and match him in the pullback department. But as his dick grows in front of me, expanding to its full blunt expression, I change my mind. I might be a princess, but I crave the simple things. The weight of a man on me. The girth of a man in me.

The stupefying pleasure of rhythmic slaps of flesh.

So, I tell him to fuck me into sweet, slow oblivion, and Morgan, bless him, does exactly what he's told.

Chapter Twenty-Two

MORGAN

I WAKE UP SLOWLY, DOPEY FROM THE WINE. I'M CRUSTED WITH COME, the skin on my back lashed and sore from the rake of her nails. Buttery fingers of light streak across the room, and I'm guessing it's close to five p.m. Hard to say. I also don't want to know. Dream worlds should go on forever, not be tied to time. If Vandana wasn't curled up beside me in the deep, endless sleep that follows godless fucking, I'm certain she'd agree.

I bury my nose, take a deep inhale of her hair spread along the pillow. It smells like her, but also like us. Despite the punishing abuse, my cock stirs to life again. Oh, where to start? It's tricky rating sex. So many factors play into it, like all the atmospheric elements of an evening that turn an ordinary bottle of wine into the finest vintage.

But this... *Her...*

I had a sense of what it would be like, but I never imagined this. My mind can't even compute a number. There is no scale on which to judge. We created our own scale.

The duvet rises and falls innocently with her breathing and I smile, remembering her at the end—soaked and cursing, crumbling in my arms. A woman's pleasure is an elusive thing, and a man can go mad in pursuit of it. But there was no shame between us. No guessing. As expected, she is a woman who knows what she wants and is unafraid to tell me.

A woman who gives as good as she gets.

Round two, that debauched damage, the heights she took me to… Whatever it is that's clogging up my throat knows.

I am totally, one hundred percent screwed.

Leaving the bed is an act of treason, although I imagine Vandana will be out for a while. With utmost care, I disentangle myself from the sheet and tiptoe to the bathroom. I knew all along the pearls were a front. Vandana is a raw, blazing diamond and this afternoon, I was her craftsman. Sculpting brightness and fire, my tongue coaxing a sparkle from deep within her quivering flesh. God, she enjoyed that. Her moan turning into a cry of sweet surrender, the bashing of the bed frame against the wall, every part of her uncoiling.

I really need to stop thinking about her.

It's impossible to piss with an erection.

Yes, I know my friend, I'm on the same page. We're not leaving this place without having her again. But for now, settle down.

Finally, my mast deflates and the plumbing kicks in. I rinse my hands and slip on a thin, cotton robe to sneak outside. The terrace is washed in shadow, although the paving stones still hold the day's heat and feel warm under the soles of my feet. Fat bees buzz around the bursting wisteria blooms, but a different buzzing draws my attention to the lounge chair. I don't want to look at my phone but I do, and twenty-one messages take the shine off my mood. There is no true down day between shows, even if the calendar says otherwise. I was supposed to be back in Monaco this afternoon but have found myself pleasantly sidetracked. Something I forgot to tell Olivier.

Strangely, his barrage of texts doesn't seem to indicate someone under the weather.

OL: Where are you?

OL: We need to talk!!!
OL: Are you ignoring me?
OL: For Christ's sake. Call me!!!

He's an abrasive little fellow about time and commitments. Surprisingly, he loses track of both when he's at the casino. I take a seat on the chair and make quick work of my replies. I confirm meetings and events, address issues and questions. Dorothy and Frankie want to meet in Monaco tomorrow. Will Vandana and I be available for drinks?

I gaze up, across the valley to the mountains, where the glow of late evening turns their green mounds to gold.

Vandana and I.

How strange.

How wonderful to be thought of as a unit.

How very apropos.

When I finally buried myself inside her in one battering thrust, when her flesh gripped me in long, shuddering spasms and my name left her lips in a delirious gasp, we fused like the thick cream and chocolate in a decadent ganache.

Minds, souls, and bodies as one.

MdRC: Yes, we are available. Lunch at the Yacht Club?

I'm not so wrung out to forget Khaled is the main event. He prefers dinner meetings, and I've skewed most other engagements to the day to avoid a potential conflict. Whenever he wants to meet, we meet. Based on his exclamation mark overuse, Olivier must have news. I consider a text, but he'll pounce and call immediately so I might as well end his misery.

He answers on the first ring. Not like he has a life or anything. "Finally," he gripes. "Where the hell have you been?"

"I took a time out."

Unseen birds begin to warble in the branches above me, prompting Olivier to ask, "Where are you?"

"Italy. In the mountains."

"Uh-huh," he says. "And she's with you."

"Not that it's any of your concern, but yes."

After a long, chilly silence he says, "You fucked her."

"That's *really* none of your concern."

"Jesus. You are so predictable. And of course, it's my concern. What did I tell you? Leave your dick out of this."

"She's not like the others," I argue. "Not at all."

"That's what every man says after they sleep with a woman for the first time!" he shouts, with really no reason to.

"I've never said that. Not once. That's why I know she's different." I reach for a lemon on a nearby tree and press the fragrant flesh against my nose. "When you meet her, you'll understand."

Nothing. Then, in a tone colder than usual, "She doesn't need to meet me."

"Yes, I'd like your opinion. I'm thinking there might be more she can offer than PR. She's an excellent people person. Curious about design. Perhaps she can assist in growing that division."

"Wow," he says, sardonically. "One screw, and you're giving her the keys to the kingdom."

"Fuck you, Olivier, I'm being serious."

"No, fuck you. Focus. Put Khaled at ease. She's supposed to be a long-term asset, not one of your disposable toys, remember? The best PR money can buy. Not the best ass money can buy."

"Very clever," I grumble. "And I am always focused."

"You are self-focused to the extreme, until a woman you haven't slept with walks into the picture. If Khaled finds out you're fucking yet another married woman…"

"That's one thing we *don't* have to worry about. She's leaving her husband."

He chuckles morosely. "And let me guess, she told you this a few minutes ago? That damn afterglow."

We've been friends for so long, Olivier's cold and uncaring nature —calculating, is how a former schoolmate referred to him—is so part of the fabric of who he is, it barely registers anymore. But I'm truly incensed at his judging flippancy. Outrage takes over, spilling out in the worst way. "Her husband is gay. He just came out. The marriage is over." As soon as the words leave my mouth, I know I've made a mistake. It's not my news to divulge. I glance at the house, feeling guilty, hoping my voice didn't carry. Turning to face the driveway, I speak more quietly. "Keep it between us, okay? Apparently, her father is in California politics and is up for an election. She doesn't want any news to rock the boat."

"Huh," is all he says. "Interesting."

"How so?" I ask, picking up on an air of scheming in his delivery.

"Nothing," he adds, breezily. "I mean, people in general. I guess you never know what's really going on."

"No, you don't," I say, surprised. Sympathy is completely out of character for him. "And speaking of that, are we confirmed yet with Khaled?"

"That's why I've been hounding you. He wants to meet on Tuesday. Dinner at an undisclosed place. His driver will pick you up at seven. I wanted to clear it with you before I confirm."

My anger fizzles, melting away into the blues and purples of approaching dusk. I'll address his attitude in due course but for now, I wiggle my toes against the warm pavers, a sense of newfound purpose filling my soul. "Thank you, Olivier."

He inhales deeply on his cigarette, blows out the smoke in a tense puff. "Thank me after you get the deal."

"Can you be at the yacht club tomorrow at one o'clock? I'd like you to meet Vandana."

"Um … Let me check the schedule. Can I confirm later?"

I swat away a pesky fly. "How busy can you be? Take ten minutes. It seems like you don't want to meet her."

"Okay, okay," he says, reticently. "I'll be there at one."

I hang up, my mind bouncing in ten different directions. Vandana, the Delmars. The award. Possibly Khaled. The best week of my life, so far. As crickets start to chirp in the long grasses and shadows start to lengthen, the only other shadow infiltrating my triumphs is a thought that percolates up from last night. To put my mind at ease, I make one more call before turning the phone off. I wish we could stay here for days. Revel in each other, getting drunk on wine and the possibility of more. At the very least, tonight can stretch out. This afternoon went down in a hurry.

I sneak back inside, sit on the landing, and watch her slumber. Eventually, her internal radar picks up on my presence.

She rolls over, blinks, and covers a yawn with her hand. "Hi."

"Good evening."

In spite of how I left her, swollen and chafed, a smile spreads on her face. "Please don't tell me we have to leave?"

"Not yet."

Shadows and light dance across the mountain range, and she's transfixed with the interplay. "This place is pure heaven," she says, her voice thick with sleep and sex. "Thank you for bringing me here." Her gaze sweeps back to me, with my elbows on my knees, chin resting in upturned hands. "You're staring again."

"I can't help it. You're my Italian dream."

She props herself up on both elbows and the duvet slips enough to reveal dark, puckered nipples, the taste of them still fresh in my mind. And so sensitive. "I feel like I have pillow face," she says, patting her flushed skin. And, after licking her lips, "And major wine mouth."

"Glass of water?"

"Please," she laughs. "The biggest glass you can find."

After fetching it, I sit beside her on the bed, watching her swallow with thirsty gulps. It's different now that I've seen her come undone. She's been so put together, but this wild tumble into unabashed naughtiness is a permanent game changer.

"Thank you," she says, cuffing a drip of water off her chin. "How much time *do* we have?"

I take the glass out of her hand and stroke her hair, fine strands like silk falling through my fingers. "We can stay until late but should be back in Monaco tonight. We're meeting the Delmars for lunch at the Yacht Club tomorrow. Frankie texted me."

She beams. "Wow, Morgan. That's great news."

"For now, I suggest a leisurely bath, some food for energy and not letting this bed go to waste."

"Look at you, organizing. Although maybe…" With a misbehaving smile, her finger winds down my torso, wreaking all sorts of havoc below. "We can tackle that list in a different order."

I strip out of the robe to join her wonderful, warm body. We cuddle into the pillows, lying on our sides to face each other. All that carefree hair and smudged eyeliner makes her even sexier. Lavender and pine, the sweet smell of us, I inhale all of it.

"It's impossible not to be seduced by this place," she says.

"I will confess, I hoped the magic might work its charms."

"I wouldn't count your charms out entirely."

I kiss the tip of her nose. "Two compliments in one afternoon. I'm on a roll."

Her hand finds mine under the duvet, fingers twining with a tight grip. Wide and dark with vulnerability, her eyes latch onto mine. The flesh of her throat pulses with a hard swallow. "I've never done anything like this," she whispers.

"Could have fooled me."

Her knee jabs me under the covers. "That's not what I meant."

Filtering her intentions, I understand the raw concern left behind. She's crossing a line for me, a client, and stepping into the unknown. But I try to keep it light because I'm in foreign territory as well. It's too soon to frame us, to put a name to something that isn't nameable, but Vandana and I, we can move mountains together.

I know it.

"I know what you mean," I say and kiss away her worry.

There's more to say, so much more, but conversation is hard to prioritize with thousands of years of human instinct coming alive under each other's touch.

The meal?

It never happens.

The bed, however, gets appropriately destroyed.

And, well, the intention was to get clean after in the bath.

I must apologize to Jean-Claude.

The Bentley's headlights illuminate the motorway, two beams searching the empty darkness of midnight. Searching, like me. Vandana's in the passenger seat, dozing. Ten minutes earlier her fingers curled around mine; now, our two hands rest on the console.

To have someone hold your hand like it means something…

I've never been much of a talker and I'm at a loss for words tonight.

So many questions.

I'm searching my soul for the answers.

I don't know what I feel inside.

I just don't want it to stop.

Chapter Twenty-Three

VANDANA

I CAN'T SLEEP.

Everything feels surreal.

The hypnotic view of the Mediterranean from my balcony, a fat moon spreading magical light on the current.

TQ's latest update only reinforces the strange vibration thrumming inside me: *Everything running smoothly. Without you two here, there's less work to do!*

And Vaughn emails, finally, from Africa. For a man worried about how many elephants would hold his attention, my inbox heaves with photos, each punctuated with a byline: *This guy was huge! Lindsay loved the baby! Amazing, right?* I scroll through pics of him happily posing with Lindsay and animals like he's Ernest Hemingway bagging big game.

Who would have guessed?

I set my phone down on the patio table to listen to the waves lap the shore in a whisper. My face glows with heat, with awareness, all my senses sharpened.

And then there's Morgan.

A man who stripped me bare, poked fun at me in the process, and left me reconsidering how any other specimens of the male species ever held my attention. The fireworks are real, not just between the sheets, but knowing his reputation makes it hard to synthesize. The fading fragments of right and wrong are still powerful enough to muddle my thoughts.

Now what?

I don't know.

I couldn't read him on the drive home tonight. He let me hold his hand, didn't pull away, but his silence threw me off. Did it feel strange for him, kissing goodnight in the car, going separate ways? I felt like Cinderella rushing home before the spell wore off. Now I'm kicking myself, wondering if I should have invited him up. I didn't feel the vibe though. He was unusually absent.

But maybe it's him calling right now, saying he found my glass slipper. I rush for my phone, the scrambled number unfamiliar. His landline perhaps?

Just answer.

"Hello?"

"Darling. It's your mother. Don't hang up."

My heart plummets. Leave it to her to be the absolute buzzkill. "Hi. What's up?"

"I'm here with Elaine Gutenberg. You remember Elaine, right?"

The Jewess doyenne who promises to guard your secrets, then sells you out when someone else's higher-priced secrets trump yours? Yes, I remember her. A fixer of sorts. In the elite OC circles my parents run in, she's the one to turn to in time of need. The female version of the Godfather. Right down to the raspy, inflected voice.

"Hi, Elaine."

"Vandana. Long time, no talk."

"We're all on speaker together," Mom says. "I hope you aren't offended, but I told Elaine about your … situation. She has ins where it matters."

"Barring any full-scale cataclysmic events," Elaine clarifies.

"And this isn't cataclysmic, darling," Mom assures me. "Not by any stretch. It's manageable, wouldn't you say, Elaine?"

"Mom," I butt in. "People come out all the time now. This isn't 1930's Hollywood. And Derek isn't famous, not in that way. No one will care."

"But you know how dirty politics is. It's bad enough your father's Mercedes is two years old."

I shake my head. Unbelievable. "Well, I hate to drop this on you, but the word's already out."

"What? So soon? How?" Her questions chirp out one after the other, and it dawns on me I never asked Stryker how he knew. He flew to Berlin yesterday for some rave and won't surface until Thursday.

"I'm not sure. Derek called me the other day because Stryker's taken him off the next movie."

"Stryker? Oh, dear god," she moans. "We're doomed." Mom knows all about Stryker's opinions. They were fast friends. I have a sneaking suspicion they also slept together, but I don't dare to ask either.

I slump onto one of the patio chairs. "We aren't *doomed*, mother. I ran into Stryker and asked him to keep it on the down low."

"And you'll do what he wants so he keeps his mouth shut?" she asks.

"Do what?"

"Sexual favors! The international currency of women. Jesus, Vandana, where did I go wrong with you?"

"Honey," Elaine grunts. "You're giving your mom a heart attack."

I feel a migraine coming on. "Okay, Mom, thanks for your concern, but I got this. Now I'm going to say goodbye because it's almost one in the morning here."

"Where are you?"

"In Monaco. Remember?"

"You went against our advice? I explicitly said you can't—"

"Wait, wait, Ivy," Elaine cuts in. "This could be good. The press can't find her in Europe. Not right away. My girl Riva, she's got a house in Israel. Haifa. Nice place. Lots of ladies I know go there after surgery. Door's always open."

Mom perks up. "That sounds ideal. What do you think, Vandana? A little Middle Eastern sojourn until the election is over?"

Oh, god. As if. "Let me be perfectly clear. I am not hiding out. Not for dad, not for you. And certainly not for me. This is my life and I'll handle it. Back off!"

Fired up, I pace back inside while mom sniffs with indignation.

"I'm telling you, Elaine. She's always been this difficult. Even at birth."

"Mom, don't you dare."

But she's unleashed and ready to tear me down. "I needed stitches to sew up my vagina after you. Your father couldn't touch me for weeks. That's when it all started."

I lose it. One hundred percent lose it. "Why don't you get your head out of your ass for one flipping second and take some of the blame? Your husband's infidelity is not my fault. You didn't accompany him on business trips. You barely took an interest in anything he did. Are you surprised he's had affairs?"

In the crackle of scratchy cell phone connection, I can picture her face, trying hard to be furious but stopped by all the Botox. "I took several golf lessons. What else was I supposed to do?"

"I honestly don't know how you've done it all these years, Mom, but being here, I realize how unhappy I've been. With Derek. My work. How you treat me. I'm not putting up with this shit anymore."

Instead of recognizing my bitterness for what it is, Mom gallops down a completely irrational, boned-in-the-head path of logic. "Calm down, darling," she says. "Just because Derek's in crisis doesn't mean you are. You're one decent marriage away from being perfectly set up. And speaking of that, Lance Shelby is still on the lookout. Like we all didn't know that Polish tart was only after him for the immigration papers."

"I never liked Lance and never will. He lit my hair on fire when I was thirteen, remember?"

"I believe we all agreed that was an accident," she hedges.

"No! His parents negotiated you out of suing them."

"Girls," Elaine interjects, trying to settle us.

But I'm so done, it's not even funny. "I'm hanging up now. And this is long overdue Mom, but please fuck right off."

Something hot and rushing sweeps over me. A stain I don't want to feel. I chuck my phone into the bed pillows and cry it out. Derek, Renan, Mom. What I'm feeling for Morgan. I feel like life is pivoting faster than I can keep up with and all my uncertainty pools into a teary wet spot on the bedspread. When I admitted my biggest fear to Morgan this afternoon, I wasn't expecting an overwrought declaration of feelings in return. We're not swoony teenagers in heat. And yes, he kissed me and smiled and said he knew what I meant, but I saw something pass over his eyes that read entirely different.

Doubt.

Like he'd made a mistake.

Did we both make a mistake? I roll onto my back and calm myself with the deep yoga breaths Flynn taught me. I can't answer any questions right now. I'm drained and in need of good sleep, but wired and restless. I need to clear my head. Morgan drove me past the Monaco casino after our lunch at the Yacht Club and mentioned it's open until four a.m. every day. Google Maps says it's twenty-five minutes away on foot. There, back and a bit of gawking in between should set me straight.

I pull on my hoodie and tights, lace up my sneakers, and head out.

Despite how late it is, I feel safe. Monaco is free from most inner-city plagues, and the flat and winding walk along the waterfront is peaceful with no one around. On Plage du Larvotto, Monaco's only beach, the outdoor restaurants are shuttered and still. At the ultra-chic Metropole Shopping Mall, workers scrub down the immaculate tile stairways leading to some of the city's most exclusive shops. Everything gleams in Monaco, but nothing shines brighter than the Casino, a Belle Epoque architectural masterpiece that oddly, Morgan told me, doesn't allow locals to gamble inside. At this time of night, the budget tourists are long gone, but big money never sleeps. Luxury cars of the high-end clients line the primo parking spots out front.

I wander inside the elegant building but only get as far as the atrium before an attendant approaches me. I laugh at how apologetic he is. First time in my life I'm called on a dress code.

But it's okay.

The extravagant locale demands a better wardrobe. I'll ask Morgan if we can come here for drinks or dinner. I do a quick lap of the atrium and wave goodbye. After all the fresh air, I'm settled and ready for bed. About to bound down the front stairs, I notice two men sitting near the bottom of the steps. One hangs his head and if he's not crying, he's close to it. The other…

Oh my god. It's Renan.

And the one crying is that strange man from Genoa.

I freeze. Shitty shit! Neither has seen me, but the only way out is past them and down the stairs. I pull the hood of my sweatshirt up, slowly and carefully, so as not to draw attention to myself, and tuck my hair inside. Push comes to shove, if they see me, I'll bolt. I can outrun them.

In the still air of two a.m., their conversation drifts toward me.

"I can only hold off Nikolay for so long. How much do you owe?" Renan demands.

"A million."

"That's pretty fucking serious."

"Thanks for the update."

"How many fingers are broken?" Renan asks. Curt and emotionless, the uncaring in his voice chills me. I glance over surreptitiously. The man from Genoa holds one hand in the other, fingers hanging at strange angles.

"Two," he says.

Renan gets to his feet and stares out into the night. With thick, folded arms and a black scowl, he was born to play the role of a heavy. "I'm not feeling confident with you. Time's running out and you have a lot more bones they can break."

"I'm trying, okay?" the other man bleats. "I'm trying! That stupid woman in Cannes didn't follow the simplest orders. I said make it public and she chose a coat room. I can't film through walls."

"You've always been a schemer, trying to get by with the least amount of effort," Renan coldly complains. "Why don't you rig his place? They're bound to end up there and you have a key, right? Or use your connections at the Bay. They'll never suspect anything."

The way he casually talks about espionage doesn't surprise me. But the mention of my hotel puts me on high alert.

"I've got something in the works," the other man insists. "It's already playing out like I thought it would. He's so fucking predictable. Just … cut me some slack. I'll figure it out." He glances up and back at Renan, and I quickly turn my head to avoid being caught in his gaze. "Can you run me to the hospital? I can't drive like this."

Renan helps him to his feet with a dramatic sigh. As they stagger down to a black Mercedes E series, I make my move, speed walking away into the shadows.

Something about their conversation doesn't sit right with me.

Nor does seeing them together.

It feels like too much of a coincidence.

I run the entire way back to the hotel, unable to escape the feeling I'm being followed.

Chapter Twenty-Four

"GOOD MORNING, SYLVIE. IS THE RESTAURANT CLOSED? THE DOORS are locked."

The young blonde at the front desk smiles apologetically, all dimples and pink cheeks. "Oui, just for today. They need to do some maintenance in the kitchen. Would you like me to order you something from the bakery nearby and have it delivered to your room? It might take thirty minutes or so."

"That's fine. Can I work in the restaurant while I wait?" I woke up late and need to catch up on some emails before lunch. I've brought my laptop with me and I'm ready to go.

"I don't see why not," she says, after giving it some thought. "The maintenance crew is delayed. I'll let you know when your food arrives."

She jots down my order—cappuccino and croissant for the win—and a bellman arrives to escort me into L'Orange Verte. The lobby restaurant has the tropical feel of a Caribbean beachside home with high ceilings, palm trees in wooden planters, and unstuffy decor perfect for whiling away the afternoon with a pina colada and nothing on the agenda. Unfortunately, it's too early for day drinking and my to-do list is a mile long. It's also windy this morning, so I take a seat at one of the inside tables and fire up my laptop. I ignore the flood of emails from my mother, but Derek's single email catches my attention. Hard to miss the all-caps headline.

FIFTY REASONS WHY YOU KILLED OUR MARRIAGE.

What follows is a dense, darkly angry spew of vitriol that glows harsh on the screen. It guts me, reading it. That he actually took the time to list my inadequacies, real or perceived. Reading my failure as a woman and wife in tidy bullet points makes me wonder how long he carried all this inside him. He ends with: *I'm seeing a lawyer this week. I'm not getting thrown out of my own house. Prepare for battle.*

Battle? Derek's always had a dictatorial streak, par for the course as a first AD, but he toned it down at home. If this is what I'm coming home to, maybe I'll reconsider extending my trip.

Or never return.

My phone starts to ring, and the sudden sound makes me jump. It's Morgan. I tamp down the rise of hurt in my throat and manage a cheery *hello*.

"Where are you?" His voice is blacker than coal.

"Down in the restaurant, working. Are you—"

"I'll be right there."

The line goes dead and I stare at my phone, confused. Although shaken when I got home last night from the casino, I fell asleep with a shimmer all over my body, courtesy of Morgan's late text: *Thank you ... for everything.*

I replied this morning, *Same.*

He didn't respond, and now he sounds pissed. Like really pissed. Like maybe the Khaled deal isn't going to happen and maybe I have something to do with it. I don't have time to consider all the possibilities because Morgan storms into the restaurant seconds later, eyes lit up with fury.

"Why didn't you tell me what happened in Genoa?" he demands. "At the awards show."

Shitty shit. He knows. It's written all over his face. But how?

As if reading my mind, he whips out his phone, waits for the facial recognition, and shoves the grainy black and white video so it's just inches from my face. "I knew you were lying," he says.

The problem in today's world is cameras. Everywhere you go, someone, somewhere, is filming you. And there I am on the patio of the hotel, cornered by Renan and fighting back.

I meet his eyes, barely. "I'm sorry. It was your night. The award … I didn't want to—"

"Fuck the award!" He flings one of the chairs as if it's balsa wood and not heavy oak, and it crashes into another table, sending place settings flying like missiles. "How do you think I felt watching this?"

Distress distorts his face and I've no idea how to handle his intensity. He's so in my personal space there's hardly room to breathe. I push out of my chair to stand and position myself behind it as protection. "The last thing we need is word getting out about that on one of the biggest nights of your career. Think about it."

"Mon Dieu!" he bellows, throwing up his hands in rage. "Your way of thinking is insanity. Image over safety? Didn't you learn anything from the party? He is cruel. He can hurt you." He snatches a water glass off the table, hurling it across the room. "Stop being so fucking American."

"What does that mean?" I ask, taken aback.

He sweeps back his bangs with an agitated hand gesture. "It means you don't have to be strong and tough and deal with shit like this on your own. I was there. I could've helped. And you ran away from me."

His voice wavers, and not once has even my own mother had the same look on her face. I'm trembling, getting hit from all sides. In the empty restaurant, it feels like I'm alone on a stage, not ready for the show, but the curtain is pulling back regardless.

The morning wasn't supposed to be like this.

"You're right," I finally say. "I should have said something. Despite what everyone thinks, I'm not perfect. I don't always do the right thing."

Morgan eyes me—how tightly I'm gripping the chair back, the

shrill rise of my voice—and dials back his anger. "You don't need to be perfect. Just be you."

"I'm trying, okay? I'm trying not to live up to impossible standards." I feel tears leaking and take a deep breath to control them. I'm revealing layers I won't be able to cover back up. "It's hard."

He moves closer, one finger feathering my trembling chin toward his. Our eyes lock. Maybe he sees my shame, my failure. Sees it all and isn't afraid. "I like you just the way you are," he says. "Maddeningly Vandana."

"Maddeningly?"

"Yes," he says, the word ringing with raw defeat. "You are driving me mad. I can't stop thinking about you."

He possesses my mouth, damn near swallows me alive in an engulfing kiss. In the crush of his arms, it's like I'm a match igniting, and my fears and uncertainty combust into an inferno of desperate, scorching need. Our hips crash together like two raging rivers of lava and Morgan groans, his tongue drilling deeper. His vital male glory throbs hard between my legs and torches my insides into a quivering, molten mess.

There are only two temperatures with Morgan: hot and hotter.

All I want to do is burn.

His mouth rips off mine suddenly and before I know what's happening, he scoops me into his arms.

"What are you doing?" I ask, breathless, legs limp and dangling.

"I'm sorry," he says, not sounding sorry at all. "But you need to be punished."

He scours the abandoned restaurant, barreling straight ahead at what he's spotted. In the mad rush, he hip-checks a chair, and my foot catches on the back of it. One of my patent stilettos falls to the floor, and I watch it become smaller and smaller until it disappears behind the swing of the kitchen door closing.

Oh my. In here?

It's dark and warm, the air thick with rich butter and slippery oil. Morgan crooks me onto one hip, and with his free arm sweeps a collection of pots and pans on the countertop onto the floor. Like I'm today's lunch special, he dumps me onto the countertop, the stainless steel counter cool and hard under my ass.

"Morgan," I say hoarsely, but his tongue silences me. He's a marauding force I submit to as he shoves my skirt up and rips the elastic of my thong with a violent *snap*.

"Those were my favorite," I gasp, watching them fly over his shoulder. And at $200 a pop, Agent Provocateur aren't exactly disposable.

"I'll buy you ten more," he mutters and yanks me to the counter's edge, the unforgiving metal robbing my bare ass of a layer of skin.

"Ow!"

Hoisting my legs into a position I thought only my gynecologist would be familiar with, Morgan grabs an empty five-gallon pail, upends it and plants his ass for a full view of my lady bits. "You're going to feel more than that," he assures me.

Without warning or pretense, his tongue takes a devastating pass and it's Fourth of July fireworks times one million, the explosion like being shot out a cannon.

"Fuck," I moan, the soles of my feet clinging to the counter's hard edge. "This is crazy."

"Tell me to stop and I will," he says.

Over my heaving chest and through the very unladylike splay of my legs, our eyes meet. The certainty of what's going to happen is undeniable. But he'll walk away if I say the word. He will not let himself be painted with the same brush as Renan.

I've never desired a man more.

Let the record show Vandana Hillman abstains from speaking.

The mute nod of my head is all the tacit understanding he needs, and the immediate, urgent suction on my clit, still tender from last night, breaks me. I'm not one to make a lot of noise, but try being silent when you're flung across the erotic universe. Morgan fucks with his tongue the way ducks paddle underwater. You can't see it happening, but man, is it effective. He works me, ripple after ripple, and I'm powerless against the pleasure, the spiraling darkness coming way too soon.

"Slow down," I plead. "Slow, slow, slow."

But he's out for destruction, on a mission, a time trial, and to speed things along, his finger drifts lower to circle on a spot he hinted at yesterday. My legs convulse and I gasp hard in response.

"Is that okay?" His lips hum against my swollen ones. How he manages to crouch on a bucket and operate so effectively without cramping is some gymnastics miracle.

"Just … on the outside. For now."

The wrong thing to agree to, in retrospect. Back door amps my libido and the dual pressure builds into a diabolical force. My hands claw uselessly on the slick stainless steel, then paw at his hair. He shakes free of my grasp, muttering he needs to concentrate, and I shudder with the thrill of knowing nothing but epic release is enough for him. So, I lie back and surrender to his carnal ways. Through half-lidded eyes, the kitchen starts to blur, reality fading. I want to forget it all, forget who I am, burn into nothing and rise from the ashes transformed into someone else.

My feet curl, blood hammering in my ears. "Yes, yes," I moan. "Fuck, yes!"

The tsunami of pleasure crests and rips through me in long, racking shudders. I bite my lip so hard it draws blood and I'm surprised I don't crush his head; that's how tight my thighs clamp around him. He shows me the side of him that has no mercy, lashing and probing until my cries weaken into whimpers.

I'm a quivering shell of a woman when he rises to his feet. He steadies himself against the counter and his eyes tell me he's not even here right now. He's in between worlds, like me, spinning.

But it can't end here.

My needs border on maniacal. I need him to ruin me and finish the deed.

I am plated and ready to be sauced.

"Can you?" I ask.

Wiping his mouth, he mutters, "I don't have anything."

What?

My condom stash is on the seventh floor, light years away. I'm achy and melting and want nothing more than the full pleasure of him driving deep into me. But I'm also smart enough to know the consequences.

Time for plan B.

"Then let's switch. Pants down." I lower myself off the counter, legs wobbly but holding. Morgan stands there with a dazed look on his face. Finishing me off seems to have finished him off. I unbuckle his belt, whip it off and unzip him. "Let's go, sailor."

"I think you mean captain," he says, reasserting his authority as he shimmies his pants and briefs down around his ankles. His naked shaft stands glorious and tall, a thick vein throbbing angrily along the length.

"Whatever." I wrap my fingers around him and let my tongue do damage with wet, slow circles on his tip.

"Fuck!" He groans and falls back against the counter. "I'm not going to last a minute."

Turns out a five-gallon bucket isn't handy for the angles I need so I kick it away, spreading my legs to steady myself. I'm prepared, unlike last night, for how completely he fills my mouth. My jaw relaxes, calibrating to the weight and girth.

"Oh, Vandana," he mutters. "You feel so good."

I like how he doesn't manipulate my head, forcing himself deeper. There's no need.

I got this.

I ease into my rhythm, bring him to the boiling point in no time. It's like an oven in here with no circulation, his male musk spiking with my rising tempo. The muscles of his thighs turn rock hard with tension, balls tightening.

It never hurts to go a little deeper.

When I do, his breathing turns into short, erratic puffs. Something inarticulate gurgles out of his mouth. When I find his eyes, they're helpless and uncomprehending.

God, I love a man on the edge.

His dick swells, testing the depths of my throat.

And then I hear … my name?

Through fluttered eyelids, it makes no sense. Tiny spasms flicker around Morgan's mouth, clamped shut to prevent an ungodly howl.

I must be hearing things.

Then, the brisk, efficient voice of Sylvie rings out a second time.

"Mademoiselle Hillman?"

Chapter Twenty-Five

WAITING FOR THE DELMARS TO JOIN US AT THE YACHT CLUB, I CAN'T help but tease Morgan. "I hope you enjoyed it. For as long as it lasted."

He swirls the deep orange of his Negroni with a straw, refusing to be egged on. "I will enjoy inflicting more punishment on you."

"You started it."

"I know. But had I known…"

That elegant jawline of his sets, and I take the hint. His displeasure has a teensy bit to do with me not coming clean about the breakfast order. (Like he even gave me a chance!) But it has more to do with being blue-balled while we scrambled to make ourselves presentable. It has a whole lot to do with how we slunk out of the kitchen guilty as thieves, me barefoot, a single Jimmy Choo in my hand, the blush on poor Sylvie's face deeper than the ones on ours.

The fact I find it amusing surprises Morgan more than it does me. Mind you, I don't have a close connection to the hotel or a general manager as a family friend. And while Morgan might think Vandana Hillman is not the type of lady to do unspeakable things in the kitchen of a luxury hotel, it's the furthest thing from the truth. Back before I was the put-together Vandana, the perfect princess, that was me most of the time. The exhibitionist courting the thrill of being

174

caught. I wanted him so badly this morning, I almost suggested he protect himself using the industrial-sized roll of Saran Wrap on the counter.

Surely it's been done somewhere.

Morgan's phone lights up on the table with an incoming text and reading it, his brows knit together. "Now what?" he mutters.

"Who is it?"

"Olivier." He snatches up the phone, reads and responds, agitation evident in his keystrokes. "I wanted him to meet you today, but he's had some kind of accident."

"Oh, no. I hope he's okay."

He blasts off another text before setting down the phone with a frown. "I don't know what's going on with him these days."

"Is he not performing?"

"He is, but…" He sits back, fingers steepled against his chin in thought.

"There they are! Hi, lovelies!" Dorothy waves enthusiastically from across the patio. She swans over in an emerald-green caftan with a matching scarf tied around her head, and Frankie brings up the rear in near identical clothing from the first night we met. We run through the usual greetings and take a seat.

"How did the Ferrari hunt go?" Morgan asks.

"Great," Frankie says. "I'm looking to add to my collection. We saw a nice one, right, hon? A vintage California."

"They were all red and nice, Bubs. Like the others in our garage." She lowers her sunglasses at him and winks.

"And how about the villa shopping?" I inquire. "Any luck?"

"Talk about everything looking the same." Frankie elbows his wife good-naturedly, getting a loving glare in return. I like their rapport. Fun, with a healthy dose of ribbing. No doubt being billionaires adds to their joie de vivre, a term Morgan explained to me the other day.

"The properties here are to die for," Dorothy swoons. "We saw two that we like. One in Cap Ferret."

"That's where my parents live," Morgan says.

"Really?" She clasps her hands together, atwitter with the reveal.

"How swish. Maybe we'll all be neighbors. Have you been?" she asks me.

"We're going to his parents place for dinner tonight, actually. It'll be my first time in the area."

Frankie eyes both of us warmly. "Meeting the parents, huh? Wedding bells in the future?"

In the slight pause, Morgan reaches for his drink, leaving me flat-footed and floundering under the very interested gaze of these two. "No, um ... just dinner."

Dorothy's mouth twitches into a smile. She's clever, this one. Good at reading people and situations. "Well, we had the best realtor experience. She knows everyone." Touching Frankie's arm she says, "Prince Khaled referred her to us, is that right?"

"You know the prince?" Morgan asks.

"He's a dear friend. He and Frankie are like this," she says, crossing her fingers. "Oil and oil."

"Very down-to-earth guy," Frankie agrees. "Tough as nails in nego-tiations, but fair and diplomatic."

Morgan and I share a sharp, sideways glance. I decide to go for it. Why not? "Morgan's one of three designers in contention to build some yachts for the prince."

"Oh, really?" Frankie's gaze cuts to Morgan. "He talked about that a few weeks ago. His sons are positioning themselves to have the biggest and the best, just so you know. Who else is he considering for the project?"

"Renan Sadik and Christof Weimar," Morgan replies.

"Hmm. I don't know either, but we can put in a good word for you, if it'll help."

Dorothy leans in to whisper, and I can see her at some high society dinner, tipsy on French 75 cocktails, spreading gossip like butter on toast. "I'll tell you a little secret about the prince. He adores his mother, and she weighs in on all the important decisions. I bet she'll have a say in this."

"Hon..." There's the Frankie warning again. TMI.

I dive back in to seal the opportunity. "Your support would be great. Morgan's meeting with him tomorrow. Make sure to mention his yacht just won the design award in Genoa."

This brings the conversation back to why we're here. Two hours later, we're full of wine, lobster salad, and yacht details. Morgan is armed with enough information to begin a design brief for the Delmars. Dorothy ran a little wild with grandiose ideas, and I suggested letting Morgan sit with all the details before committing to anything.

After they leave, we soak in the good fortune of a multimillion-dollar commission. "I really like those two," I say. "They're solid."

"You are incredible," he says, his head shake more admiring than his words. "How you handle people. Far better than me."

I smile shyly, caught off guard by how this warms me. "Thank you. It's all about knowing when to push and when to pull back."

He finishes up the last of his sparkling water with a telling smile and I understand where his mind just went. Mine's been there most of the day.

"How did you figure they were in the market, that night at the yacht party?" he asks. "I couldn't get past the jeans."

"The diamonds she was wearing were real. And she had a Coomi. It's a thirty-thousand-dollar handbag."

He nods approvingly. "Good eye."

"And the way she looked at all the details … I just had a hunch."

"You're very interested in the details. Knowledgeable, too. It makes me think you've done design work."

"I have. I took a design course after Stanford. The plan was to pursue interior design and then I met Vaughn. But I designed our house and Sevruga's offices."

After hearing *our house,* his expression flattens out. A beat passes as he fiddles with his napkin, folding it, unfolding it. "I'd like to see your work. I'm sure it's impressive. Have you ever thought about pursuing design?"

"Not as a full-time career. I'm too busy with PR."

"And you enjoy it?"

"It has its moments," I answer truthfully. "Although I find the creative aspect of interior design fulfilling. Having something concrete at the end to show for all the work."

Folded into a perfect fan, he plunks the napkin in front of me and smiles. "Agreed."

The waiter comes around and asks if we'd like anything else. The lunch crowd has thinned, enough time passing that the light outside has changed. With the bill paid and bellies full, there's no reason to linger.

I gather up my handbag and make a motion to leave. "I should finish up the press release for your award. I'd like to get it out before four. Do you mind dropping me at the hotel?"

"Before we go…" His head swivels, taking in our immediate perimeter. I can tell from the lines around his mouth he's got something on his mind. "You'll probably disagree, but I'd like you to think about bringing some sort of action against Renan. He's known for that kind of behavior and with the video, you can present a case."

"Oh." Wasn't expecting this. "Well, I don't know the first thing about Italian law."

"Finding a lawyer isn't a problem."

It's a thing for him now. Only I don't want it to be. Yes, I'd love Renan to face the bleak walls of an Italian jail cell, but he'd probably get served Chianti and the finest cheese. And I've heard the rumors. On the surface, Italy is a beautiful wonder. Underneath is a chaotic, bureaucratic mess. I have no aspirations to get stuck in the mire.

"Is this even a case to them?" I ask. "From what I know, Italy is all about macho men. I kneed one of their kind in the balls, and that's clearly on the video."

"Yes, I know," he says. "I saw."

"Can I think about it?"

It's not what he wants to hear but he says yes anyway. On the elevator ride back down to collect the car, the frequency humming between us is almost physical in its force. I want to stay on the right side of it. I planned to ask him about what went down at the Casino last night. If my description of the other man might trigger something for him. But with him bringing up legal action, coupled with the fury of his outbreak this morning, if he hears that I wandered the streets of

Monaco alone at two in the morning and stumbled upon Renan, he might flip.

When we're back in the car, I focus on tonight. "What can I bring for dinner? I don't like showing up empty-handed."

"My parents have everything," he says. "Including a wine cellar to last two generations. Just us is fine. I'll pick you up at five. We'll take the scenic route, so I can show you around the Cap before dinner."

"That sounds great."

He glances over. "You're ready for Maman?"

"She knows we're just working together, right?" No time like the present to ensure our stories match, although what exactly our story is, I have no clue. Chapter one is still unfolding.

"Yes," he says, "and I don't want to give her any false hope."

He leaves it at that, although the tension in his voice makes me wonder if this dinner is stressing him out. He looks out the windshield in a way that makes me think he's not seeing anything. The entire drive to the hotel, he talks about the Delmars and his initial thoughts about the concept, but my mind's elsewhere. After what went down this morning and the look in his eyes when he said he can't stop thinking about me, there's more than just work going on.

But maybe it's plain foolish to imagine a distant world where he and I make sense.

Maybe it boils down to his dick in my mouth, a couple flashes of erotic mayhem, and nothing more.

Monkeys on a tree.

Chapter Twenty-Six

FOR MOST OF THE DRIVE TO SAINT-JEAN-CAP-FERRET, I'M IN spellbound silence. Bathed in the late afternoon sunshine, each town and hamlet along the seaside route glows with a luxurious ambience. Morgan points out the home of Bono in Eze, says Beaulieu-Sur-Mer is full of boring Swiss. I can't get over how beautiful it all is.

"You're lucky to live here."

"It's my favorite part of the world," he says. "Perfect climate. The ocean."

"Like LA, only more manageable, less smog, and a hundred times more picturesque."

He looks at me sideways. "I take it you aren't missing it."

"Right now?" I laugh. "No." The reality is, stepping away has given me some perspective. The beat of life of here is less intense and more my speed. Mind you, it's hard not to see life through rose-colored glasses driving around the Cap. The stately homes are full-blown manors in the Downton Abbey sense with price tags in the tens of millions, if not higher.

"Could you live somewhere else with the work you do?" he asks.

"Not really," I say. "So much of what I do is about being there. I imagine your line of work is similar?"

"I could be elsewhere and manage," he says unconvincingly. "Have you thought of developing a European client base?"

"No, but maybe we should."

The idea is tempting, although I can't see Vaughn thriving in Europe. He survives on Philly cheesesteak sandwiches, keeps a pistol in his briefcase, and would consider the tiny espresso shots they serve here a joke.

But I could get into a groove here.

Our cruise around the neighborhood slows to a crawl and Morgan stops in front of an intricately scrolled gate. The property stretching behind it is so vast I can't even see a home. During our tour, he's been name-dropping people I don't know but who sound important, so I'm curious.

"Who lives here?" I ask.

"My parents," he says, and rolls down the window to buzz an intercom embedded in the rockwork girding the gate. After an exchange in French, the double-sided gate swings open and the wheels of the Chiron crunch in the pea gravel.

"Be prepared for a tour," Morgan warns. "Maman is all about her jardin."

No kidding. It's as if we detoured to Versailles. The manicured opulence goes on and on. Flower beds the size of swimming pools are inlaid into a lawn so green it looks fake. I have a vision of Morgan's mother plucking errant leaves from the trimmed boxwood lining the driveway with her tweezers and possibly hair spraying the shrubs after the fact.

"It's incredible," I say. "How long have your parents lived here?"

"The property has been in our family for generations. I used to play endlessly in this yard," Morgan says.

"This is where you grew up?" For some reason, I imagined a smart city home, not a sprawling mansion where aristocrats lounged in the shade and drank Absinthe. (If that's a thing. It feels like a thing.)

"As my father will no doubt remind you, I have yet to grow up."

I smile back. "Right. I'll keep that in mind."

Maison de Rohan-Chabot finally appears, a rambling French

Country affair with pink roof tiles and tall rectangular windows flanked with louvered shutters painted a fresh periwinkle blue. A maid dressed in traditional black and white smiles at us from the front steps. Morgan parks and introduces me to Josie, who escorts us inside.

I've been to many Beverly Hills parties on some of the city's most exclusive real estate. I don't know what it is about Europeans, but they do everything better, including wealth. Morgan's family home is stylish, without an air of being overly curated. Huge rooms allowed to breathe with simple, modern design.

"Did you do their home?" I ask, admiring a bold chandelier the size of a sedan.

"I helped out with sourcing and a few things. As you might have gathered from meeting my father, he's very much in charge."

I hear Alix's voice before I see him, his laughter drawing us into the kitchen filled with a fatty smell of beef and butter. An elegantly dressed woman stops stirring one of two Le Creuset pots bubbling on the Wolfe range and rushes over to embrace Morgan.

"Bonsoir, bonsoir, ma douce!" She kisses him exuberantly before turning to me. "And you must be Vandana," she says with a warm smile. "Welcome. My name's Cèline and please, call me that."

Blonde, regal, and owning her age, Cèline could be Catherine Deneuve's twin sister. Together, she and Alix are a beautiful couple. I immediately see how the best of their DNA has shaped Morgan. Cèline's lustrous, windswept hair and inquisitive tiger's eyes play softer than Morgan's versions and Alix's classic bone structure formed more precise angles on his son, but as a trio, they are equally stunning.

"Thank you for having me," I say. I have the kiss thing figured out and execute like a pro on both her and Alix. "Your home is beautiful. And it smells delicious in here."

"Beef Bourguignon is Morgan's favorite." Cèline's tone suggests I take note, her accent stronger than Morgan's. "You eat meat?"

"Oh, yes. And I have a healthy appetite."

This pleases her. It pleases every mother I've been introduced to. But behind her smile is the appraisal Morgan warned me about. I wore the white eyelet dress with a knee-length flared skirt for this very reason. Demure, not flashy. Paired with a headband and black flats, it strikes the right tone. She'll never suspect her son spent most of his Sunday afternoon buried between my legs.

"Morgan mentioned you're an avid gardener."

"Oh," she says, sharing a look with him. "You like to garden?"

If paying my gardeners to visit twice a week counts, then yes. "My thumb isn't as green as yours."

"While they prepare aperitifs, would you like to see my roses?" she asks.

"I'd love that," I say, while Morgan masks a smile of *I told you so.*

"What would you like to drink, Vandana?" Alix asks. He looks very fatherly today in a short-sleeved dress shirt and pressed pants. But he carries himself with confident, outlaw energy. I bet he and Vaughn would get along like a house on fire.

I touch Morgan's arm. "What did we have in Genoa that I liked?"

"Aperol spritz," he says. "We'll start with a round of those."

Cèline glances at Alix with a sly smile before herding me out of the kitchen and onto the sprawling patio that overlooks a little slice of heaven. Birds of paradise and hibiscus plants in full bloom surround a turquoise pool the length of the house. Beyond that, a verdant lawn stretches down to the rocky shores of the Mediterranean. With the heat, humidity and the smell of jungle greenery, I wouldn't be surprised if a peacock or streak of tigers showed up.

"Is this all you?" I ask. The maintenance here is seven days a week, for sure.

"Mostly, but where we would we be without a little help, no?" She smiles and her hand is warm enveloping mine. "Come, we'll go this way."

From the elevated patio, a stone staircase spirals down to pool level. I follow Cèline's lead to a hard-packed dirt path meandering us past the pool to a hidden garden teeming with vegetables, herbs, and rows of fragrant roses. She chitchats about varieties and fertilizers and weather concerns and when that line of conversation peters out, she makes her move.

"How did you and Morgan meet? Alix mentioned you work in Los

Angeles?"

"I believe his Vice President Olivier found my firm. He set up the meeting."

"Mon Dieu," she mutters. "We've been encouraging Morgan to get rid of him for years."

"I thought they were old friends?"

Her mouth flattens into a disapproving line. "Olivier's made sure they've remained friends. He's been riding on Morgan's coattails far too long. But there's only so much parents can say, no?" She stops to smell a wide-petalled rose in shades of pink and canary yellow, offering the bloom to me.

"Wow." The scent is rich and complex, layered and sweet. "It's like perfume."

"Roses are my hobby," she says. "They keep me busy. Sounds like your work keeps you busy as well. Now that Morgan's a client, will you set up an office here?"

Here we go. "He's our first European client, so it's early days. Something to consider though."

She thinks on this, goes for strategy number two. "It must be hard on your husband and family if you're traveling all the time."

"I'm recently separated and don't have children. I never felt the pull of motherhood."

"Ah, I see." She's careful to keep any judgment in check, but I can tell it's one point for being single and two demerits for not wanting kids. And a gold star for me, letting it all hang out. It's getting easier to say words like *separated*, and one day my chest won't tighten. "Yes, well, Morgan feels the same about children," she adds. "I blame myself and his father for that."

"How come?"

She pauses at an immaculate bush and squishes a decent-sized bug between her fingers, flicking away the carcass. A ruthless killer dressed in a silk tunic and Valentino kitten heels. "We were at sea for much of his early life," she says. "He never had a lot of interaction with other children. Became very singular and focused as a result. Those qualities help in business but he's never had much success with relationships."

"He's very talented," I say, steering clear of her minefield. "You must be proud."

Cèline smiles. "Yes, of course. He's accomplished so much on his own. He never wanted Alix's help. But we're so glad he hired you. He could use a woman's hand in his affairs." Her grip on my arm is firm, and if we're alone much longer, she'll be offering me a permanent room here.

In the nick of time, Morgan calls us up for drinks. Gracious, practiced hosts, Alix and Cèline make me feel right at home. Morgan relaxes with his mother's obvious seal of approval of me. Dinner is exceptional, and when Josie clears the table for coffee, Cèline encourages Morgan to watch the sunset with me from the gazebo. "We'll have dessert when you come back."

More directive than a suggestion, Morgan knows the drill. We refill our wine glasses and make our way to the gazebo.

Once we're out of earshot, Morgan asks, "How did it go?"

"She trod lightly."

He laughs. "Why do I not believe that?"

The property line narrows into a round of grass pristine enough to be the eighteenth green at Augusta. Right in the middle sits the gazebo, painted white and commanding a breathtaking view.

"We can watch from here," Morgan says and leads me to a swinging bench hanging from two sturdy cables drilled into the support beams. I curl up beside him, legs tucked underneath me. A few yards ahead, the land falls away, suddenly and steeply, and I can hear waves crash below as droplets from the spray shimmer in the sun. Morgan drapes his arm around my shoulder, and we rock back and forth in companionable silence, wine glasses slowing draining. I stare out at the sea, as I did so often as a child, curious what lies beyond the horizon. My thoughts drift, and I burrow closer to Morgan, his body heat comforting.

"Are you warm enough?" he asks. "There's a blanket here."

I gaze up at him. The sun slowly sinks to the west and a wash of perfect magic hour light illuminates his features. "The temperature is perfect. The meal was perfect. Everything here is perfect."

Morgan smiles and pulls me closer. "I agree."

Our gentle kiss melts my bones, turns my body into jelly. Instead of the frantic dominance of this morning, the slower tempo highlights how good of a kisser he really is. He tastes like wine and heaven, his tongue soft and jousting with mine. My nipples start to swell with anticipation, and I moan a little into his mouth. I've been waiting all night to kiss him.

"You feel wonderful," he mumbles. "I need more." We set down our wineglasses and fall back onto the bench, him on top of me.

"You feel rock hard," I tease, grinding against him.

"We can do something about that."

I peek through the slats of the bench, at the pink roofline in the distance. "Can they see us?"

"No."

I want him bad, feel the heat funneling between my legs, but didn't plan for this. As if reading my mind, his hand rummages for whatever's in his pocket. "I've learned from the best," he says, holding up the condom with a boyish grin. "Be prepared."

"You have one in every pocket now?" I joke.

"No. Good idea though." He sits up, laughing, and pats his lap. "Here, like this." He helps me position myself, knees on either of his thighs. The billow of my skirt covers both of us, allowing him to unbuckle and get ready in privacy.

"You don't even have to look," I marvel.

He nibbles on my lower lip, his scruff tickling my chin. "The best view is right in front of me."

"Don't rip it off," I warn him, his hands now free and roaming under my thong.

"I'll work around it," he promises. "But I need some help. Up."

I rise onto my knees, abs tightening as the bench sways. Morgan tugs my thong lower, just enough for access. I warm and bloom under his first touches and I can smell myself, ripe with need. My hands slide down the flat planes of his back muscles to grip the firm curves of his ass.

"I love it when you touch me there," he says.

He starts to flower me open, my heartbeat thudding out of control. If fingering a woman is art, Morgan is Renoir. No hard lines or stark realism. The strokes of a master. My head sinks into the dip of skin where his shoulder and neck meet, and the smell of him goes straight to my head.

"I don't think this is what your mother had in mind, sending us down here."

"I think it's exactly what she had in mind."

"What about not giving her false hope?"

He leans back, our faces shrouded in a tangle of my hair. A silence hangs heavy before he finally says, "Oh, she is smitten. Of that I am certain."

We kiss again and he drills a finger deeper. I can feel myself slipping toward the edge. Morgan pushes me to the breaking point faster than anyone with just his fingers, but I'm hungering for him to be deep inside me.

"Hold on," I say. "Let me."

I find him under my skirt, his thick vein pulsing and angry beneath my fingers. I angle him into my hot, wet warmth and he bites his lip with a strangled sound. My inner muscles also groan, but become pliant, now familiar with the intruding dimensions. I ease myself lower, each pulse a delicious sensation. He lodges himself in place with a final thrust, his balls tight and pressing against my ass. I wrap my arms around him, pleasure in how we lock together like puzzle pieces.

"Good?" he asks. With my nod, he pushes one foot against the concrete slab. We start rocking on the bench, on each other, and he whispers into my ear, "I can't think of anything better than making love to you overlooking the sea."

Later, when the sky is thick with stars, and our bellies are full of rich espresso and sweet cherry clafoutis, we drive back to Monaco and hold hands in the Chiron. The gazebo feels like a dream; a sway of building arousal, the setting sun on our skin, and the pounding waves louder than our muffled cries into each other's shoulders.

Chapter Twenty-Seven

MORGAN

IT'S A BEAUTIFUL MORNING, WAKING UP TO A TONGUE LICKING MY face.

If only it belonged to Vandana.

"Yes, yes," I mumble, scratching Asterix behind his ears. "I'm getting up."

From the slant of light pouring through the window, I'm guessing it's 7 a.m. or just past. I forgot to roll down the blinds last night. Forgot to brush my teeth. I stumbled into bed on cloud nine and have woken up a glorious ruin of a man. Vandana blew my mind yesterday and I pet Asterix absently, trying to make sense of it all.

The paradox of Vandana is more than the unholy combination of angel and devil, sinner and saint. She is a woman I can make love to, truly make love to, not just satisfy some animal urge. She wants and gives it all, unafraid to fly high and far. Lost in her sweet warmth, I feel like I can do anything, be anything. Impossible not to feel like a god with her heart raging against mine.

And speaking of raging…

Lust is addictive, nonsensical, and most of all, uncontrollable. Asterix headbutts my chin again, nagging and hungry, but I have other priorities. He watches the rhythmic pump of my hand beneath the sheets with a bored, superior expression.

Can your manhandling possibly wait until after breakfast is served?

I push him farther away. "Get a move on, you dirty old man. What are you going to do when Vandana comes over? Sit and watch?"

With a flick of his tail, he jumps off the bed, padding across the floor to join the rest of the troops sunning themselves on the rug. I power on to the finish line in degenerate beast mode, not nearly as satisfying without the heat of Vandana pushing me to the outer limits while ocean waves pound in my ears. Freshly emptied, my thoughts refuse to organize in the thick, muggy cavern of my mind. I need a second opinion. I shush the meowing masses, grab my phone from the nightstand and plug in my earbuds.

"Good morning," Olivier answers.

"It is indeed, my friend."

"Do I dare ask?"

I plump up my pillow and rest against it. "I need your advice. I'm falling for her, Olivier. Hard."

After a heavy pause, he says, "Surely you jest. It's been what, six days?"

"God created the world and man in a week," I remind him.

He spits out a laugh. "It was only a matter of time before you compared yourself to the creator. My advice? Back off from the wine."

I kick at the sheet, the old frustration rising quickly with his snark. Can he relate? Feel the magnitude? Operate outside his normal range of lampooning? All the emotional equity I've put into our relationship feels like it's come to this moment. "I'm confiding in you. You're my oldest friend. She's set me off the deep end. Our connection is … powerful."

"This *power*," he says, skeptically. "What does it translate into? Is she moving here? Are you moving to LA?"

I ignore Asterix and his death stare. "We haven't gotten that far."

"Not to rain on your parade, but she's in Monaco, all caught up in the glamour. You're a rich boy toy. If what you said about her husband is true, maybe you're an easy out for her. Have you substantiated her situation?"

"She's successful in her own right," I argue. "Not some backwoods Estonian hooker on the prowl." Olivier and his continuous pessimism. He belongs in the Medieval Ages, when no one trusted anything but the man in the sky.

"Morgan," he says, in a tone of numbing truth. "I've known you since we were fifteen. You've never spoken about a woman like this, aside from Tatiana. And we both know she scarred you. You were in a funk for months. Years. I don't think you've ever recovered. You've shut yourself in a room, emotionally speaking. Plundering into your first whiff of romance feels perilous. Don't get so easily attached."

Of all times for Olivier to bring her up. We don't talk about Tatiana for a variety of reasons. Hearing her name, my heart pinches, long-suppressed memories balled tight and unwilling to loosen.

I ran into her two years ago, in Paris.

She's married, with two little ones, exact replicas of her with unruly red hair and milky skin, running around with endless energy. Her lawyer husband barely cracked a smile. Tatiana spoke formally, keeping her distance, content now to live with a tired-eyed man who doesn't carry the taste of salt in his skin and hair. It's funny seeing someone after so long with not a glimmer of what fired between us evident.

"I don't love the sea, Morgan. Not the way you do."

That's how she ended it.

She did try very hard to love the sea, but a wicked storm, one where we almost capsized, was the final nail in the coffin. Since her, it's been an uphill battle. Plenty of women are happy to lounge on a yacht; I can round up fifty this morning without trying hard. But once the afternoon sun dips and the art of suntanning is revealed to be their only skill, it's in their eyes. *Okay, this was fun; now get me back on shore.*

When Vandana and I stood together on the prow of *Catch Me,* I don't profess to know what she was thinking. Don't want to flatter myself into believing any of her thoughts involved me. But her body language spoke volumes. I can tell if a woman is comfortable on a boat. With that, and the capacity to understand me, Vandana's already leaps and bounds beyond anyone else.

Now comes the challenge. The ultimate test. Being out on the water.

Because loving me means loving the ocean.

"You're right, my friend," I say. "About substantiating. I'll ask the hard questions on Wednesday. We're taking *Liberté* out for the day."

"You're skipping the first day of the show?" He's in shock.

"One day away won't make a difference."

"Where are you off to?" he asks.

"Toward San Remo. Away from the crowds. I've arranged it all. Your only task is making sure tonight runs smoothly with Khaled."

Olivier clears his throat. "I have full confidence the best man will win."

Later, I'll think back on this conversation. Was bringing up Tatiana his roundabout way of warning me?

"How's the hand doing?" I ask.

"Oh … Uh, fine. Just a sprain."

"Overuse does have its consequences."

"Ha, ha," he says, dryly. "Talk later."

I hop into the shower, feed the troops, and start my morning the usual way: an espresso on the deck while watching fair Monaco come alive before me. It makes me ache for Vandana's presence. I'm tingling with all the things we have yet to do to each other.

It's not too early to send a message.

MdRC: Good morning. I hope you slept well.

VH: Hi! I slept like a baby. Thank you for last night. Very special.

MdRC: C'etait parfait.

VH: I hope that's a compliment.

MdRC: I have to teach you French.

VH: Good luck with that. Your parents are lovely BTW.
MdRC: They said the same about you.

Maman's actual words to me before we left? I'm a flying idiot if I don't pursue Vandana. *A boat will never love you, Morgan;* her well-oiled argument was trotted out yet again. She offered to take Vandana out for lunch today, to meet some of the Cap Ferret ladies. Not even a day and she's revving in fourth gear. As bad as those Regency-era mothers pawning off their daughters to the highest bidders.

VH: You excited for tonight?
MdRC: Yes. And a little nervous.
VH: Me too.

We banter back and forth about nothing and everything, and I feel lighter as I set down my phone. I've already forgotten last week, when living one day at a time was all I could look forward to. No point dreaming about the future if you step into it and nothing's changed.

Suddenly, the future is full of promise.

I kick my feet onto the table, humming U2's *Beautiful Day*. The tuxedo twins join me on the chaise lounge, each picking a side; black and white purring machines rumbling against my thighs. I'm already thinking of all the ways I can spoil Vandana. A spa weekend at Cap Estel. Docking at La Guérite in Cannes for a candlelight dinner. Grand Prix. Nikki Beach in Saint Tropez. The madness of drunken table dancing at Anjuna Beach. So much to share. Monaco is an elite kingdom for those who can afford it, and I love everything about my surroundings. Tonight, after the meeting with Khaled, I'm taking her to the Hotel de Paris for drinks. I think she'll get a kick out of being an American in the Bar Americain. If the timing feels right, I'll test the waters with a few questions. While I don't wish Vandana any more grief or heartbreak, that fool husband of hers makes one part of this easier. If he prefers men, their marriage is irreparable. But how do I convince her to leave a thriving business behind? Or relocate here? It's a near impossible task, but I'll never forgive myself if I don't try. When Olivier brought up the past, it was a reminder of all the things missing from my life.

I'm tired of being alone. I can do better. I can have better.

Vandana is as close to the best as I've ever seen.

If she'll have me, I'll rearrange my life to make it work with her.

And, if I can teach her to caress the dark, intimate hole of my ass at just the right moment, then maybe there truly is perfection in this world.

Chapter Twenty-Eight

VANDANA

IS THIS WHAT RAPUNZEL FELT LIKE, TRAPPED ALONE IN HER ROOM, waiting for word from a prince?

It's nine p.m., and not a peep out of Morgan. His meetings in Genoa barely topped an hour and he's been with Khaled for over two. Barefoot in my strapless Marchesa cocktail dress, I pace around the hotel room. Apply lipstick to the layer already chewed off. Watch more TV in a language I don't understand. Check my phone again. Khaled's security took Morgan's phone for privacy reasons, and he's gone dark until they finish up. But I'm dying to know how it's going and can't handle another minute cooped up in here. Time passes faster with a distraction, and there's an outdoor bar by the pool that has a seat with my name on it.

I need a drink. Or three.

I worked all day in my room catching up on the backlog while Morgan spent time with his staff, prepping them for the show. Not being part of his day, the sense of FOMO is real. And disconcerting.

My emotions are all over the map.

It's one thing to sleep with a man. It's entirely another to have his family welcome me into their fold. And yet another to share a moment as magical as last night. As we dissolved into one, I never wanted it to end. Morgan fucks like the man of my dreams, and his bag of tricks is a nod to David Copperfield, the Kama Sutra and, I'm sure, given the opportunity, the Marquis de Sade. He's got it going on in every department and then some. For the first time in years, I have no clue how to proceed.

How does this work? Can it work? Do I want it to work?

No surprise, every question ends with work. I can't do my current job remotely, even if I wanted to. Clients demand in-person handling of events and managing the media in real-time, not Europe time. With Morgan's career planted firmly here, the other question is, how would it work for him? And is he even thinking about it working? He dropped enough questions yesterday to hint at yes, but maybe I'm getting ahead of myself. Letting the hormones cloud my judgment.

Relax, Vandana.

But the anticipation of another night with him makes me jumpy, my legs restless as I wait for the elevator. When one car arrives, a petite woman swathed in a long black gown shuffles over to make room for me. Only her eyes are visible in the slit of her niqab, and they are bright and inquisitive. I'm not familiar with the customs of Islam, such as if she can talk to me, but it's my nature to engage with everyone.

"Having a good night?" I ask.

She shakes her head, the universal sign of *I don't speak your language.* But women, regardless of provenance or upbringing, speak a universal language of fashion. Her enthusiastic thumbs-up at my ensemble brings a much-needed smile to my face. My dress is flirty and fun—sandy beige organza with tiny pink rosebuds circling a hem that shows enough leg to get Morgan's mind off Khaled.

I hope.

When the elevator reaches the lobby, I hold the doors open, allowing my new friend to exit first. But she doesn't move. She's statue-like in her stillness, completely unnatural. The wrongness of it sends a jolt up my spine.

"Are you okay?" I ask.

From out of the folds of her gown, a hand gnarled as a piece of ginger reaches for me. A muffled cry spills out her mouth, head banging against the mirrored wall.

A dead, black sensation blooms in my chest. "Oh my god. Do you feel faint? Are you—"

Her eyes lose vibrancy, glass over, and she collapses at my feet.

For a handful of seconds, time stands still. Distant elevator Muzak unfurls in my ears while a still-warm body lies motionless on my satin Manolos. The shock of it runs ice-cold in my blood, my entire body humming with a faint tremor. I recall some long-ago advice of not moving someone who's collapsed, but someone needs to move her, or she might not move again. I maneuver my feet out from under her with a horrible taste in my mouth. Heart racing, I peer into the lobby. The front desk is just visible, manned by a lone, male clerk deep in an administrative stupor.

"Help!" I shout. "We need an ambulance." With the sound of my piercing voice, his head snaps up. "Yes, you! Call an ambulance! Now!"

I point at the elevator and pantomime the hand gesture of a phone call. Instead of making a call, he dashes over only to stagger backwards at the sight of the crumpled body. His name tag reads FABIAN, although Babian is more like it. Unprepared for any emergency beyond a paper cut, his eyes blink non-stop behind thick glasses.

"Uh … Un moment, madam," he says. "I need to get my supervisor."

And he takes off, me yelling in his dust. "We don't have a moment!"

Jesus Christ, what is wrong with him?

The elevator doors bump against me, trying to close, and I won't let them because it feels too final. The woman isn't moving. I can't tell if she's breathing. It feels like I have a rock in my stomach. Screw these idiots. I pull out my phone, fingers trembling to punch in 911. Argh. Of course that's not the emergency number here. As with their electrical outlets, Europe just has to be different.

God, Morgan, I curse under my breath. Of all the times to be unavailable.

I'm about to Google the Monaco version of 911 when the clerk reappears with his supervisor. Heavy-set and long past fitting in his suit, his cold eyes seem locked in permanent disapproval. He speaks with a voice reserved for panicking children.

"Madam. This is a very exclusive guest and—"

"Did you call an ambulance yet?" I interrupt. "Because if not, she's going to be an exclusive, dead guest."

"Please, Madam," Fabian pleads, holding up both hands to calm me down. "We've sent a message."

"Message? I said you need to call an ambulance. Jesus!" I barge past them and sprint through the lobby, an unfamiliar metallic taste rising on my tongue. If that lady dies on my watch, it will haunt me forever. With my focus tightened, I zone in on a trio of skimpily dressed Barbies leaving the patio bar.

"Excuse me. Pardonne. There's an emergency. A lady collapsed in the elevator. What's the number for the ambulance? 911?" I'm rushing, words tumbling on top of one another. The women huddle protectively in their couture, peering at me like I'm a mad, begging homeless woman. One of their faces reads as familiar, but the hot-pink wig throws me off.

"Vandana?" Perla asks.

Lord. Of all people.

"Oh, hi. Perla, yes, it's me. This woman … she was in the elevator with me. She just collapsed and needs an ambulance, but the hotel staff are dragging their heels and I don't understand why they're not doing anything."

I glance over my shoulder, Perla and her friends absorbing the scene first-hand. A small crowd has formed a cautious circle around the elevator, no one wanting to get too close to someone else's disaster.

Perla's eyes narrow. "You say hotel staff do nothing?"

"They said she's an exclusive guest, whatever that means. And it doesn't matter. She might be dying."

Clocking my panic and that it's real, Perla snaps open her handbag. "I'll call. Wait minute." Composed, speaking clearly and calmly in French, she gives details to the operator. When she's done, she tells us, "Five, ten minutes. They rush fast as possible."

"Thank you. Thank you." I grab her arm and she flinches, either from my sweaty palm or the unexpected camaraderie. Likely both.

"Okay, okay," she says, breaking free of my hand. "Let's go talk. We find out what scoop is."

We're a glamorous battalion of four marching across the lobby. Perla butts right into the conversation of the two employees, letting go with a tirade of French. Fabian waves down her hot-headedness and explains, by the sounds of it, the lay of the land. Her eyes widen and she nods, before pulling me aside to explain.

"She is Prince Khaled's mother, Ayasha. They need to talk to him first. Strict protocol."

Oh, god. "He's meeting with Morgan right now, going over the yacht commission. I don't know where. I can't get a hold of him."

She lowers her voice, angles us away to prevent them from hearing. Her breath reeks of triple-strength vodka. "It's very sensitive. All scared, these people. No backlash wanted."

"Backlash? This is life and death. A person is a person. It doesn't matter what their profile is." I glare at the employees, who find some-place else to look. Getting stripped down by a tangle of hot women isn't usual Tuesday night decorum at The Bay.

"I know, I know," Perla says, calming me. "But you know too. You deal with important clients."

Of course, I do. And I know it's all bullshit—people afraid of repercussions from someone wealthier or more powerful than they are. It's part of my business I don't like.

The Cruiser

"Fuck," I mutter. "The ambulance better get here soon. You told them we called, right?"

Perla nods and we stand on the sidelines, reduced to spectators. I can't even look in the elevator. Perla's friends are antsy, don't want to hang around for the drama. They're gossiping amongst themselves, making pouty faces and snapping selfies, when the scream of an ambulance siren draws closer. Two paramedics, beefcake ex-soldier types thick with muscle, roll in with a gurney. They make quick work of strapping the woman in. Seeing her still body makes the stone in my belly heavier.

"Is she going to be okay?" I ask.

Fabian approaches me warily, asks me to explain to the paramedics what happened. I speak slow, measure my English to appear like I'm not frightened, when in fact, any more nervous energy running through me and I might collapse. The older paramedic takes it all in, thinks it's a heart attack. They need to get her into emergency asap.

I nudge Perla. "Can I go with them?"

"Not good chance," she says. "But let me ask." It's a firm no, redoubled with some explanation and a shake of a bald head. "Only family," Perla reports back.

"But I should go to the hospital, just in case. What if she snaps back and starts freaking out?"

"Is *okay*," Perla says, shutting me down. "The prince will go."

"It's not okay! Someone needs to be there. She can't go alone." I watch the retreating paramedics roll the gurney across the lobby and into the night. I'm in this now. No way out of it. Her warm body lay on my shoes minutes earlier, and damned if I'm the type of person not to manage a situation to its conclusion. "Do you mind giving me a lift?"

For some reason, this request is more outrageous than asking her to call 911. Her lips tighten and she glances at her friends. They stealthily tip their hair sprayed heads—*let's get out of here.*

I get it. We're not friends. Not even frenemies. But sometimes, all it takes to change things between two people is one person trying.

"Please?" I beg. "I've never been there and don't know my way around. I need someone who can speak French, to help me explain things at the hospital. A taxi driver won't do that."

Perla might be in no condition to drive, but whatever she sees in my eyes breaks her. "Okay," she sighs. "Let me get car."

Chapter Twenty-Nine

BUILT HIGH INTO THE MOUNTAINSIDE, PRINCESS GRACE HOSPITAL IS A labyrinth worthy of *Lord of the Rings*. As suspected, navigating the complex is as easy as navigating French bureaucracy.

"Idiot," Perla mutters, turning to me in disgust. "In Belarus, we don't have this problem." Unmoved by her beseeching-turned-belittling, the clean-cut orderly manning the emergency desk gets back to pushing paper.

"But is she okay?" I ask. "Can he tell us that?"

"He says he tell us nothing," she huffs. "We not family. So stupid. If not for you, she may be dead."

"Don't say that in here. It's bad luck."

She puts her eyes back on me. "Anything with Morgan?"

I shake my head. Still nothing, after checking on a near constant basis. I don't want to send a bunch of morbid texts because there's nothing more unnerving than reading bad news. "I'm going to call and leave a message. Tell him we're here."

Morgan's phone clicks to voicemail on the first ring. My message is short, covering all the necessary details and for him to call me as soon as he can.

After I hang up, Perla drags me to the waiting area. "You look tight. Let's sit."

For all of Monaco's wealth, very little of it appears to be funneled into the hospital and its appearance. The only chairs to sit in are plastic and uncomfortable, the dull tangerine color a breath of fresh air compared to the rest of the decor. The departure area of La Guardia Airport resonates more charm.

Perla watches my hands clasp and unclasp in my lap. "On bright side, dinner must be well. Khaled doesn't linger if he's uninterested."

I glance at her, surprised. "You know him?"

"I know everybody, cheri." With fluid grace, she crosses one fishnet leg over another. We're quite the pair, dressed to the nines in full make-up and hair. Thelma and Louise, Monaco edition.

"Given you know everyone, what can you tell me about Renan Sadik?"

Her head tilts. "What you want to know?"

"There seems to be some bad blood between him and Morgan. I wanted some context."

"He not tell you?" Her voice sharpens with disbelief.

"There's always two sides to every story."

She considers this. "What was his story?"

Okay, fine, I'll play her game. I summarize Morgan's story and she nods knowingly, like someone holding a trump card.

"All very true," she says. "Only one piece missing. No surprise, a woman. Olivier and Renan and Morgan all like Tatiana, and she choose Morgan. Understanding to everyone, except Renan and Olivier."

"They're all friends?" I ask. Morgan never mentioned this.

"Long time. Before Renan's mother pass way. After that, nasty time, as Morgan say. Morgan clings to Olivier; they old, old friends. Only good friend I think. Olivier…" She makes a face. "He's weasel. Desperate man. His family lose everything in stock market crash. He always follow the money, so he stick with Morgan." She shrugs, sequined shoulders rising up and down. "Renan go down tubes. Now mafia tough guy. How you say … man drama?"

"Was that recent?" I ask. "The woman?" I think back to their fight.

How personal it felt. I'm not giving Renan a free pass by any means, but losing out at love and losing a mother shines a light on his attitude toward Morgan. And women.

"No, cheri. Many years ago. But you know men. How they are. Morgan better, at everything. Renan and Olivier always second. Or four."

I sit back, unsure with this news. "I haven't heard a lot of good things about Olivier."

"You not meet him?" she asks. "He like plague. Always hanging around."

My phone, dark for so long, finally lights up. The relief is like shrugging off a bulky sweater. "It's Morgan," I say. "Hold on."

As soon as I answer, he apologizes for missing my call. "I was on the phone. We're ten minutes away. How are you?"

I stand up and walk, to shake off the jitters. "We're fine, but they won't give us any updates."

"Khaled's on the phone with the hospital right now," he says, tension hardening his voice. "Tell me what happened so I can relay." I give him the rundown and of all things, the first question out of his mouth is, "Perla drove you?"

I glance over. Perla's not close enough to hear but trying her damndest to do just that. "She's been helpful. Just get here in one piece, okay?"

Knowing he's on his way, my beating heart starts to slow inside its crumpled cage. I drink deeply from a water fountain and rejoin Perla, filling her in. In the stretch of silence after, I take stock of the emergency room, the whole evening turned on its head. How any of this will play out is a crapshoot. I hope it doesn't blow Morgan's chances.

"I read your press release about his award," Perla says, out of the blue. "Very good piece."

"Thank you." Note to self: she reads more than Instagram feeds.

"Sounds like things run smooth with him?"

"So far," I say. "Tonight's the only blip."

She fiddles with a giant hoop earring. I know what she's really asking, but nope. Not giving it to her. "Well, I think you good fit for Morgan. He need someone strong."

"I have a lot of experience handling tough personalities."

She shoots me an equally sly look. "Yes, I'm aware."

I smile and rest a hand on her leg, girl code for *we're cool*. "Thank you for driving me. I appreciate it."

"Welcome." She touches up her askew wig, clearly not ready for female bonding. Not with me, anyway. But like I said, sometimes all it takes is one person. "So you know," she continues. "Nothing happen with Morgan and me. I mean, yes, I like him, but sometimes not meant to be. He was drunk and not good mood at party… I offer drive him home. One kiss. That all."

She shrugs it off, but I know it's not easy, admitting defeat to the competition. I've been there.

"I'm sure he appreciated the gesture," I say, gently.

Toying with her cocktail ring, she smiles, a little bittersweet, a little self-conscious.

And that's how Monaco's gossip queen and I bury our swords.

For now.

In my mind, I built Khaled into an imposing Middle Eastern figure. All-powerful, infused with centuries of male superiority, a permanent trench between blazing coal eyes. Instead, a man shorter than June rushes through the emergency doors, looking more like a lost trick-or-treater in a ghost costume two sizes too big.

Morgan's right behind him, the worry in his face retreating when I approach him. He embraces me hard, our collective anxiousness draining away in a small gesture of comfort.

"What a fright for you," he says, talking into my hair. "You're okay?"

"Yes. A little rattled."

"Morgan!" Khaled waves him over. "Can you help translate?"

"It's Prince Khaled, by the way," Morgan whispers as we walk over. "He has some questions for you."

Khaled wears the traditional white gown and headdress of Saudi men and nods politely but vacantly when introduced. He's got other things on his mind and Morgan jumps in to translate French into English. Ayasha isn't out of the weeds yet, but not in critical condition either. A doctor will arrive shortly to fill in the gaps. Visibly relieved, Khaled turns to me. Skin like leather, but no longer pinched with anguish, he lifts both hands into prayer position.

"I cannot thank you enough. My mother loves The Bay. Insists on staying there despite my wishes. Next time I'm keeping her with me." He shakes his head and I guess parents are the same everywhere—frustrating their children. "Your act of kindness and fearlessness will be generously rewarded," he adds.

"Oh god, no," I say. "Please. I don't need any reward. I did what any human would do."

But Khaled's having none of it and overrules me by addressing Morgan instead. "You and I will discuss how to handle this. I'm very sorry our evening was interrupted. It's been a great pleasure getting to know you. And if this is the woman you mentioned," he smiles at me, "your team is rock solid."

At this point, the doctor on duty appears through a set of sliding doors. Bleary but poker-faced, blue scrubs stained with blood, he treks straight for us in his Air Jordans. Introduces himself as Dr. Broussard.

"How is she?" Khaled's voice tightens.

"Stable," he says. "We have her on oxygen, and her heart's weak but strengthening. She made it here in the nick of time."

Khaled lifts both hands to his mouth and asks quietly, "Can I see her?"

"Yes, but only you." The doctor gives me and Morgan a sideways glance. "And from the viewing room."

Khaled shakes Morgan's hand one more time and insists we use his driver to take us home. He thanks me again with a solemn nod and I get the sense this isn't a total departure for him, females orchestrating the night's biggest pieces. I guess Dorothy's bit of intel about his mother proves right after all. Given what I've heard about Saudi men and their controlling tendencies over women, no wonder Frankie wanted Dorothy to keep that tidbit on the down low.

Image is everything.

After Khaled and the doctor disappear into the bowels of the hospital, Morgan rakes both hands over his hair and exhales loudly. "What a crazy night. I can only imagine what it's been like for you."

"I haven't even told you about the ridiculousness with the hotel staff."

"You should see her in hotel," Perla chimes in. She's filing her nails, watching the drama unfold. "Tough girl. Not taking no for an answer. Directing everyone, including me."

Morgan gazes at me, full of warm respect. "I want to hear the whole story over drinks. Or have you even eaten yet?"

On cue, my stomach rumbles, loud enough he hears it. "I haven't and I'm starving. I've been waiting all night on pins and needles."

"It went well tonight, really well," he says, and reveals that Frankie Delmar shared some last-minute insider info that he spun to his advantage.

"And all this?" I ask. "It won't set things back?"

He kisses me softly on the lips. "If anything, you might be the winning card."

Across the room, Perla smirks at me. Cat's out of the bag. Let the gossip commence. Morgan, noticing my smile, cranks a look in her direction. She sticks her tongue out and makes a funny face.

It's a night of truces, for old battles and new.

"She's not so bad after all," I say.

Maybe they won't be full friends, but halfway there is better than being enemies. Finding my hand, Morgan squeezes it tight. "Let's say goodbye."

Khaled's driver drops us off at The Bay. Morgan had plans for us to paint the town, but we're content to chill and regroup. I'd prefer not to show my face again in L'Orange Verte, but as luck would have it, its the only restaurant that can seat us. After bringing me up to speed on tonight's meeting with Khaled, Morgan watches my demolition of a rib eye and pommes frites in quiet astonishment.

"I thought you were just being polite eating two bowls of Maman's bourguignon," he says.

I swirl a last fry through the remaining steak juice on my plate. "Are you kidding me? That was delicious. I almost asked for thirds."

By now it's late, and the restaurant is cleared out except for a few stragglers. Two pimply-faced busboys start clearing nearby tables. They're having a good old time talking about something.

When a laugh bubbles on Morgan's lips, I nudge him. "What? What are they saying?"

He brings a finger to his mouth, a silver cufflink refracting light into my eyes. "Shh."

The busboy with bad posture yanks out my Agent Provocateur thong from his pocket, dangles it from his finger like it's a stinky fish, and then chucks it across the table. His co-worker picks it up, sniffs it, and laughs uproariously.

"Oh shit!" Horrified, I burrow my face in Morgan's shoulder. His chest ripples from the effort of trying not to laugh. "Don't you dare say *anything*," I threaten.

Their crude laughter and discussion continue, and I don't ask for any translation. Not based on Morgan's endless chuckling.

"You're certainly leaving your mark everywhere in Monaco," he teases.

"Hey!" I slug his arm, with juice.

"Ow," he says, rubbing at it.

"You're the one who ripped them off me. Thanks to that and what happened tonight, I'm probably banned from this hotel forever."

He glances down at me, eyes alight with humour. "You can stay at my place tomorrow night. Subject to an approval process."

"Your feline friends?"

"You'll need to be on your best behavior."

I roll my eyes. "Right. After all this, I wouldn't keep your hopes up."

I stay curled in his arms and let the hormonal fantasies of two horny teenagers play out. This is one for the record books. Hard to believe I can outdo some of my worst Stanford antics. Best I keep this story to myself.

Forever.

Morgan fingers the silk roses stitched on the hem of my dress. "You won't need anything this fancy tomorrow. I wish we could stay on *Liberté* until you leave, but she's scheduled for maintenance Thursday."

In the chaos, I've totally forgotten we're on his yacht tomorrow. I ask him if he wants to cancel, given the circumstances, but he's adamant we go.

"I've been looking forward to this all week. But only if you're up for it."

It's all I can do to put the night, the whole week into some sort of perspective. It feels like I've lived a year and during that time, became someone else. Or maybe, I've become myself again. One painful blowup at a time.

"At this point," I say. "I think it's time I keep a low profile. Sea level sounds about perfect."

Morgan settles the bill and we wait for the best opportunity to slip out undetected. He suggests we both get some sleep instead of him keeping me awake all night in my room. He wants me well rested for tomorrow. I'd love to fall asleep in his arms, but Morgan's right. Sleep would be low priority. I ask him what I should bring for our day at sea, and he says just a bathing suit.

After a dreamy kiss that curls my toes, he adds, "Although you might not be wearing it all that much."

Chapter Thirty

HIGH ABOVE THE AZURE MEDITERRANEAN, MORGAN'S HELICOPTER allows for a bird's-eye view of *Liberté's* deep scarlet hull.

"I love the red," I say, talking over the chopper noise.

"It's my favorite color," Morgan replies. "Same red as the company logo and Monaco's flag."

With the yacht show underway and all available dock space at Port Hercules spoken for, *Liberté's* anchored offshore. As the pilot circles overhead, I take a closer look at the rear deck of the yacht, unsure if what I'm seeing is an illusion.

"What's going on with the pool? It looks like the bottom of it is rising."

"It is," Morgan says. "I designed the pool so the base rises to become the helicopter landing pad. On a smaller yacht, it's all about maximizing space."

"What happens to the pool water?"

"It drains into holding tanks for reuse." As he explains the mechanics to me, the pool floor, painted with a giant black H, becomes level with the deck.

Wow. That is something else.

The pilot lands expertly on his mark, we disembark, and a smiling young man in red shorts and a crisp white polo offers us chocolate-covered strawberries. He's one of the skeleton crew for our day trip. Morgan wants maximum privacy.

"The tour begins here," he says, licking chocolate off his fingers. "This is the main deck. Beach club down the stairs."

Beach club refers to deck space closest to the sea. An area where you can dive right into the ocean, which is what I plan to do today. It's a perfect ocean play day: warm with just enough breeze to keep the heat at bay. I'm as giddy as a teenager on her first date. Helicopters. Yachts. Chocolate on platters. It's like living in a dream.

And *Liberté* is appropriately heavenly.

I like to compare great design to the notes of a perfume. Both are layered sensory experiences. As Morgan walks me through his paradise, the top notes of his interior design are the things that hit me first—bold pieces of furniture and modern art splashed with his favorite shade of red. The mid-tones are the textures and patterns, all the details that tie everything together. The bottom note, the foundation to it all, is where the magic is. Morgan sculpts space and light in a singular, signature way that leaves a lasting impression. His design vibe is streamlined and structural but also tactile and intimate with thick, silk rugs under our feet and back-lit onyx walls that glow like my face after he's had his way with me.

Upstairs, his bedroom on the top deck is what the cool kids call *extra*. A palatial spread with a bed facing east and nothing but endless ocean outside the windows. The Mark Rothko hanging over his desk is probably an original. Tucked in a corner is a cat tower, a whimsical addition that makes me smile.

"Morgan, seriously." Out on the adjoining deck, a buffet fit for a king awaits. Necks of wine and champagne bottles poke out of crushed ice piled high in a silver bowl. Pink crab legs stacked high. Fruit and cheese, crackers, crudité, and of course … "Caviar," I marvel. "You didn't need to do that."

He shrugs, smiling. "I know it's your favorite."

"Everything about this boat is so you," I say, noticing a rendition of Rodin's *The Thinker* on his dresser, the muscled legs just like Morgan's. "Now I know why you spend so much time out here."

He draws me closer, a smile growing wide and wicked. "All that's been missing is a certain raven-haired vixen."

I wrap my arms around his waist and laugh. "Do I know her?"

"I'm hoping to learn more about her today."

"Such as?"

"Her capacity for pleasure."

His hands slide behind me, deep into the valley between my cheeks. His preferred stomping grounds, I've come to realize. I return the favor, gripping the hard orbs of his ass. Was it just last week I fantasized about touching him? I've lost all track of time.

"Hmm," I say. "I think she's open to suggestions."

He raises a brow. "Are you allergic to mangoes?"

Another laugh slips out. I did notice the spears of deep orange amongst the buffet. "That sounds very specific."

"I always eat fruit for breakfast," he says, the twinkle in his eye just like his father's. He tugs at my dress, wanting me out of it. "And I'm very hungry."

He's loose today, a kid playing hooky. I get it. The zing in the air is palpable. I peel off my dress, toss it on the bed and shake out my hair. Based on Morgan's devious smile, the small squares of mesh that qualify as my bikini won't be on me much longer.

I hold my hand out coquettishly. "Lead the way, sir."

While he pops the cork on a bottle of champagne, I settle onto the thick mat designed for serious lounging and create a little nest out of the scarlet pillows in my immediate vicinity. Morgan returns with our bubbles and hands me the flutes. He strips off his shirt and shorts right in front of me without a stitch of self-consciousness. Under the wattage of bright sun, I realize he has no tan lines.

His hard, tight body is perfectly bronzed.

Everywhere.

And he's already rising to the occasion.

"Is that my breakfast?" I joke.

"Before we both eat," he says with a cheeky smile, "I want to talk about some ideas with you."

He grabs the platter of mangoes from the table and sits beside me. We both smell like kids on the beach from the Coppertone Morgan massaged into our skin while we waited at the heliport.

I run my fingers through his hair. Soft, no gel today. "What's on your mind?"

"I know your client base is in the US," he starts. "But what if I made you an offer you can't refuse?"

I glance at him, the surprise in my expression hidden by sunglasses. "Like what?"

"Whatever it is you want. Money, responsibility."

"You mean, work for you exclusively?"

"That would be ideal," he says. "I don't know how that works with the rest of your business. Or with Vaughn."

The enormity of that concept sends a shot of nerves into my belly. "I'm not interested in being an employee."

"How does consultant sound?" he's quick to add, and I know he's thought of every angle long before this conversation. As I think on my response, his hand brushes the top of my thigh and he starts massaging the tight muscles, finding all the right pressure points. "I don't expect a definitive answer right now," he says. "But I think you'd be a great addition to the team."

"If it means moving here, that's a big shift. A major decision."

His hand slips into the warmth between my legs, and it's game over. I'm moist and blooming even before his thumb pad starts shamelessly circling my clit. "I understand," he says. "But will you consider it?"

The depraved pleasure of his tactic rushes through my blood. It's electric, unstoppable and most of all, ingenious.

"Is this your idea of negotiation?" I ask.

He laughs and kisses me deeply. "Didn't I tell you the de Rohan-Chabot men are known for their persuasiveness?"

"I can still say no."

And if I ever wondered what zero conviction sounds like, voilà.

"Let's talk more after breakfast," he says, his smile turning base as he sets his sunglasses off to the side. "Can you slide lower?"

Morgan's already taken me places I've never been, and the wanton part of me knows there are plenty more destinations ahead. With my every muscle twitching in anticipation, I do as he asks. On my back, looking skyward, I catch a glimpse of the satellite navigation gear squatting on top of the captain's deck.

"The captain can't see us here, can he?" I ask.

He undoes the ties of my bikini bottom and whips it off me. "Not the way I designed it."

As he wedges a pillow under my ass, a bird hovering high in the sky catches my attention. It makes a strange sound, a low hum, air over wings, I think. Or maybe it's the satellite. All that technology can't run silently. I'm about to ask Morgan if he hears it, but he's busy setting up his morning buffet. He lowers himself onto his stomach with a spear of mango in hand and tells me to close my eyes.

I swallow hard and let my eyelids drop. I know it's coming. But I don't expect the mango to be so deliciously cold.

My breath catches in my throat, eyes flashing open. "Woah!"

"Refreshing?" Morgan asks, and pulses it deeper to the point removal requires some special extraction skills.

A shudder runs over me, head to toe.

Never get between a man and his mango.

His mouth hard, a little rough, it's insanity, how good it feels. Literally and figuratively eaten out. One spear after another, he devours flesh, turning mine into a bundle of sweet, sticky arousal. At one point, he squeezes a mangled piece, letting the juice pool like liquid sin in my belly button. He tongues it out, lapping and growling like a mad dog. The tickling sensation leaves me giggly and gasping and feeling all of fourteen. His face is a mess of orange and smeared with my cream when he comes up for air.

"I can't get enough of you," he pants and starts all over again.

Morgan's tongue is a reckless creature and my hips buck wildly, his hand strong and pressing down on my belly. I'm vibrating, wound to the breaking point, the high-pitched whine no longer contained in my body. It's high above me, its own thing, so alive and real I flutter my eyes open, certain to see the sound waves.

But there's nothing.

Only a shockingly bright sun and his savage destruction of my clit.

Both are blinding me.

The spreading, hot wetness of desire between my legs is like a volcano erupting.

And he's so on fire, ready to plunge deep before I come down from the stars.

A sharp, cutting rip of packaging between teeth bleeds into a snap of rubber onto skin. He hoists both my legs onto his shoulders, a bruising torpedo tip pushing my trembling parts wider. He buries himself completely, groaning like a beast in heat.

"Fuck, Vandana. You are heaven and hell."

A properly fueled man can cover miles in a single day, and Morgan's hell-bent on breaking any marathon record. I rise above the dark edge of pain and pleasure, absorb the marauding blows. Let the planets spin behind my eyelids, drift off into the purple cosmos. I'm boneless, lost in shadows, his ragged breathing coming faster and faster.

Whatever that bird is flying so high, I can feel the air pulsing off its wings, swooping and diving.

Feel the freedom.

I arch into the surrender of it, Morgan's final assault accepting of my defeat. We shatter together in a way that defies re-piecing, fragments of us drifting up into the endless blue sky.

Drifting back into the real world, I'm a sticky mess of mango juice and sunscreen, limbs glued to Morgan's. He's lying in stillness beside me, his breathing slowly returning to normal. Words escape me, the very basics of speech in general.

Our heads turn at the same time, eyes meeting in silence.

He, too, is at a loss as to what just happened.

"Did I hurt you?" he asks.

"I might need a breather," I reply, gamely. Ridden and raw, muscles I didn't know I had are achy and screaming.

"I'm sorry." He kisses me softly. "I lose myself around you. It's dangerous."

You can say that again.

"How about you don't starve yourself before dinner?"

He lifts my limp hand and brings it to his lips. "I'll eat two lunches," he says, with a lazy, wrung out smile. "That should help."

It's late afternoon when we crawl out of bed for an ocean dip. Morgan swims naked and his disregard for swimwear comes as no surprise. (I'm not there yet.) With the coastal town of San Remo in our sightlines, we bob in the water and talk about where we want to travel (me —Africa, him—Vietnam). Our favorite bands. (Maroon 5 and U2, respectively). Things we want to accomplish. He drops another hint about me working here but lets it slide when I swim in silence beside him.

Right now, I want to be in the moment.

Enjoy the peace while I can.

On our way back to the yacht for an early dinner, Morgan stops and treads water, squinting at the horizon with a frown.

"What do you see?" I ask.

"That one boat's been close all day."

"Do you recognize it?" From here, it looks like your average yacht; white, mid-sized with no distinctive features.

"No," he says. "And I know most of the boats."

I pinch his bare bottom. "Maybe it's time to put some shorts on."

He smiles distractedly. "Never."

Our meal will go down as one in my top five list, for sure. Sable-fish and Niçoise salad and lemon soufflé served on the beach club deck, sparkling waves right at our feet. Sunbaked and thirsty, the wine goes down too easy and Morgan slips upstairs to grab another bottle. Left with my thoughts, ten different emotions swirl and try to land. This life. His life. It's almost too perfect to be real.

But I could live this life, no problem.

He asked the questions.

Now it's up to me to figure out the answers.

"Vandana!" Morgan's voice bursts with excitement, carrying down from the top deck. I swivel my head as he bounds down the stairs, breaking stride to scoop me out of the dining chair.

"Woah! What? Tell me."

"Hold on," he says and leaps off the deck, me shrieking in his arms. Airborne for what feels like an eternity, we cannonball into the sea with a gigantic splash.

I break the surface, sputtering air and shock. As big as Florida, Morgan's smile could warm the entire state if the sun went missing. "Khaled just texted," he says. "We did it. We got the commission."

"Oh my god. That's amazing!" Our kiss is big and sloppy, technique out the window. "I can't believe he came to a decision so quickly. How's his mother?"

"Recovering well. Khaled sends his thanks again. You have to decide on a gift. He refuses to let the matter go."

"What do you think I should ask for?"

His eyes are bright, the sun turning his golden skin into a luminous canvas. "An apartment next to mine?" he suggests.

"I'm being serious. I need your guidance. I don't know what's right." I'm treading water with effort, arms tired from the long swim and too many glasses of Pinot Gris.

"Wrap your legs around my waist," Morgan says. "I'll keep us afloat."

I do as he asks and become weightless in the water. We wrap our arms around each other while his powerful legs churn underneath us. How crazy is it to be a mediocre swimmer in the middle of the sea and somehow feel so safe?

I hug him tight and Morgan whispers into my ear, "This is what's right. Anything else is gravy."

Chapter Thirty-One

IT'S STRANGE TO BE BACK ON LAND.

Confining, like a too-tight dress.

I felt it immediately in the helicopter, the Chiron intensified it and now, riding up the elevator to Morgan's apartment, it's like the walls are closing in. Once you've tasted the playground of open waters, it's addicting. Morgan's more relaxed than I've seen him, arm slung around my shoulder, humming a familiar melody. It's hard to imagine being back in LA, waking up without him around.

After the high day at sea, I don't want to think about it.

On the top floor, the elevator doors open into his private hallway. As he unlocks the front door, he says, "We have to be quick. The committee tries to escape every now and then."

We're inside for all of three seconds before a furry squad comes trotting across the open concept floorplan. Down on one knee, Morgan greets his cats in French while they wind through his legs and bump his hand with their heads, each one wanting attention. He introduces them one by one: Asterix, the leader. Josephine, the sleepyhead. Vlad, the bully. The tuxedo twins, Fox and Freya.

He encourages them to say hi to me with a sing-song voice I'd never associate with him. "Oui. C'est Vandana. Elle est très belle, no?"

Huddled protectively around Morgan, their silent observation of me is comical. Other cat owners advise the trick is to let them come to you, so I lower my hand. Tentatively, a fluff ball of white, Asterix, comes sniffing around.

After the welcome headbutt, I look up at Morgan with a smile. "I guess I'm approved."

He excuses himself to feed them, suggesting I take a spin through his place, check out the view on the deck. I expected his apartment to be grand and it doesn't disappoint. It's like walking into a modern opus of architecture where Italian furniture designers have been hoarding their finest creations. And the space. An entire family could spend the day avoiding each other on the main floor. Never mind the staircase spiraling to the second floor.

"You have your own swimming pool," I say, although *pool* is more of a suggestion. It's a Grecian bathing center right off the living room, complete with Venus de Milo in the corner. Jesus.

"Every apartment has one," he says, like this is somehow normal. "It's one of the reasons I bought the place."

"The swimming naked part?" I ask.

He laughs. "Precisely."

I wander onto the deck and feel light, floating high like the view. A full moon shines bright in the sky and city lights twinkle along the dark caw of the Mediterranean. We're so high up the stars feel within reach. Behind me, the sounds of Morgan shushing his meowing cats softens something in my heart that's been hard for too long.

A reminder that one week is enough to complicate my life for years.

I don't love him, I tell myself. I can't love Morgan without knowing him fully, and that takes time. Time eventually creates love, slowly and sweetly. But Morgan is a man I can love. And that's scarier than being in love, because the path to love is unknown.

Formless and measureless, like the night around me.

"Thank you for a wonderful day," he says, joining me outside with filled wineglasses. Another prime selection from a master sommelier, the bouquet is intense and ripe, full on the tongue. We sip in silence, gazing into the night.

"It's like opposite worlds," I say. "Land and sea."

"You enjoyed yourself today, no?"

"No. I want a full refund."

He laughs, and I like how his face rearranges with lightness. His eyes skim mine, and whatever passes between us, I can't see it. But I sure as hell feel it.

"What a week," he says, summarizing my thoughts perfectly.

This time last week I was a woman with undying scruples. Welcome to this week's Vandana, breaking every boundary I swore I wouldn't. It doesn't feel as wrong as I imagined it would. I don't know if that's good, but something else bothers me more, and I give voice to it. "When we flew back this evening, I thought about the stupidity of last night, the drama with Khaled's mother."

"You did the right thing," he assures me.

"I know, but if I didn't turn into a crazy, ranting woman, who knows what the outcome might've been. And for what? Some privileged guest no one wants to get into any trouble over?"

He sips his wine, studying me. "Feels like there's more to this than Khaled's mother."

"I've been struggling with the craziness of PR," I admit, words measured and careful. "How we have no control. Putting out fires in the middle of the night. The media just running with whatever and not even caring about whose lives they destroy. Shoot first and ask questions later."

"Imagine if you only had one client and full control over them," he says.

I bump him with my hip and laugh. "I wonder how long that would last. The control part."

"I mean it," he says, "what we talked about." His eyes turn serious and search mine. "You could accomplish so much here, whether it's PR or pursuing design."

Everything he has offered me is the right side of the Cinderella story. The promise of it is so enticing. But playing for keeps this early in the game has bitten me in the ass one too many times. And I still have to untangle myself from Derek.

"I think so too," I say, adding the disclaimer, "in time."

I hear his hard swallow, how he chases it away with wine. "How soon do you think you'll be back?"

"I can't answer that right now," I say, being gentle with the truth. "There's a lot to sort out, and it can't happen from here."

For a long time, he says nothing, his focus on the dark water. It strikes me this is how I first laid eyes on him—side profile, illuminated by the moon, lost at sea.

"But it's over, no? You and him?" He asks this without looking at me.

"Very much so."

I lean against him, finding comfort in his strong frame so intent on punishing me in all the right ways. He makes space and brings me into the fold of his arm. It feels like I'm breathing and somehow not, and the magic of it isn't surprising because if magic exists, this is it, a moonlit night in Monaco, after a champagne blur of tangled limbs, floating on waves, and yacht design dreams coming true.

"You smell great," he says.

"Like what?"

I look up at him, thinking he means the scent of his sweater I've borrowed. It drapes on me like a cozy, second skin.

"Like us."

He kisses me sweetly before his wayward tongue opens me up with unabashed clarity of intent. Absolutely naked is how that tongue wants me. In no time at all, we find ourselves in his bedroom, on the platform bed, leaving each other breathless with only one thing on our minds.

Until a mournful meowing starts.

Morgan pulls back with a borderline embarrassed smile. "Can you give me a minute? I need to say goodnight to my team. They get funny when I lock them out of the bedroom."

I bite back a laugh—Morgan at the mercy of his cats. "No problem. Can I pop downstairs while you do that? I forgot my bag in your car."

"What do you need out of it?" he asks. "I have an extra toothbrush and all the toiletries."

Crooked up on one elbow, his eyes are dilated, the swirling intensity back with a vengeance. I know what that means. And I have no interest in missing a minute of it.

"I can grab it in the morning."

While he sorts out the cats, I brush my teeth with his loaner and wonder what it would be like to wake up every morning and walk right into his open shower. Wash my hair with a view of Grace Kelly's former palace. Get wet with him and put the tiled bench to good use.

Maybe we can give it a test run tomorrow.

When I come out, Morgan's in bed texting. At the sight of me, a smile of pure wonder takes over his face. I'm going for broke, leveling up to his game in the nudity department. Venus de Milo, eat your heart out.

"Where did you come from?" he says.

I toss my hair, go for the full effect. "La-la land."

He laughs, sets the phone aside, and opens up the duvet for me to climb in. We spoon under the covers and he's warm as a furnace, heartbeat slow and steady against my spine. My body melts, ready to relax, but after seeing Morgan on his phone, my mind jumps ahead to tomorrow. A full day of meetings and, after the show closes at five, it's off to the Royal Morgan Yachts office to meet the team.

My first Olivier encounter.

He intrigues me in that I'm not sure what to expect. Few photos of him exist online. None, to be precise. I looked the other night. His only social profile is on LinkedIn, a yacht instead of a personal picture. Everything I've heard so far points to negative, but maybe he'll throw me for a loop and be an absolute charmer.

"Are things back on track with Olivier?"

Morgan, who's been breathing lightly and quietly, stills. "Why do you ask?"

"Monday at lunch when he texted you seemed … bothered."

"I'd rather not talk about him right now."

He sounds put off that I'm bringing him up, so I quickly backpedal. "No problem. I don't know why he popped into my head."

I snuggle into him, trying to tamp down any remaining ruffled feathers. His energy softens, and silence settles around us, Tuesday night in Monaco soundless as a graveyard.

"Amazing how quiet it is up here," I whisper.

He kisses the back of my head, a smile returning to his voice. "We could change that."

Full and warm and pressing behind me, he's not quite ready for the starting gate, but not far off. A flutter of excitement skims my chest. I can still feel the shock of cold mango and the heat of his mouth devouring it.

"What do you have in mind? Or dare I ask?"

He nuzzles my ear and quietly asks, "Can I have all of you?" My heart skips a beat, or maybe it stops altogether. Tension gathers between my shoulder blades and he feels the apprehension. "I'm in no rush," he says.

I'm not surprised he's asked because the message has been clear. Where his hands automatically go. A girl always knows. Morgan is one hundred percent an ass man. Asking is a requirement in my books, but I've never gone down this path so early with anyone. And he's a different caliber.

I take a deep breath and let the scales tip back and forth in my mind. I've done it before. Don't mind the simple, dark pleasure. What am I scared of, other than wanting him more than any man I've ever wanted? So I burrow deeper into him, curl up tight in a way that says I'm ready to be unwound.

Communicate without words.

And that's how it starts.

His fingers drift over me like sensory dust, writing invisible love letters on my skin. We tumble in the sheets that smell like sunshine and he suckles my nipples, refusing to relent until I writhe and beg. Then he moves lower and finds new ways to send me down the rabbit hole of bliss. And when I'm a whimpering ragdoll misted in sweat, he flips me over and readies himself before readying me with a cold smear of foreshadowing from the tube he procures from his bedside table.

"Tu es mon ange. Mon ange parfait," he murmurs and pinions my wrists above my head with one capable hand.

Face down and defenseless, the pounding of my heart takes over and all other sounds disappear. Morgan's undemanding and gentle but I still suck in the pillowcase, tremors triangulating into a bright white pinpoint. Then it's me moving instead of him, because it's easier. Bodies on a slow crawl, funneling together, I'm dimly aware of sensations and textures. Black and white shadows slivered on the wall, the soft chafe of his linen sheets against the rise of my nipples. His invisible scent. He asks if I'm okay and my answer is absorbing him until no room is left.

I hear the breath catch in his throat. I can feel him inside me, throbbing in the tightness. All I ask of him is to go slow.

"Tell me if you want me to stop," he says. "At any time."

Dominant and tender, strength in check, the intrusion, the shock of him, gives way to a particular thrill no words can describe. He ebbs and flows slowly, like low tide drifting in and out, his moans cresting like waves. And when we're long past the point of joining, my fists buried in the sheets, I dissolve into a shadowy world deeper than the ocean, where nothing else matters except this—to exist for the pleasure of a lover.

Chapter Thirty-Two

MORGAN

"MORGAN!"

A door slams, the sound tumbling me out of a deep, REM sleep. Wrapped in my arms, Vandana stirs, a sound of sleepy satisfaction humming on her lips. My morning wood throbs against her, the sublime wreckage of last night burnt permanently in my memory.

"Morgan, if you're in there, get up." Three crisp knocks ring out on the bedroom door. "We need to talk."

My eyes slit open, heavy and thick with sand.

Olivier? What's he doing here?

"Who is it?" Vandana mumbles.

"Uh … It's nothing. The cat sitter. Go back to sleep, I'll be right back."

I untangle myself from her limbs, from the sheet snaked around my leg. Olivier has looked after the cats on occasion, when my housekeeper is on vacation and I'm out of town; dropping in unexpectedly, however, is not part of our arrangement. I shrug on a robe and find him in the kitchen, leaning against the counter with a sour expression. Bags under his eyes and fingers in a splint, he looks as rough as I feel.

"Since when do come over without notice?" I ask.

"When did *you* get so careless?" he demands. "I told you to keep your dick out of it. But no, you had to invent a new Olympic sport in broad fucking daylight." His phone clatters onto the counter. "Take a look."

The tone of his voice unnerves me. I pick up his phone, the taste in my mouth fouling beyond red wine and morning breath. I scroll. And scroll. Scroll until my stomach drops out.

Vandana and I on *Liberté*.

In every position.

And I do mean every.

"Fuck," I mutter.

Olivier snorts. "That's the understatement of the year."

"This is a total invasion of privacy. She'll be humiliated."

"That's your concern?" he asks, incredulous. "When Khaled sees this, he's going to have a heart attack."

I swallow hard, the scope of this ballooning beyond my comprehension. "I can make this go away. I just need some time."

"You're out of time, friend," he says, his usual scowl sinking into something far uglier. "I told you to keep your hands off her."

"What's going on?" Vandana pads barefoot into the kitchen, wearing nothing but my sweater and a look of confusion. She shields her eyes from the bright sun, sees Olivier and stops suddenly. "Hi. Again."

I look sharply at Olivier, who stares back unblinking. "I didn't know you had company. And I'm very sorry," he continues, addressing Vandana. "I don't think we've met."

"Yes, we have," she says, adamant but wary. "In Genoa. You were talking on your phone. On the dock. You're a yacht broker."

"This is Olivier," I tell her, reluctant to inform her she's mistaken. Not when she radiates with such certainty. "He didn't come to Genoa, remember? He was ill."

Vandana stills, the way people do when told improbable facts that tilt their entire world. "You're Olivier?"

"I think there are more pressing matters to deal with," says Olivier as he tilts his head toward the phone.

Vandana's soft, trusting eyes find mine, searching for understanding. She gave herself to me last night in a way few women do, a passage into surreal depths I'm still spinning inside of.

"We can manage this," I say lamely, handing her the phone.

One lewd photo at a time, she absorbs the full, hellish ride. "Oh my god," she whispers. "Are these everywhere?"

"Unfortunately," Olivier replies.

The phone drops out of her hand like it's on fire, and all the color drains from her face. She no longer sees me or the kitchen. Hers is the faraway look of complete devastation. "This is going to destroy my business. Your deal with Khaled."

Apropos of nothing, Olivier chimes in. "Your father's campaign should be okay. If anything, this might distract the press from you and your husband."

In slow motion, Vandana's head swivels to meet mine. "You told him?"

"It slipped out … by accident." Accident. Like how my fist will land on Olivier's face. Why the fuck is he is bringing this up?

"*Accident*." She walks backward, as if she doesn't want to be close to the word. Asterix starts his morning yowling, the others joining in. We all jump at the sudden morning orchestra, and her eyes flick to them, to me. I can see the rapid-fire calculations as she tries to piece this together. She turns to Olivier. "What did you mean by, *I told you to keep your hands off her?*"

"Didn't you tell her?" Olivier asks me innocently.

"Tell me what?" Vandana's voice jumps an octave lower.

"I did tell you, remember?" My voice jumps an octave higher, trying to hold this oiled catastrophe together. "That it was Olivier's idea to hire you."

"It was my idea, but I also told you she was married and to keep your hands off," Olivier states, matter-of-factly. And, crossing his arms like a prig he adds, "I knew I couldn't trust you."

I turn to him and hiss, "Would you shut up already?"

But it's too late. Vandana moves farther away, her reality warping. "Trust? Why would you…" Cold realization dawns over her face. "Is this all a setup?"

"No, of course not," I say and shoot Olivier a suspect look. Did *he* set me up?

Vandana shakes her head as memories spool back. "Jesus. I *knew* it. You *were* propositioning me that night." She laughs, a crazy, I can't believe it laugh. "I thought I was losing my mind. And you let me believe it. This has nothing to do with PR, does it?"

Olivier sighs. "More or less, right, friend?"

"What the hell is wrong with you?" I yell, shoving him hard.

"It's more like what the hell is wrong with both of you?" Vandana says with a look of disgust. "What are you two? Hustlers?"

"It's nothing like that, I swear." I reach for her arm, but she yanks it away.

"Don't touch me. I don't know what's going on with you two, but I saw him in Genoa." She glares at Olivier. "We had a conversation on the dock. And I saw you with Renan at the casino the other night. Someone broke your fingers because you owe a million euros. And…" Her voice thins to almost nothing. "Oh my god. You were talking about me. Rigging my hotel room. That we'd never suspect anything." Shock and hurt crumple her beautiful face. She can't even look at me. "This *is* a setup."

It's too much, all at once. The casino? Olivier and Renan? Rigging her hotel? What is going on? Vandana's insistence on knowing who Olivier is feels overblown, but no way would she make up these details. A dark pit of wretchedness in my soul yawns open.

I pick up Olivier's phone, hand shaking. "Don't tell me you did this."

"I don't know what she's talking about." His beady eyes flick back and forth. "And I haven't seen Renan in weeks."

"You two are liars," Vandana says. "Sick, twisted liars." Tears start to wet her eyes and she bolts for the bedroom, slamming the door behind her.

I need to calm her down, explain, but I don't know what the explanation is. Not all of it. But I do know some of it. It's why Olivier edges left, putting the kitchen island between us. He's friends with all the drone guys, hires them to film our yacht promos. I knew I heard something strange yesterday. And that damn boat floating too close to mine.

"No one else knew we were going out on *Liberté*," I say, my voice wavering on the edge of fury.

"Everyone knows the red hull," he counters, but in his flat, blank stare I see the truth I've been unwilling to believe.

"Why?" I ask. "For the money? Renan's offering you more?"

"Don't say money like it's a four-letter word."

"In the end, it means nothing."

He laughs tonelessly. "Why do only rich people say that?"

I move so quickly Olivier has no reaction time. I fist his shirt, dragging his eyes to meet mine. "Do you know what Renan did to her? Do you know what this is going to do to her?"

"Do you actually care what's going to happen to her?" he scoffs, unafraid at my posturing. "You treat women like Kleenex. It's disgusting. Even if they could hold your attention, it's all about you and your fucking boats." He shakes his head. "You almost killed Tatiana, but she would've left you anyway. You never deserved her."

"That's what this is about? Tatiana? That was fifteen years ago."

"She liked me," Olivier says. "I had a chance with her, but no, you couldn't handle it. You have to one-up me all the time. You've fucked a million women in the past fifteen years, and I still pine for her." His voice finally cracks along with his facade. "I'm glad you fell for Vandana. Glad you can finally feel what it's like to be on the losing end."

I feel like I'm having an out-of-body experience. I'm numb, a dull vessel of nothing, when I should be beating the living shit out of Olivier. All his pumping me up and feigned understanding has been a ruse.

I shove him away, disgusted. "Give me my key and get the fuck out before I break the rest of your fingers."

He rummages for the key, lays it on the counter. The intensity of his stare slowly hollows out to match the shell of the man he's become. "You could've helped me," he says. "But you're a filthy rich bastard who only cares about himself."

"*Get out!*" I yell, the force of my voice sending Vlad flying off the couch for the safety of the deck. The tuxedo twins blink blankly at the front door slamming shut behind Olivier, heads swiveling like they're at a tennis match as my bedroom door bangs open seconds later. Vandana storms out in her flip flops, purse bouncing on her shoulder, nipples poking through her tiny mesh bikini.

I try to block her, and we dance back and forth as she steps right to left. "Vandana, wait. This is all Olivier."

"Don't be a coward, Morgan," she says, eyes spitting sparks. "Take responsibility for your own actions."

"I'm not—"

She silences me, holding up a finger. "I'm going to ask you one question. It's a simple yes or no. Did Olivier tell you to keep your hands off me?"

"It's—"

"Yes or no!"

I knuckle my fingers into my eyes and sigh. "Yes."

"Great. So, you come to LA with some dare on the table. See if you can bag the married lady? Some bored, sexed-up yacht boy pretending to need PR."

"I wasn't pretending. That part's the truth."

"That part," she says, with a tart laugh. "And what about the part that's out there?" Her arm flings toward the terrace, indicating the endless infinity of the internet. "You and me, looking like goddamn porn stars! And I *knew* it! I knew you were trouble. I should've known better."

She shoulders past me, leaving me to jog after her. "Where are you going?"

"The hotel. And then home."

I starfish myself across the front door, a last-ditch desperate attempt. "Home? But the show…"

"Show? Are you kidding me? Move!" Surprisingly strong, she tries hard, palms flat and pressing against my unmovable flesh.

"You can't go outside in just a bikini," I plead.

"I can do whatever I want, Morgan. You better move, or I'm going to smash your balls to high heaven. And don't think for a minute I won't."

Chapter Thirty-Three

VANDANA

By the time the elevator dumps me onto the ground floor, I'm a bawling, bikinied hot mess. The concierge, flabbergasted at the sight of me stumbling across the lobby, leaps to his feet

"Mademoiselle! Est-ce que ça va?"

"No," I yell, shoving the front door open. "Whatever you asked, the answer is no."

I power along the walkway onto the street, half-blind with fat tears. It's too overwhelming to process. CNN, all the talk shows on which I'll be the joke of the day. Worldwide coverage of our naked asses. I, of all people, know there is no privacy anymore. One of our biggest clients, the CEO of a company everyone knows, got raked over the coals six months ago for a morning skinny dip. With his wife of twenty years. At their remote lakeside cabin. He was devastated with how his closest allies dropped him like a hot potato. Blamed me for not controlling the story. I clench my fists, nails digging into the soft flesh of my palm.

That whole scenario sank my spirits and ever since, I haven't had my head in the game.

Shitty shit!

Vaughn is going to kill me.

"Hey babeeee."

A car whizzes past, some loser giving me a hubba-hubba out the window. I flip him the finger and Morgan's right, of course. Walking the streets of Monaco in a bikini is very déclassé.

But at least I'm wearing something.

I reeled out of Morgan's apartment with my travel bag still in the Chiron, but screw it. I don't need a bag full of tainted memories. I don't want to see Morgan ever again. I want to pretend none of this happened.

I want to go home.

Head down, I march as fast as I can. Passing pedestrians give me long looks and wide berths. I dare them to say anything, happy to start a fight. But knowing my luck, I'll be squealed on and arrested by one of those cartoon cops. The ones standing on Monaco's streets in short-sleeved white shirts and fancy pants.

They don't even know how to do real police here.

Fake, spit-shined Monaco, where the sun shines every day, relentless and bright.

Like now.

I dig out my Dior sunglasses, grateful to hide behind something. Save for the odd car roaring past, it's disturbingly quiet, the slap of my flip flops carrying far and wide. I wish I had my Nikes because the farther I get away from Morgan's, the more I realize how far the hotel is. Rush hour, it if exists in Utopia, will start soon, and I don't need any more exposure. At the next apartment alcove, I dig out my phone and Google taxis. Call the first company on the short list. The dispatcher asks the question of the day: where am I?

Hell if I know.

There are no flipping street signs. Visible ones, anyway.

"Hold on," I say, moving further down the block. I squint up at a small plaque carved in a tiny gothic font on the side of the building. "I'm on Boulevard de Jardin Exotique. Close to…" I squint at an awning stretched over the café patio across the street. "The Azur Bar and…" Spinning around to see what's behind me, my voice deflates. "A Volvo dealership."

I hate Volvos.

"Ah, oui," the woman says. "Ten to fifteen minutes, madame."

Fifteen minutes? This place needs Uber, big time.

Whatever.

I'll just be right here, with the coffee drinkers across the street wordlessly admiring me. For some coverage, I position my straw bag over my torso.

Nothing to see, people. Nothing to see.

Only an unmitigated fuck-up that we'll lose clients over.

Sex scandals are for reality TV stars, Hollywood girls famous for being famous. June and Flynn and I poked fun at the last one, some bottle-blonde ditz who later blamed her drug-addled boyfriend for selling the footage for cash. We sat on my couch laughing at the TV, righteous with our glasses of Chardonnay.

That will never be us, we crowed.

Ha!

I don't even have the excuse of a cash-strapped boyfriend to hide behind. I'm doing the nasty with a guy so rich he can afford to play games with people's lives. So rich he can afford three-million-dollar cars and chase me with them. The familiar roar of the Chiron's engine growls closer and Morgan banks down the corner on squealing tires, coming to a lurching stop when he sees me. The passenger window slides open.

"Vandana," he says, voice quiet but still ballsy with authority. "Please get in. I'll drive you to the hotel."

"No. I called a taxi. It'll be here shortly."

With a frustrated sigh, he says, "I know you don't believe me, but this is mostly Olivier. He's the only person who knew we were on *Liberté*. He's the only one I told."

"First of all, that changes absolutely nothing. Second, you should keep your damn mouth shut. How dare you tell him about my father and Derek!"

Cars start to line up behind the Chiron, horns tooting and beeping. Morgan motions for them to drive around him, except a bus squats on the other side of the road at its stop and, like everywhere else in Monaco, there's not enough space.

"Please get in," he pleads. "You can't leave like this."

"Like how? In a bikini? Or with my tail between my legs? Every online pervert in the world is ogling us as we speak. Don't you understand? I just spent the past week trying to help you land the deal of your life."

"I don't care about Khaled!" he shouts. "I care about you."

This hits me in all the wrong places. Places I don't want to feel it. Judging from the look on his face, he doesn't know what to do with that statement's impact either. But I'm not giving him an easy out. He's already played me. "You should care about Khaled. You should care more about the public, your peers, your enemies. The collective that determines your fate, whether you like it or not. Just because you're rich doesn't mean you don't have to care. You not caring put me in the path of Renan."

The driver in the Audi directly behind Morgan pokes his head through the sunroof. "Hey, asshole! Move it along."

"Vandana." Morgan's voice is tight with tension, hands clawing the steering wheel. "Think about things for one second. Would I put you in harm's way with Renan on purpose? After everything I've told you. Do you really believe that?"

"I don't believe anything you've told me. How can I? Even last night I asked you about Olivier and you shut me down. Why?"

"Because I planned on firing him," he says. "That's why I asked if you'd consider moving here. Among other reasons."

I bite my lip, absorbing this. "Maybe that's true, but you're far from innocent. You just told Olivier to shut up because he was spilling the beans about something shady. There is some seriously screwed-up shit going on, and I don't even think *you* know half of it. Do you want to know why I kneed Renan in the balls? He told me we're all just puppets and whores and not to think I'm above either. I thought he was calling me a whore. But you know what? He must know you pretty damn well. He knew you were using me. A puppet in whatever stupid game you're playing."

Plain as day, the look on Morgan's face is utter heartbreak. "That is the furthest thing from the truth," he says. "I wasn't … I'm not using you. Yes, Olivier and I talked about you in advance. Yes, I saw you didn't have your wedding ring on. Yes, I did proposition you. Can you blame me? You're the most beautiful woman I've ever fucking laid eyes on."

"That's no excuse!"

"I know," he yells back. "I know all about my weaknesses. And thank you for indulging them. But I didn't know Olivier was deliberately setting me up to fail."

His backhanded comment about last night infuriates me. That I let him indulge. Like I need a reminder sitting on a plane for the next twelve hours isn't going to be easy.

"You're blaming Olivier again, but you want to know why *you* failed? Because of who you are. In here." I smash my fist against my heart. "I heard what Olivier said to you. All the women you chase. Do you know what people call you? *The Cruiser.* So you know what that means? It means I've just been cruised."

His body deflates, eyes blank and lost. I know it's a low blow. Know I'm being a bitch and not owning up to my weaknesses. I made the first move, knowing his reputation. And I didn't tell him about seeing Renan and Olivier together. My lack of transparency is just as damaging. But I need him to hurt. Need him to know what it feels like.

On the other side of the road, the bus finally chugs up the hill. The backed-up line of cars starts to stream past, choice comments hurled out the windows.

"Nice ass."

"Idiots!"

With a cacophony of horns and yelling disrupting the neighborhood, a mother with her tot in hand points at me as the cause, a powerful look of disgust on her face. The downfall of Monaco, playing out in front of her.

Ignoring the upheaval, Morgan jumps out of the Chiron, my travel suitcase in one hand. He's barefoot, only in jeans, and might as well be carrying the weight of the world on his shoulders, that's how crushed he looks. I want to hate him. Don't want to think about how gently he sudsed me clean last night in the shower. Don't want to think how he's turned me inside out so completely.

"Vandana," he says, with infinite weariness. "Take an hour, the day. Let it all settle and we can figure it out. Just don't leave."

Another car sidles up to the curb and I'm about to tell whoever it is to beat it, when I realize it's my taxi. I wave at the driver—*one sec.* Composing myself, I face Morgan like I'm in my favorite Cavalli suit and best heels, not see-through mesh.

"Forget about our contract. Forget about any of it. I'm going home. And don't follow me to the hotel." I grab my bag out of Morgan's hand, yank the taxi door open and stuff it inside. I slide in after it, slam the door and bark my instructions. "The Monaco Bay Hotel, please."

The stunned driver, senior citizen of the day, finds my eyes in the rearview mirror. He takes in my bikini and tear-streaked face. Glances at Morgan staring forlornly from the sidewalk, then back at me. Jesus. Is he really wearing a fucking beret? I can't be in Monaco a minute longer.

I don't need his judgment.

And I sure as hell don't need his pity.

"Move it!" I yell.

Chapter Thirty-Four

THREE HOURS AFTER THE DEBACLE AT MORGAN'S APARTMENT, I'M slouched in a chair in the departure lounge of Nice airport. Hair up. Sunglasses on. A sour taste in my mouth. I've paid far too much for a last-minute business class ticket but would slap down fifty grand if teleporting was an option. Morgan keeps texting, telling me his jet is on standby, begging to talk. To put an end to it, I finally text back.

VH: I've arranged a flight.

MdRC: Please call me. This is not what you think it is.

I hit DELETE and block his number. It's childish, but I need to feel in control of something. It's starting. The North American news feeds picked us up, and I'm scrolling through the commentary damage on *Huffington Post* when TQ calls.

It's three a.m. his time.

"Hi."

He hears it in my voice, clucking with sympathy. "Oh, sunshine. I was really, really hoping you had a doppelgänger."

"What's the destruction level? Honestly."

"Nothing horrendous ... yet. Although I just got back from clubbing and haven't done a full scour. But before we get into that, can we talk about how Morgan isn't your husband?"

238

Shame rises in my heart, swift and all consuming. Of all people to keep in the dark. "I'm sorry. I should have told you."

He gets the quick and dirty version, absorbing it all in absolute silence. "The fact you didn't tell me is criminal, lady," he finally says. "I don't know what to say, other than I'm sorry. I'm crying on the inside."

"I know. It just all happened so fast."

As the perfect mournful denouement, a young Asian traveler starts to play *Für Elise* on the piano inside the terminal. Beautiful, but not the heart-lifting tune I need right now.

"Where are you?" TQ asks.

"At the Nice airport. I'm coming home."

"What? Why?"

On the verge of blubbering, I take a deep breath. "I screwed up. Big time. Got taken for a ride."

"Well, yes, I can see that."

Leave it to TQ to find humor in the most devastating situation. Despite it all, I can still laugh. A good sign. "You are horrible! What I mean is, this whole trip…" I stop before the words spill out. I still don't fully understand what happened and need time to comb through every conversation from the past two weeks before calling anything.

"If you need a minute," TQ says, "breathe it out."

"I'm good. The bottom line is, the shit is going to hit the fan. We need to be ready."

He blows out a foreboding breath. "Copy that, boss."

Over the loudspeaker, last call for my departing flight is announced. Travelers around me start to collect their bags.

"I gotta run, babes," I say. "I'm in the air for the next seven hours. When I land at JFK, I'll check back in. Keep everyone at bay until then, please. As best you can."

"You want me to pick you up at LAX?"

"No, I'll grab an Uber. Don't tell anyone I'm coming home," I warn. "The last thing I need is a swarm at the airport."

"I hate to inform you, sunshine, there's going to be swarms everywhere." He yawns, tiredness leaking into his voice. "I should really get to bed. I'm going to need my wits about me."

I can only blame myself for my loss of face, and now he's tasked with helping me manage it. His tirelessness in keeping Vaughn and me afloat, always being there for us, makes the whole thing more shameful.

"I'm sorry, TQ. This is a major bad."

"Well," he says, ever hopeful, "if it makes you feel any better, seeing photos of you naked is almost enough to turn me straight."

"I really should be strangling you right now,"I say, as lovingly as I can.

"Don't kill me just yet. An idea popped into my head, and this might be late-night, five-cocktails-deep-spit-balling, but maybe we approach the mango industry. They won't know what hit them, this sudden demand. We can take credit. Maybe get a new client?"

Just when I think there isn't further to sink. I shut my eyes against the horror of a reputation shot to pieces. "Can you really tell it's mango?"

TQ sighs. "Damn those zoom lenses."

The transit at JKF starts uneventfully.

In the slow-moving customs line that tests my patience, two bratty children pelt M&Ms at the wiener dog sniffing around bags for contraband fruit while their clueless father surfs on his phone. The airport policeman taking the dog for a stroll shoots me a loaded look as if I'm the negligent mother. If he wants a fist fight, I'm ready. I paced the aisles non-stop on the Atlantic cross, my brain is this close to exploding, and I'm one snippy comment away from an emotional meltdown. I can't wrap my head around the duplicity of Morgan. Is he the cat-loving, brilliant designer who turns me into mush? Or is he a calculating sleazebag who forgets the basics of humanity while searching for new conquests?

I need a session with June and Flynn to help me dissect this. Before leaving Nice, I sent them a group text and brought them up to speed. I should check my phone and respond to their inevitable shock—last they heard I was going out on Morgan's yacht——but I'm too scared to turn it on.

After the air train drops me at Terminal 7, I grab dinner and pick a dark corner to sit in. I stab half-heartedly at my wilted chicken Caesar salad and wash down the rubbery chicken with a pinot noir so nasty it could peel paint off the walls. It's like the universe reminding me I'm not in Morgan's curated world anymore.

Yeah, thanks. I get it.

Time to forget.

But as the TV mounted above me sputters to life and CNN starts to blare, all hopes of forgetting come to a screeching halt. One of my least favorite newscasters seems to be staring right at me as she finishes a piece on Middle East politics and unloads the heavy artillery.

The internet is lighting up today with news of Vandana Hillman, one of North America's most respected public relations figures. Risqué photos of Hillman and a mystery lover surfaced out of Europe, and we caution viewers the images are explicit and may be offensive.

Of course, they show the close-ups.

Hillman is married to Derek Slaughter, and both are connected to Hollywood enfant terrible director, Stryker Talone. Talone's latest movie, Tangled Roots, recently wrapped filming in South Africa. Rumors of infighting and creative differences plagued the set, with tensions running high between Talone and Slaughter, his first assistant director. Deadline, one of Hollywood's breaking news sites, revealed earlier that Slaughter has been removed from Talone's upcoming superhero movie. And last night, Slaughter was photographed at a West Hollywood gay bar with a man who allegedly worked with him on Tangled Roots. Given Talone's outspokenness over the LGBTQ community, Hollywood is buzzing with the news…

The half-digested chicken starts to spin counterclockwise in my stomach.

Welcome to the PR apocalypse.

I might never turn my phone back on.

On the final descent into LAX five hours later, I watch the endless stream of cars on the 405, moving slowly like blood through clogged veins. I'm restless in my seat, imagining luggage in hand, wheeling toward the exit. When I step outside, will it feel like home? Or will I feel lost and rootless? A passenger traveling through someone else's life?

It's hard to believe so much can change in a week.

The 747 touches down and around me, phones light up, everyone keen to see what they've missed. I'm half-drunk and dehydrated from too much champagne. I bought a New York Yankees ballcap at JFK, jammed all my hair inside, and flew to LA with it low on my eyebrows, sunglasses on. I know how to avoid being recognized. This girl has never worn a ballcap in her life. As the usual announcements come on—welcome to Los Angeles, stay in your seat until we reach the gate—I find the courage to power on my phone. Waiting for the system to connect, I overhear two flight attendants chatting in their jump seats. Dinner reservations and an overnight layover. Then,

"Did you see those photos on *Pop Sugar*? The ones with the super-hot Euro guy on the yacht?"

"Holy shit, I know! His dick…"

"She must be *dying*."

Their comments chip away at all my cross-country positive self-talk. And the fireworks going off on my phone nix whatever's left. I can't keep up with the flurry of incoming messages and emails.

Reporters wanting comments. Clients asking me to reach out.

My mother is near total collapse.

Twenty texts and counting.

IH: Have you lost your mind? This is your idea of "handling your life?"

IH: (a forwarded article from Perez Hilton) *Frenchman eats Miss America.*

IH: I can't even, Vandana. How am I supposed to show my face at Nordstrom?

Jesus. My ladies know how to rein it in, at least. June and Flynn understand the scope.

FD: We're here for U! Anything, call. Xoxo

JA: I love you, you naughty bitch. #poundtown

Thankfully, nothing from Vaughn. It's wrong to hope he meets an untimely demise so I don't have to face him, but that would almost be better. Hunkered in my seat, I make one call to TQ.

"It's not earth-shatteringly bad," he lies. Not even a hello.

"I've had texts from Missy, Rupert, and Elijah," I say. Powerful clients we know by their first names who might not be clients much longer. "They want to talk."

"Oh, shit. They spoke to me too. I didn't want to tell you right away."

I chew what's left of my manicure off. Bits of Essie Ballet Slippers pink litter the floor under my feet. "The whole office knows, right?"

He sighs. "Honey, the whole world knows."

The plane takes forever to taxi and when we finally lurch to a stop at the gate, a bustle of activity breaks out. Overhead bins click open, coats get pulled on. The flight attendant's voice crackles once more over the speakers. It's time to collect our bags and get on with our lives.

What's left of them.

I think of how perfect it all felt on Wednesday when Morgan and I kissed in the waves, together in his world, limbs liquid as the sea.

Very quietly, I start to cry.

Chapter Thirty-Five

WHOEVER SAID BEING TALKED ABOUT IS BETTER THAN NOT BEING talked about must be a narcissistic fool. Or a sadist. In any event, they have never spent a Friday morning watching their life blow up on a laptop screen from the comfort of their home office. To remain sane, I've stopped Googling my name. Turned off commenting on my Instagram account. My focus now is on the grim client correspondence clogging up my email inbox.

It's been a pleasure working with you, but in the light of recent circumstances…

Thank you for all your hard work. We've decided to pivot with our PR strategies…

We've enjoyed our working relationship and best of luck…

More surprising is a note from Perla, who must've tapped Sevruga's website for my email.

I hope not so bad for you. Here is crazy. You two big news. Like BIG news. Ha, ha. Keep touch, Perla.

I could live out the rest of my days in here, I think. Shuffle around in fuzzy slippers, surviving on takeout. It's easy enough to disappear in a city of thirty-two million people. Morgan's not so lucky. On a good day, Monaco's population flirts with forty thousand.

If it's as nuts as Perla says, Morgan's no doubt captive in his apartment. Or he's yanked *Liberté* out of maintenance and is speeding toward Vietnam. I keep checking for an email from him, but there's nothing.

By the time four p.m. rolls around, I'm done. Eyes burnt from screen time and still in my pajamas, I slam another espresso shot to stay awake. June and Flynn arrive shortly for the debrief, and I'm gearing up for how I'm going to start. We all joked about it, me having a fling. Never did I guess it would end up being a Code Red. Even my sloppiest affairs at Stanford ended better than this.

Flynn arrives first with steaming hot pho and June (late, of course) with enough bottles of Cabernet for all of us to black out. They circle the wagons around me and blow by blow, I give them the whole enchilada.

Minus a few spicy peppers.

June, looking a bit ragged from overwork but rocking a skin-tight Alexander McQueen dress, tries to make sense of all the pieces. "Let's start at the beginning, that first night in LA. He admits to propositioning you, but also claims wanting PR wasn't a total ruse?"

"That's what he said, but who knows." With no appetite for rich broth and slippery noodles, I set my bowl down and cozy into the couch corner. We're camped out in the living room, gas fireplace blazing.

"Not to play devil's advocate," Flynn says, even though it's what she does. All the time. "How many guys did we talk about sleeping with? Long before we actually did."

June flashes a careful look at me. "True. That in itself isn't a crime."

"Yes, but we never misrepresented our intentions in the process," I add, prickling just a little. Whose side are they on?

Flynn fills her wineglass, emptying bottle number one. She's about to embark on a two-month speaking tour and I notice she's drinking more. It might have to do with the stalker she acquired after last year's tour. He eventually backed off, although the residue of the situation hasn't faded away so easily for her.

"Has Morgan said anything else since you left?" she asks. "Sounds like you stomped outta there without hearing him out."

Trust Flynn to turn my pity party into a self-reflection session. And she does it so smoothly. Never assume a headful of wild curls means there's chaos in her brain. She is ruthlessly efficient in uncovering the lies we tell ourselves.

"No," I say. "But I blocked his number, so even if he did reach out…"

I glance at June, knowing she'll sympathize. When it comes to relationship blowups, she's at the top of the podium. Raising ten million dollars? Easy. Intimacy with men? Better odds buying a lottery ticket. She has a heart of gold but hasn't found the right guy with the tools to mine it.

"Well," she says, drawing out the word. "You're always saying there are two sides to every story. Maybe you need to hear his."

The lame thing is, I thought the same thing last night. Now, with some distance, two things are clear. Olivier is one hundred percent a giant shit, and Renan is a mafia goon funneling bitter teenage trauma into bloodthirsty adult drama. Those two losers aside, the ultimate question still hangs: did Morgan really need PR? He was so disinterested in what I had to say, and he and Olivier talking about me beforehand shades everything, no matter what my heart says.

"Sure. Fine," I say. "I'm willing to listen. If I'm important enough to him, he can make the first move." My flippant, superior tone doesn't quite match the purple pajamas and Yankees ballcap and the hole in my heart, but hell if I care.

The trouble is, I do.

And it's written all over my face.

Flynn's inevitable next probing question gets preempted by my ringing phone. It's TQ. We haven't spoken live all day.

I force myself to sound breezy. "Hi. How's it going."

"Fine," he says. "Just tidying up after World War Three."

But there's something else. He wouldn't call otherwise. "Whatever it is, just tell me."

"Um, yeah," he says, confirming my fears. "I just forwarded an email to you. It's the Royal Morgan Yachts contract, voided. I wasn't sure if that's what was discussed."

My spine stiffens. "What does it say? The email."

"Nothing. It came from their accounts payable department."

"Nothing?" My toes clench in my slippers. I can hear myself telling Morgan to forget about the contract. To forget about everything.

"Do you want me to respond?" he asks.

"No. I mean, I guess that's that, right?" My voice catches, and I wish June and Flynn would stop eyeballing me like I'm an alien in drag.

"I'm sorry, sunshine," TQ says. "It's probably not what you wanted to hear." He doesn't know the whole story and doesn't need to, because he knows me. When we've lost clients or I've blown a pitch, or for all the times I turned to him for advice about Derek when things were tricky, he knows the Vandana voice of uncertainty and sorrow.

But I find my resolve, buried as it might be. If anything reinforces the subtext behind Morgan's first move, it's this. "You know what? Wire back all the money. Every cent."

After a heavy pause he asks, "You sure?"

"One hundred percent."

After I hang up, June uncorks another bottle. In the silent gloom, she tops up the glass I just emptied. "Care to share?"

"Morgan sent back our contract," I say. "Null and void."

Flynn and June share a look. "How do you feel about that?" Flynn asks.

How do I feel? Like I've been run over by an ice cream truck. Like everyone on Planet Earth knows my wax job of choice is a Brazilian. Mostly I feel abandoned, which is nonsensical, because I was the one who jumped ship.

June sits beside me and slides an arm around my shoulder. She's our den mother and will go to the ends of the earth for us. "You don't have to pretend. It's us."

My head drops and all the tears I've been saving make an appearance. I swipe at them angrily. "Maybe I liked him. Maybe I liked him more than I thought I would."

And I shut down, because if I don't, I'll break in half and there's no glue strong enough to hold me together.

Time and distance, I remind myself for the umpteenth time. Time and distance.

All of this will pass.

Life is full of regrets, and I can't let one drag me down.

Even if he is a regret I'll remember for the rest of my life.

Chapter Thirty-Six

Come Saturday afternoon, the storm finally settles. I'm still standing, and the damage isn't so bad. We've lost nine clients but have inquiries from a dozen new ones. The news outlets move on to a new scandal. Vaughn had his freakout and even that came with a light, if not impressed, hand.

"Jesus, Vans," he said, his voice crackly and far away on the sat phone. "You're making me feel old. Every muscle I have would seize up if I attempted half of that shit."

It's better he's not here. Better that I not stand in his office and watch his eyes drift between my fully clothed body before him, and his computer screen where I'm testing the boundaries of penetration with Morgan. The fact he's staying in Africa to complete his holiday is music to my ears.

I wrap up the week from hell with a hot bath and chamomile tea, topped off by sleeping like the dead.

Assuming the dead wake up on Sundays at five a.m.

It's too early for light. Too early for birds. Too early to call June, who was probably late for her own birth, and yet manages to rise like clockwork at six-thirty every day.

But it's never too early to be caffeinated.

I shuffle downstairs and promise myself today is the day I will wash my hair, put on makeup, and wear something other than flannel. All achievable goals.

One step at a time.

I grind up my favorite beans and sit in the dark, listening to the coffee machine burble to life. After the two-day onslaught with no time to catch my breath, I relish the stillness. I can hear what's bubbling inside me. In the end, maybe having things end this way with Morgan was for the best. Better than uprooting my life and chasing a dream only for things to not work out.

It's obvious where he stands, so moving on.

Only it's not so neat and tidy in my heart.

It's a great big mess.

Beep-beep.

The door alarm goes off, and every hair on the back of my neck stands at attention. I slide off the stool, scan the counter, and palm a chef's knife. Really? Now this? Can't a girl catch a break? A mudroom separates the kitchen from the back door, and with the approaching footfalls I raise the knife. My heart pounds like a tribal drum. I can squash a spider no problem, but stabbing another human?

When Derek steps out of the shadows, equal parts shock and relief flood over me. "Hi," I say.

"Jesus fucking Christ!" he yells, jumping back, not seeing me in the dark. With a hand over his heart, he watches me warily, slowly recovering from the adrenaline jolt. "Fuck, V. You scared the shit out of me. What's with the knife?"

"Sorry, I wasn't expecting you. I thought…" I slide the knife back into the holder, suddenly feeling very stupid. Our property is gated, in one of LA's safest neighborhoods, and the most we've ever dealt with is someone narcing on us watering the lawn during restricted times.

Derek flicks on the under-cabinet lights, and in the ghostly glow he looks tired. Rings of black under his eyes, two or three days of growth on his face. In his usual on-set attire of Dickies, a black shirt and base-ball cap, it's all familiar, and at the same time he feels like a stranger.

Under my watchful gaze, he must think I'm about to rail on him. "I thought you weren't back until tonight, otherwise I would've texted. I'm just here to grab some files."

"It's fine," I say. "Go ahead. Grab what you need."

It's rare I sit in the kitchen in a robe and rarer still what he comments on. "I don't think I've ever seen you awake at this hour," he says.

I shrug. "The joys of jet lag."

He crosses his arms, awkwardly stuck between me and the hallway to his office. Is there anything more uncomfortable than seeing your estranged wife after she's been a global, naked sensation? "How are you?" he finally asks, his tone telling me he knows everything.

"Could be better."

"I guess Sevruga doesn't need any PR right now, huh?"

A week ago, I would have ignored his lousy humor. But maybe my habit of ignoring things has a lot to do with why he's here, sneaking into our kitchen in the half-light of early morning. "Can you believe we've had more phone calls in two days than the last three months?"

"You seem..." He pauses, searching for the right words. "Okay with it."

"Now that I literally have nothing left to hide, it's kind of liberating."

He looks at me sideways. "Is he your new boyfriend?"

"More like a man-stake," I joke, and immediately feel the discord. How it's not the right way to describe Morgan. What I want to ask is does it feel strange for Derek to say the word *boyfriend,* now that it's taken on a different meaning.

"You looked pretty cozy for a mistake," he says.

"Don't tell me you looked."

He sighs, examines the floor before finding my eyes. "You always had an amazing body, V. Still do."

It hurts, hearing that. Knowing that whatever forces brought us together are no longer. Walking through the house yesterday, nothing felt the same. When love leaves, all the things surrounding us, and the passage of time they mark, take on different meanings. It's not the sofa we bought together in Chicago and the snowstorm story that goes along with it. It's not me hammering a nail with a jar of mayo until Derek came to help. It's not the dinner party where everyone got drunk and stayed over, the living room a makeshift Bedouin community, talked about for weeks after.

It's just a sofa, a nail in the wall, and a dinner.

The coffee machine beeps and I get up to pour myself a mug. "You want one?" I ask.

"Sure."

I fix his coffee the right way, adding the sugar. A silence opens up and we sit on the edges of it, coffee mugs wrapped in our hands, unsure what to say next.

Derek finally clears his throat. "I'm sorry, V," he says. "I really am. I could've handled this way better."

I find his eyes, guilty and dark. Feel darkness gathering in me. "It's okay."

He sets down his mug and shifts closer. The cologne we fought about two weeks ago is light on his skin. "It's not okay. The email I sent was super shitty. I don't want it to be ugly, V. I'm putting you through enough shit as it is. If you want to stay in the house, we can figure all that out."

"It's your house too," I note.

"You made the down payment." He looks away, emotion clotting his voice. For the first time, I consider all the shit he's waded through. All the negative talk from my mother. Me dropping hints to dress better. Stryker's high maintenance personality running him ragged. The constant pressure to be more.

"I don't want to talk about this right now, okay?" I say.

This is what I do. Keep it all in. It's so damn tiring and I'm exhausted with myself. With everything. I bite my quivering lip.

"No one's perfect, Vandana," Derek says, more softness in his voice than I can bear. "Not me and not even you. Don't beat yourself up."

"Is that what killed us?" He's blurry, my vision washing with tears. "Me wanting everything to be perfect?"

"Oh, babe," he says. "C'mere."

He takes me in his arms, and being in the embrace of the man I married with the best intentions finally breaks me. There are things you share with girlfriends and co-workers, but husbands and boyfriends know us at our intimate worst and best. They know our bad moods, the days we forget to shave, how we haven't forgiven ourselves for silly things done or said. I tell Derek I'm gutted, embarrassed, and scared. I voice all the things I've admitted to no one else and he holds me the entire time, stroking my hair, knowing it calms me.

"You always told me this stuff blows over eventually, V. You're in the worst of it right now. Chin up."

I look out the window over his shoulder as light starts to seep into the morning sky. I think back to the night we met, at a club in West Hollywood called Concorde. How the sexual electricity between us was so intense. That after slow dancing, his dick hot and hard, we'd slipped outside and didn't make it more than half a block. We got down and dirty against the courtyard wall of an unsuspecting apartment building, and just before coming, I remember the landscaping lights, how they made the night sky look dreamy and surreal, like it is now.

It's a great memory and a reminder of what needs to change. I used to believe sex held a relationship together, but long-term happiness is a combination of things. I never found the courage to leave Derek because it's easier to pretend life is perfect then it is to face your mistakes.

Coming out of our embrace, I sniffle and wipe my nose. Derek rips off a piece of paper towel for me and says nothing when I honk loudly into it, disposing of a half-ton of snot. I apologize and he laughs.

"Don't ever be sorry for being you, V. And fuck 'em if they can't take you for who you are."

I dab at my eyes, swollen and wet. "I'll get through it. One day at a time, right?"

He finishes his coffee and puts the mug in the dishwasher instead of the sink, something I always asked him to do but he never did. "I had my own hell day telling my parents last week," he admits. "All sorts of fun."

His parents, both sets, are the kind of Happy Americans who never question what goes into a hot dog. They don't want to know all the ugliness. How we can be put together in different ways. Judging from the mainly hostile answers on any question I asked that interfered with their vision of God and humanity, I doubt Alistair will suffer through a similar Christmas fate.

"I'm just waiting for the phone call from your mother," he adds with a rueful smile. "It's gonna be epic."

"Can you talk to her for me?" I ask, half-joking. I'm keeping Mother at bay for a looong time. Until the next Presidential election if possible.

"Anyway," Derek says, brushing hair out of his eyes. Still not cut. "I should get my files. I have a meeting with my accountant in Van Nyus at seven."

"It's good to see you," I say, tightening my robe belt.

He kisses my cheek. "Good to see you too, V."

When you've been together with someone for so long, it's hard to see yourself without them. Hard to define yourself without them. Derek and I are on different paths now, but it's for the better. In Monaco, I caught a glimpse of who my future self might be. Whatever the next step is, the next phase, I'm ready for it.

I'll do it on my terms, and it will be okay.

Derek turns for his office and then stops to look over his shoulder with a funny smile. I crushed his heart but he's going to be okay, too.

Apparently.

"If it doesn't work out with that guy," he says, "you mind giving me his number?"

Chapter Thirty-Seven

TWO MONTHS LATER

"Vans?" Vaughn knocks on my office door, pokes his head in. "You busy?"

I push back from my computer with a smile. "I always have time for you."

He steps inside, surveying the minor mess strewn across my desk. This whole morning has been an art direction show-and-tell from hell. A new client wanting feedback on their branding switch-up.

"How did the open house go this weekend?" he asks.

"Great," I say. "The realtor created a bidding war. It'll probably sell this week."

"Amazing," he says, tossing a manila envelope on my desk.

"What's that?"

"A courier just dropped it off. Probably some samples. You're still the hot ticket." He perches on the edge of my desk, grinning.

All sorts of packages arrive out of the blue these days. We're busier than ever. Weeks after my Monaco mess, it still blows my mind. What kind of crazed world do we live in when a naked scandal does more for your bottom line than a year's worth of marketing? I shake the envelope. It has bulk, but whatever's inside isn't heavy. My name is typed on front in capital letters. Nothing else.

I'll get to it later.

"So what's up?" I ask, spinning in my chair.

"I'm looking at December and wanted to check in with you. Lindsay's itching to do a getaway to Cabo over Christmas. You mentioned some time off. Anything concrete yet?"

I'm still getting used to the new Vaughn. The one who comes to my office to talk instead of yelling down the hall. Who takes two hour lunches with his wife. Who leaves the office earlier than me. His safari kick started this welcome renaissance and every aspect of his life is benefiting.

"If the house sells, I'm thinking December. Get out of dodge for Christmas. Destination wise, I'm thinking Europe. Three to four months."

He lets out a deep breath. "Okay. So ... lots of time. Like you said."

"You'll be fine?"

"It's never the same if you're not here, but I've got TQ. Holly's ready to step up to the plate. We'll get 'er done." He smiles, although I see the creep of worry in it. The same worry that's inside me. I might not ever come back. After a beat he says, "Seeing as how you've chosen Europe, what's the story with yacht boy?"

"I don't know," I say, shrugging off his question. Vaughn and I don't talk much about Morgan, primarily due to me not wanting to.

"All this time, nothing?"

"He did send the contract back," I remind him. "That pretty much says it all."

Vaughn flips one of my pens back and forth between fingers. "If he did reach out, would you talk to him?"

I sit up in my chair. It's been crickets from Morgan's end. Sweet nothing. "Probably. Why?"

He looks past me, at the retro Monaco poster gracing my wall. Boats in a blue harbor. I found it at a tourist shop the day Morgan was busy with his staff. I couldn't leave it behind. "You're a big girl, Vans, and you don't need me to tell you what to do."

I smile. "But you will?"

"Let's put it this way. I'm not saying what he did was right, but from what you told me, you can't really blame the guy for trying. You're the whole package. Smart. Ballsy. A stunner. Men are weak. Fuck, look at me. Chasing skirts. Chasing you."

"Is this your way of apologizing?"

He considers this. "Maybe."

"Accepted. And I know what you're saying."

"I'm saying it because the past couple months, you've been walking around like a lost deer. Every time your phone rings, I see the look in your eyes. You made me drive back to Burbank in rush hour because you left your Yacht Club pen on a table. I also know, very well, how you conduct yourself in business. You would not have gone down a path with him if there wasn't something."

Leave it to Vaughn to pile drive home the message. Surrounding myself with people who know me well is getting to be a real drag.

"So, what? You think I should reach out?" Butterflies erupt in my stomach at the mere suggestion.

"At the very least, thank him for getting rid of the photos."

"You still think it was him?"

"I know it was him. It takes serious money and clout to vaporize shit off the internet."

A few days after we became international stars, all the photos vanished. It doesn't erase what everyone saw or how many screen shots still exist. Ironically, mango sales did rise.

Thanks for that tidbit, TQ.

Vaughn stands and sets one loafer on my coffee table to stretch out his calf. He's casual about a lot of things around me, but I doubt he'd swim naked. "I think it will do a lot for your head and your heart if you clear things up with him," he says. "Don't sit here and wait for him to reach out. Like I said, men are weak. He's probably watching the sunset from his yacht, crying into his foie gras."

I chuckle. "You certainly know how to paint a picture."

"It's what we do, right? Spin the story, tell the tale. We're in the business of manipulation and illusion. I don't know if you gave me the whole story, but it sounds like there was some BS with one of his employees. Maybe you thought he was a certain kind of person, but he might prove you wrong. You'll never know until you peek behind the curtain. And," he says pointing his thumbs at himself, "don't look any further for evidence that people can change."

He kisses me on the cheek and before he ducks out for lunch, we discuss a couple of upcoming events, the pros and cons of a new client. TQ and I plan on gathering in my office for a salad and catch-up so I tidy my desk, coming across the envelope Vaughn left behind. With no return address or any type of logo, curiosity gets the better of me. I slice the top clean with my letter opener and upend the contents onto my desk.

It's not the Agent Provocateur panties—I know, without counting, that there's ten inside the bag.

It's not the cream-colored stationary from the Fairmont.

It's my name, written in his distinctive script.

Like the bold vertical lines, my heart starts to jump all over the place. For several minutes I don't dare open the card. All I can think about is how our contract came back with *VOID* stamped in bitter red above our signatures. No message. How much it hurt.

Two months is a long time to sculpt the ultimate *piss off* letter, and I'm not sure I want to read it. But like Vaughn said, I need to clear my head and heart once and for all.

I tip it open.

Dear Vandana,
   I am sorry for everything.
   I'm here until Saturday morning.
   Every night at 7 I'll be waiting for you.
   Please come.
   Morgan

. . .

I plug my mouth with two knuckles, holding down the throb of emotion. It's so very Morgan, minimal and to the point, but it's a three-novel set to me. I trace the elegant lines of his writing and something inside me loosens. Remembering how, at his apartment, the soft brush of his fingertips left a glow on my skin. Remembering the taste of salt on his lips, kissing in the Mediterranean. Remembering our embrace at the hospital. How I never wanted him to let go.

I want to make him wait, all the way to Friday.

But I can't wait that long.

Damn you, Morgan.

I'm never in control when it comes to you.

It gets cold in Los Angeles come December, despite what everyone thinks. I'm in dark jeans and slouch boots. I wore my favorite cashmere sweater to fend off the chill, but it feels scratchy instead of butter-soft from all the nerves dancing on my skin. Morgan sits on the same sofa as before, in jeans and a light jacket, a linen scarf nattily tied. But he's not wearing socks. That will never change. My bravado shrinks seeing him, although it's too late to back out. He sees me and stands—or gets up awkwardly is more like it. I can tell he's unsure whether to greet me his usual way.

"You came," he says. No kisses.

"I can't stay long."

"Of course. I'm sure you're busy. One glass of wine?"

"Half, for now."

The same Barolo from last time stands on the table. We take our seats and he fills my glass exactly halfway. It's busy tonight despite the weather, and having more people around makes me feel secure. My resolve is a slippery slope, and the mere act of breathing him in pushes me toward the wrong side of the slide. It's hard enough to find his eyes.

"À votre santé," he says.

I clink his glass. Take a careful sip. He's thinner. Wound very tightly. "What brings you to LA?"

"Another client, by way of Texas. Dorothy and Frankie say hello."

"Things going well with them?"

"As expected," he says, the ghost of a smile inferring Dorothy. "And you? How are things going here?"

"Business is good. Great, actually. Busier than ever."

"Good to hear."

His smile disappears as he takes a long pull of wine and re-arranges himself on the sofa. Repositions his scarf and wipes imaginary dirt off his jeans. He's fidgety tonight, more so than I remember. What I remember with absolute clarity are those strong hands—perfectly manicured and perfectly capable of tying ten different types of knots. Perfectly capable of tying me into knots.

"I heard through the grapevine Khaled kept his word," I say as if I saw a random headline and haven't been online stalking him. "Must be exciting times."

He stares at me with a strained look. "I have you to thank for the Delmars and Prince Khaled, among other things. Their yachts will make my career."

"Your work is amazing, Morgan. I didn't have to do much."

"You did everything," he insists.

"If you're hoping to hire me again for PR, the answer is no."

His laugh is flat and humorless. "That's not why I'm here."

A fluttering sensation starts at the back of my throat. He exerts the same gravitational pull as always, and knowing what it's like to fall into his black hole is a scary thing. I inch backward and cross my legs to stop the jitters. "What are you hoping for, coming here after all this time?"

His eyes flicker off mine to look at the ocean as if it somehow holds the answer. "What every man hopes for," he finally says. "That the woman of his dreams doesn't slip through his fingers." He finishes his wine and turns to face me. "To answer your question more thoroughly, I came here to ask for your forgiveness. Every waking minute of every day I think of you, and I go to bed miserable, with the hope that maybe I'll wake up and stop thinking about you. If I had the guts to come sooner, I would have, but I also needed to clean up the mess I created."

He says it simply and candidly, no clue it's the reason behind my sleepless nights of self-doubt. "So what exactly was the mess?" I ask.

"My behavior, for one," he says. "I've made many mistakes and I'm sure you can guess most of them. As far as Olivier goes, it was far uglier than I imagined. He was drowning in debt and running side deals, siphoning money from the company. Renan knew Olivier was in debt and knew the mobster who could forgive it. He also wanted the Khaled commission, so he strong-armed Olivier to bring him into the mix, and it all spiraled into a messed-up scheme. The worst thing is you got dragged into it, and I'm so sorry." He looks at me, gutted. "I can't believe how blind I was. I trusted him." His jaw squares, holding back what's trying to break through, and I catch a glimpse of the wreckage, what he's overcome in my absence.

"Trust is pretty important between people."

"I know," he says. "And I abused yours at the beginning. There is no excuse for my actions that night, and please know the intention was to hire you. That is the honest truth." He leans forward, setting the wineglass down to clasp his hands together. "If you can forgive me, I'd love to start over. If it means I need to get a place here, I'll do it. You can continue to do your thing. No pressure."

The beautiful amber in his eyes starts to swirl and fighting against the pull of it is hard. But I've had time to think things through and it makes what I have to say a whole lot easier.

"It's been an emotional couple of months for me, too. I think about you all the time. The thing is, I've been doing my own thing for too long. Living a life without my partner in it. I want someone in my life. *With* me. And honestly, I don't know if that's going to be in LA."

He's not expecting this. "What do you mean?"

"I'm not sure what it means," I admit. "I'm taking time off to figure it out. Three or four months. Derek and I separated. We put the house on the market. Lots of changes."

"And your business?" he asks.

"Vaughn and the team will cover for me."

He swallows hard, tries for casual. "Where will you go?"

"Don't laugh, but the plan is to charter a boat. Cruise the Mediterranean. You piqued my interest."

"Have you decided on a boat?"

"Not yet. Once the house sells, I'll map things out."

"I'd be offended if you didn't use *Liberté*," he says. "No charge, of course, although I may have to drop in now and then."

His generosity stokes a flame in my heart, as does the subtle need for control that comes along with it. But there's a different Morgan here, too. One who has apologized, played his emotional hand with such frankness, and is clearly hoping for more. It would be so easy to say yes.

"That's very kind of you to offer but, no. *Liberté's* yours, and I need space to think about next steps. I haven't even told Vaughn, but I'm considering starting fresh. In design. Maybe in a new city."

"Vandana," he says, not missing a beat with my news. "I don't care if you need a month, six months, a year. Take whatever time and space you need. Eventually, you'll be ready. If you tell me there's a chance with us, I will wait. Patiently. Faithfully. I promise."

"A year's a long time, Morgan."

He swipes his bangs back with a frustrated sigh. "Don't you understand? I've waited my whole life for a woman like you. What's one more year?"

Something in his face. I recognize the same nervous hope that rattled through me on the drive over. I chew on my lip, would gnaw it off if it could tell me whether I'm doing the right thing.

"I don't give a lot of people second chances."

"If you offer one," he says, "I will fall to my knees and weep."

He's serious, about to leap to the ground. I hold up both hands to stop him. "Please don't," I say. "The last thing we need is another video going viral."

Funny how the thing that wedged us apart is what brings us back together. When I say it out loud, our silly smiles turn into chuckles at the absurdity of being international gossip for all the wrong reasons.

And maybe there's a sliver of pride because damn, we did look good.

"I think I'm done with videos," Morgan says, ruefully.

I make a cringey face. "What did your parents say?"

"My father. He's a man." Morgan shrugs, no further explanation required. Only bucketloads of embarrassment the next time I see Alix. "At the very least, you put my mother's biggest fear to bed."

It slowly dawns on me. "She thought that?" Wow. Morgan playing for the other team is like the Pope being a polygamist. Maybe Cèline needs to get out more.

"And your parents?" Morgan asks. "I heard your father didn't win the election."

"No, he didn't. It might be the best thing that ever happened to both of them."

He tilts his head. "How so?"

"Their marriage wasn't a happy one. My mom finally packed it in." During her phone call to me two weeks ago, she cited me of all things as her inspiration. *If you can weather a global scandal and come out on top, I can leave Lorne and survive. Screw these miserable OC bitches and their gossip train.*

"I hope she's doing okay," he says.

I eye him across the table. "I don't know if I should tell you this, but both she and my ex asked for your phone number." Morgan bursts out laughing, loud enough to draw attention from guests at a nearby table. "I'm not joking," I insist with a small smile.

"That would be a very awkward ménage à trois," he says, a twinkle back in his eye.

And then I'm laughing too, because why not?

Morgan suddenly stands, arcs one long leg over the table, then another. He sits beside me, and I can feel his body heat, warmer than the heat lamps. See the glow of his tanned skin that I remember feeling like heaven against mine. Our eyes hang together in deep, longing silence.

"I want nothing more than to have it work out between us," he says. "I know you have a lot on your plate, but if the timing works, think about Monaco for Christmas. It's magical. I'd love to have you there." He reaches for my hand, brushing a kiss on top. Then he lays my open palm across his cheek with so much tenderness, the gaping hole in my stomach tightens right up. "I've missed you so much."

All this time, it's what I wanted. To be face to face and do what I should have done in the first place: given him the chance to explain. I didn't dare dream of an optimistic outcome.

The only thing missing is my belated amends.

"I'm sorry for leaving you high and dry in Monaco," I say. "Not my finest hour."

He kisses my palm, weaves his fingers with mine, lets our entwined hands lie in his lap. The spark of mischief in his voice is unmistakable when he says, "I have all sorts of punishment in mind."

His phone suddenly lights up on the table, and the lock screen photo is us at Dolce Aqua. Our gazes pivot off the phone and back to each other in perfect synchronicity. Before his sheepish smile disappears, I kiss him, knowing full well Saturday will be the next time I set foot outside this hotel if he has his way.

Our waiter, who has been doing the rounds, comes to a sliding stop beside our table. "Whoopsie! Sorry for interrupting." I break our heated kiss and Morgan glares rather unforgivingly at the poor guy who takes it all in stride. "But while I'm here, do we perchance need another bottle of wine in this cozy nook?"

Morgan looks at me questioningly. There is ground to cover and much to say. But desire shines in both of our eyes. Hope, too. One day, maybe love. It's too soon to call. All I know is the next few months are wide open.

An adventure awaits.

Liberté.

I look up at the waiter and smile. "We'll have another bottle."

Thank you!

I hope you enjoyed *The Cruiser!*

Revews are the lifeblood of an indie author's success. I'd be honored if you took a moment to post a review on any of the sites below. If you're not comfortable putting your thoughts into words, a star rating works just fine. Merci!

Amazon

Good Reads

Book Bub

Interested in behind-the-scenes, giveaways, and first dibs on future books? Join my VIP newsletter HERE. If you are reading the paper-back version of this book, link below:

https://rowanrossler.com/vip-club/

The Hustlers Trilogy - Book Two Teaser

Book two of *The Hustlers Trilogy* continues with the story of Flynn Dryden. Vandana and June both make appearances, and wait until you meet the beautiful man who storms into Flynn's life!

Hot stuff, people!

Release date TBD but teasers will start later in 2022. Can hardly wait to share.

xo

RR

Acknowledgments

Every book leaves a permanent mark on a writer's heart and *The Cruiser* is no different. As a method writer, I slip under the skin of my characters in such a visceral way sometimes, admittedly, it gets a bit weird. But it's the only way I know how to do them justice. My characters always help me understand something about myself, and the duo of Vandana and Morgan materialized the moment I needed them most. A shout out to them for shepherding me through the murk, one word at a time.

A question I get a lot is why I chose to write a story about a yacht designer. As a voracious reader, I'd never come across a romance story that featured this profession. The yacht world struck me as an intriguing backdrop worthy to explore and damn, how right I was. I had so much fun researching this story (as you can imagine) and I encourage everyone to spend one September on the glittering shores of the European Riviera to experience yacht show season. You will not be disappointed!

My thank you list is wide and varied and I'm forever grateful to the following individuals who offered me support and encouragement.

Number one in Team Monaco is Bex Mathias. Lady, you outdid yourself in every department. From suggesting Le Simona apartments for Morgan's residence to arranging apartments for me to the parties and lunches and social events, and being best friend material, I am forever indebted to your kindness. (And for helping me source the most fabulous trench coat ever.) I consider myself an honorary Mathias if your mother Patricia and sister Julia will have me. Number two on the list is Jen Jacotine, my soul sister. You are the right amount of crazy and provided wonderful inspiration. I will never forget you and your ex-husband arguing over details about Morgan ... like he was a real person! We are the Bentley babes and Monaco Yacht Club superstars.

Number three is Richard Lambert of Burgess Yachts. Richard is the yacht broker to the stars and made my VIP Monaco Yacht Show experience one I will never forget. Number four is Elizabeth Charlier. We shared a great lunch at Casa del Caffe and you imparted excellent tidbits for someone not directly involved in the yacht industry. A million kisses!

Team Italy consists of the ever-fabulous Lara Paoletti, Press Officer for Confindustria Nautica. Your insight into the history of Salon Nautico and the award components were instrumental to my story. Sorry, we never had the chance to meet in person at the show—had to dash off early to get to a seaside villa dinner, as you do in Italy. Ha!

Now, it's all about the boats. The following individuals in the yacht design industry graciously shared their time and expertise with me.

Ron Holland is nothing short of a boating legend. One of the old school designers that transitioned from the simpler world of boat design to the high-stakes world of luxury superyachts, he's now working on his last commission. It was an honor to have lunch with you and hear your wild stories.

During the Monaco Yacht Show, I spoke to several key players in the industry. Bjorn Benecke from Abeking and Rasmussen yachts supplied some great insider intel and also referred me to Christian Schäfer, a yacht designer with Focus Yacht Design GMBH in Bremen, Germany. Our zoom call was very interesting and don't worry ... your secrets are safe with me. Props also to Christian Oliver from Delta Marine Industries, in Seattle, Washington. I never did get on board *Invictus* (damn those ladies on the dock behind podiums) but she looked very impressive. Sebastian Rheineck from Lürssen Shipyards, one of the world's biggest shipbuilders. You patiently answered all of my questions and had wonderful stories to tell.

Not directly involved, but still deserving of recognition, is *Alfa Nero*, my all-time favorite yacht. The description of *Liberté's* swimming pool/heli landing pad, and the mechanics behind it, is modelled on the aft section of this luxury superyacht designed by Nuvolari/Lenard out of Venice, Italy. Bigger and more opulent yachts have been built since, but there is something about the lines of *Alfa Nero* that hold a special place in my heart. She's sexy, like Morgan! I had to give a shout out to her in this story. She's available to rent for one million euros a week through Burgess Yachts. If you ever book a trip with her, please, and I do mean please, call me! I'll even swab the decks…

Aside from thanking all my high faluttin' European teams, my local peeps are equally deserving.

Jen Rainnie, your endless support and reading of anything I send you is so appreciated. Your input helped me order the books in *The Hustlers Trilogy* properly and I am forever grateful. You are a kick-ass business lady, a bona fide hustler, and I'm proud to call you a friend.

While my family might not know what to do with me some of the time, you are always there for me, and that's what matters in the end. Props to my eldest niece Sylvia for giving me the phrase "pound town." I use it in a slightly different expression than you do, but either way, the term rocks, so thank you!

Last, but certainly not least, my dear friend Tracey Rogers. This book is dedicated to her and it breaks my heart she can't be here to share the publishing moment with me. I spitballed the idea of *The Cruiser* in her Monaco apartment while she was undergoing chemotherapy. Tracey battled breast cancer for a decade and eventually succumbed to bone cancer in June 2020. She worked as a yacht charter broker for many years and we had many good laughs and adventures every time I visited Monaco. Tracey brought me to the fairy tale town of Dolce Aqua and I had a bit of a cry going back there during my final research trip in 2021. Girl, I miss you terribly. I know you're feeling all of this somehow, somewhere. Thank you for always believing in me and you were right … there was something in Monaco for me.

About the Author

Rowan is an award-winning storyteller whipping up contemporary romance tales. *The Hustlers* is her first trilogy and is inspired by all the beautiful men and women who grab life by the cajones and make the world a better place. She lives in Vancouver, Canada but her heart belongs to Europe.

Ingram Content Group UK Ltd.
Milton Keynes UK
UKHW012024190623
423702UK00006B/700